Before Queer Theory

BEFORE QUEER THEORY

Victorian Aestheticism and the Self

Dustin Friedman

Johns Hopkins University Press
Baltimore

Johns Hopkins University Press
2715 North Charles Street
Baltimore, Maryland 21218-4363
www.press.jhu.edu

Library of Congress Cataloging-in-Publication Data

Names: Friedman, Dustin, 1982–, author.
Title: Before queer theory : Victorian aestheticism and the self /
Dustin Friedman.
Description: Baltimore : Johns Hopkins University Press, 2019. | Includes
bibliographical references and index.
Identifiers: LCCN 2018054660 | ISBN 9781421431475 (hardcover : alk. paper) |
ISBN 1421431475 (hardcover : alk. paper) | ISBN 9781421431482 (pbk. : alk.
paper) | ISBN 1421431483 (pbk. : alk. paper) | ISBN 9781421431499 (electronic)
| ISBN 1421431491 (electronic)
Subjects: LCSH: English literature—19th century—History and criticism. |
Aestheticism (Literature) | Literature—philosophy. | Self (psychology) in
literature. | Homosexuality and literature—England—History—19th century
Classification: LCC PR468.A33 F75 2019 | DDC 820.9/92066409033—dc23
LC record available at https://lccn.loc.gov/2018054660

A catalog record for this book is available from the British Library.

*Special discounts are available for bulk purchases of this book. For more
information, please contact Special Sales at specialsales@press.jhu.edu.*

Johns Hopkins University Press uses environmentally friendly book materials,
including recycled text paper that is composed of at least 30 percent
post-consumer waste, whenever possible.

To the memory of my grandparents:
Ann and Leo Friedman
Frank and Judy Mitchell

CONTENTS

ACKNOWLEDGMENTS

This book could not have been completed without the generosity of many people in many different countries and continents. It began life as a doctoral dissertation completed in the Department of English at UCLA. I could not have asked for a better advisor than Joseph Bristow. His "Aestheticism and Decadence" graduate seminar in the spring of 2005 set me on the path that led to this project. The quality of his teaching, the time and effort he spent on his students' professional and personal well-being, and his high scholarly standards made him both a superlative mentor and an inspiring professional role model. I will be forever grateful to have been his student. Jonathan Grossman's seemingly endless amounts of energy and enthusiasm were something I could always rely on for inspiration. Besides giving incisive and detailed comments on my writing, he paid me the highest compliment a faculty member can give to a student: he always took my ideas seriously. Eleanor Kaufman's knowledge of modern French thought provided a decisive intervention at an early stage of this project, and Johanna Drucker kindly stepped in at a later moment to offer her expertise in aesthetic theory. I am also appreciative for the guidance provided by Ali Behdad, Chris Chism, Helen Deutsch, Arthur Little, Chris Looby, Sianne Ngai, Felicity Nussbaum, and Amy Richlin. For the quality of my day-to-day life in graduate school, I am thankful for the efforts of Jeanette Gilkison, Mike Lambert, and Chris Mott.

The comradery of my fellow graduate students was indispensable. I especially want to thank Noelle Chao, Will Clark, Noah Comet, Vivian Davis, Matt Dubord, Beth Goodhue, Laura Haupt, Amanda Hollander, Eric Newman, Val Popp, Sam See, Maureen Shay, Erin Suzuki, Anne Stiles, and Dennis Tyler for their friendship. Sam See's comments on an early version of chapter 1 changed the trajectory of this project, and his intelligence, wit, and kindness are sorely missed by all who knew him.

I am lucky to count many colleagues, both in Victorian studies and beyond, as friends. Lee Behlman, Daniel DeWispelare (who read the entire draft of this book), Neil Hultgren, Kevin Riordan, Richard Sha, and Marion Thain offered valuable feedback on various aspects of this manuscript. Elisha Cohn, Lindsey Green-Simms, Nathan Hensley, Kristin Mahoney, Benjamin Morgan, Patrick O'Malley, David Pike, Anne Thell, and Danny Wright offered vital feedback and advice for navigating the publication process. Diana Maltz and Josephine McDonagh have been incredibly generous with their professional wisdom.

I never expected to move halfway around the world for my first full-time academic job. What could have been a difficult adjustment was made easier by the warm welcome I received in the Department of English Language and Literature at the National University of Singapore, especially from Jane Nardin and Anne Thell. Nele Lenze, Petrus Liu, Lisa Onaga, Kevin Riordan, and Walter Wadiak also helped make a faraway place feel like home.

The decision to move back to the United States to take a position at American University is continually confirmed by my wonderful colleagues and friends in the Department of Literature. I am thankful every day to work with Amanda Berry, Fiona Brideoake, Kyle Dargan, Erik Dussere, Stephanie Grant, Lindsey Green-Simms, Despina Kakoudaki, David Keplinger, Keith Leonard, Sarah Marsh, Jeff Middents, Marianne Noble, Patricia Park, Dolen Perkins-Valdez, Deborah Payne, David Pike, Tom Ratekin, Roberta Rubenstein, Richard Sha, Anita Sherman, Kathleen Smith, Rachel Louise Snyder, Linda Voris, and Lily Wong. I am happy to have started at AU at the same time as M. J. Rymsza-Pawlowska and to be following in the footsteps of Jonathan Loesberg. My professional life would be considerably more difficult without the assistance provided by Mike Burgtorf.

While working on this project, I have relied on the moral and intellectual support provided by the UCLA English Department's Nineteenth-Century Group, the Aestheticism Reading Group at the William Andrews Clark Memorial Library (convened by Joseph Bristow and consisting of Elisha Cohn, Renee Fox, Neil Hultgren, Patrick Keilty, and Simon Reader), the Southeast Asia Society for Eighteenth-Century Studies (consisting of Samara Cahill, Leung Wing Sze Evelyn, and Anne Thell), and the Nineteenth Century and Beyond Group at George Washington University (convened by Maria Frawley). Financial support for this project has been provided by the Departments of English, Gender Studies, and LGBT Studies at UCLA, the UCLA Center for Seventeenth- and Eighteenth-Century Studies, the William Andrews Clark

Memorial Library, the Department of English Language and Literature at the National University of Singapore, the Department of Literature at American University, and a Mellon Faculty Grant from the College of Arts and Sciences at American University.

At Johns Hopkins University Press, I have had the honor of working with the brilliant Catherine Goldstead on this project. I am also grateful to James Eli Adams and the anonymous reader of this manuscript for their detailed and incisive commentary. This book is undoubtedly better because of them. Thanks go to Carrie Watterson for her care and attention copyediting this manuscript, as well as to managing editor Juliana McCarthy and the whole team at the Press.

Portions of chapter 2 appeared in an earlier form as "Aesthetic Cosmopolitanism: Euphuism, Negativity, and Genre in Walter Pater's *Marius the Epicurean*," © The International Walter Pater Society, 2009, in the *Pater Newsletter* 55/56 (2009): 31–49. An earlier version of chapter three appeared as "Negative Eroticism: Lyric Performativity and the Sexual Subject in Oscar Wilde's 'Portrait of Mr. W.H.'" © Johns Hopkins University Press, 2013, in *ELH* 80, no. 2 (Summer 2013): 597–626.

Lara-Beye Molina has been a constant presence in my life since our first year of college at UC Berkeley, and I have long relied on her keen appreciation of the absurd to help me through the trials of academic life. Elizabeth Donaldson's friendship has been vital since our first days in the UCLA English graduate program together, and our shared enjoyment of the campy, the outré, and the bizarre has cemented a lifelong bond. Patrick Keilty has been a loyal friend ever since we met at the Clark Library; his intensity and exuberance have been a bracing influence on my intellectual life, and morsels of our conversations about sexuality, gender, and philosophy are sprinkled throughout these pages. Special thanks also go to his parents, Eileen and Tom Keilty, for frequently offering their home and hospitality to me, as well as to Clay Doyle, Michael Logan, and Eric See for giving me a warm welcome and a place to stay during my travels back to Los Angeles.

This book is dedicated to the memory of my grandparents, Ann and Leo Friedman, and Frank and Judy Mitchell, whose boundless love colors my very earliest memories. Throughout my life I have drawn inspiration from my mother, Gail Mitchell, whose wit, personal fortitude, and effusively unconditional love have always helped me keep things in proper perspective. My father, Richard Friedman, and my stepmother, Carolyn Johnson, have long been the bedrock of my support, and their constant faith in me has been sustaining throughout many challenges. The gratitude I have for all of them is immeasurable. My siblings, nieces, nephews, and grandnephew always keep life fun and interesting. Finally, I offer the utmost gratitude and thanks to my husband, Karim Shah. His influence shows on every page of this book. The amount of happiness he brings to my life cannot be measured, and his laughter and love fill my days with joy. Without him, none of this would have been possible.

Before Queer Theory

Introduction

> For nearly ten minutes he stood there, motionless, with parted lips
> and eyes strangely bright. He was dimly conscious that entirely fresh
> influences were at work within him. Yet they seemed to have come really
> from himself. The few words that Basil's friend had said to him—words
> spoken by chance, no doubt, and with willful paradox in them—had
> touched some secret chord that had never been touched before, but that
> he felt was now vibrating and throbbing to curious pulses. . . . Yes; there
> had been things in his boyhood that he had not understood. He under-
> stood them now. Life suddenly became fiery-coloured to him. It seemed
> to him that he had been walking in fire. Why had he not known it?
> —Oscar Wilde, *The Picture of Dorian Gray*

At this moment, the hero of Wilde's novel goes through in an instant a process that takes many of us much longer. Dorian Gray's realization occurs while
he attends the last sitting for his portrait. As Basil Hallward, the painter who
loves him madly but secretly, puts on the finishing touches, Lord Henry Wot-
ton provokes Dorian with elegant conversation and self-consciously crafted
"aesthetic" language. He exhorts Dorian to "live out [his] life fully and completely," by which he means committing "sin," and tells him to yield to "passions that have made you afraid, thoughts that have filled you with terror,
day-dreams and sleeping dreams whose mere memory might stain your cheek
with shame." His speech brings Dorian to a fever pitch of fear, excitement, and
confusion. "Stop! You bewilder me," Dorian cries.[1] Lord Henry's beautiful
words have made him capable of finally understanding his desires—desires
that, given his alarmed response and the narrator's tumescent rhetoric of
vibrating, throbbing, and pulsing, hint strongly at his possession of "sinful"
homoerotic impulses. Although this thought has apparently never occurred
to Dorian before, he recognizes its truth immediately.

Dorian's reaction to Lord Henry's provocative words seems, at first, paradoxical. He believes entirely new "influences" to be at work upon him, yet
he also feels that these come not from any external force but entirely from
within his own mind. Lord Henry has not given him new information about
his sexuality, exactly. Instead, his words have shifted Dorian's perspective,
making him capable of seeing in a new light desires that have been part of his

consciousness since "boyhood," even if he has not been aware of them. This shift in optics changes not only Dorian's self-understanding but his entire way of perceiving the world. "Life" now appears to him "fiery-coloured": lively and passionate but also mutable, unstable, and dangerous.

The upheaval in perception required for Dorian to see his desires anew profoundly rearranges the contents of his consciousness and sets the stage for his eventual rejection of the moral strictures of bourgeois Victorian life. Soon after this moment, he will embrace Lord Henry's "new Hedonism," the philosophy of exquisite sensation and transitory beauty Wilde based loosely on the writings of Walter Pater, his mentor in aesthetic philosophy, who famously enjoins readers to "burn with a hard, gemlike flame" in pursuit of sensual pleasure in art.[2] This experience marks the birth of a new sense of self for Dorian, symbolized by the picture that captures the exact instant of this revelation and forever changes his life.

Scenes like this are paradigmatic in the writings of Victorian aesthetes who, like Wilde, possessed stigmatized sexual desires. A character, a narrator, a lyric persona, or even the author him- or herself encounters a work of art and then realizes his or her desires are not what the culture says they should be.[3] Though this revelation is, at first, profoundly unsettling, aesthetes soon find themselves harnessing that sense of fear and alienation and transforming it into a liberating sense of detachment from oppressive social norms. This experience elicits a version of subjective autonomy that allows them to envision new modes of seeing, thinking, and living that expand the boundaries of contemporary social and intellectual structures.

This study's central claim is that aesthetes such as Walter Pater, Oscar Wilde, Vernon Lee (Violet Paget), and Michael Field (Katharine Bradley and Edith Cooper) showed art to be a realm where queers can resist a hostile social world by developing an autonomous sense of self, one that is inspired by their sexual difference and grounded in the ability to resist dominant power relations. This sense of freedom follows from the realization that the discourses causing feelings of alienation are not absolute and unquestionable, but historically contingent, and therefore can be imagined differently. Although queer aesthetes realized their homophobic culture put obstacles in the way of becoming self-aware of their desires, they also realized those obstacles could become, in their own way, aesthetically enabling. Their writings demonstrate how encounters with art could be crucial for gaining sexual self-knowledge and, in turn, how queer desire could bring into being radically new ways of perceiving the self and the world in and through art. As

Brian Glavey has recently stated, "the power of the aesthetic" for queers "stems in part from the way it offers . . . a space where creativity, cooperation, and surprise might be conjured within the cramped restraints of a repressive and often unsurprising social world."[4] One does not need to aspire to the practically impossible goal of liberating one's mind entirely from social authority to be able to see the world differently. Instead, aesthetic experience allows one to gain a sense of personal independence while still enmeshed within structures of oppression, granting access to a domain where repressive laws are not always strictly enforced.

The process depicted by queer aesthetes has been described by Georg Wilhelm Friedrich Hegel, perhaps the nineteenth century's most profound theorist of subjectivity. Philosophical idealism, and Hegelian thought in particular, was in vogue in English cultural life during aestheticism's heyday. His influence dominated British academic life from the mid-nineteenth century until the early years of the twentieth century. In the cultural sphere, almost every author writing seriously on art and literature during this time knew at least the broad strokes of his philosophy. The queer aesthetes discussed in this study had at least some direct knowledge of his writings, but its reception was always mediated through the writings of Walter Pater, the Aesthetic Movement's most philosophically astute theorist of art and sexuality. Pater knew Hegel's body of work as well as anyone in Victorian England, and he disseminated it widely through his popular writings on art history, literature, and aesthetic theory. His effect on later queer aesthetes was immense, as they continually defined their projects in relation to his own.

This intellectual climate is key for understanding the aesthetes' theorizations of sexual subjectivity. Unlike most Victorian intellectuals, who were interested in Hegel's dialectic as a theory of historical progress and harmonious reconciliation, queer aesthetes were drawn to an aspect of dialectical thought most Victorian commentators neglected: the concept Hegel identifies as "the negative."[5] This term has also played an important role in recent developments in queer theory, in the so-called turn to the negative or antisocial thesis. Mari Ruti writes that queer negativity valorizes "self-destruction, failure, melancholia, loneliness, isolation, abjection, despair, regret, shame, and bitterness" as a corrective to the relentless positivity and productivity that define the social and political order of Western modernity.[6] Yet this turn to the negative in queer theory is not Hegelian in origin but instead derives from Lacanian psychoanalysis. It participates in a poststructuralist tradition that, Diana Coole explains, explicitly rejects the Hegelian dialectic, defining negativity instead as "excessive productivity and multiplicitous antagonism," and that understands the notion of coherent, autonomous selfhood to be merely a chimera created by the Enlightenment notion of sovereign subjectivity.[7]

Hegel's *Negativität* follows a very different logic. For him, the negative is the destructive force powering the dialectic. He writes in the *Phenomenology of Spirit* (1807) that "the life of the spirit is not a life that shuns death and bewares destruction, keeping clean of it; it is a life that bears and maintains itself in it. Spirit only gains its truth by finding itself in absolute rupture. Spirit is that power . . . only in so far as it looks the negative in the face and dwells in it. This dwelling is the magic force which converts the negative into being. That power is what we called . . . the subject."[8] Negativity describes how consciousness, upon encountering an obstacle, destroys and subsequently rearranges itself to accommodate that obstacle. This process paradoxically encourages, rather than hinders, individual self-development. By causing one's subjectivity to disintegrate, the negative does not destroy it entirely but instead allows it to be reworked into a more self-aware and sophisticated configuration. While, for Hegel, the logic of negativity can be found in all realms of human existence, including art, for the aesthetes it is fundamentally and primarily an aesthetic phenomenon. As Wilde states in his essay "The Truth of Masks" (1891), just as "it is only in art-criticism, and through it, that we can apprehend the Platonic theory of ideas, so it is only in art-criticism, and through it, that we can realise Hegel's system of contraries."[9]

"Erotic negativity" is the name I give to one of the foundational propositions of the queer aesthetes: that negativity describes the process through which value can be found in the possession of homoerotic desire not despite but *because* one lives in a culture where such feelings are condemned. By transforming the painful recognition of one's queer desire into a profoundly consciousness-transforming experience, erotic negativity allows one to tarry at the very limits of what is thinkable in one's culture. The aesthete, when he gazes upon the masculine beauty of an ancient Greek sculpture or when she regards a painting of an exquisite woman, undergoes a shock that is at once intellectual and visceral. This fearful and startling revelation shatters and radically reconfigures the very structure of the mind itself. For queer theorists of negativity, such as Leo Bersani, desire's shattering of the self leads to the conclusion that sex is not necessarily a "struggle for power" between the subject and object of desire, but instead provides an arena where the destruction of one's subjectivity is experienced as pleasure.[10] For the aesthetes, however, fragmentation of the self is not the end of the process. It marks the moment preliminary to an inchoate collection of erotic impulses crystalizing into a distinct sense of sexual difference, of being at odds with prevailing cultural norms. The cultivation of what Pater calls the "temperament, the power of being deeply moved by the presence of beautiful objects," allows one's shattered subjectivity to develop into a newly open and dynamic form of consciousness (*R* xxi). This disposition militates against both society's homophobia and visions of the self and the world that threaten to become static, limited, and moribund.

Erotic negativity grants queer aesthetes a limited yet powerful sense of independent self-direction, of partial freedom from preordained metaphysical, social, and biological orders. In an era when advances in philosophy and science, such as the psychological discourse of associationism and the growing acknowledgment of the fluidity of the natural world found in the works of Charles Darwin, John Tyndall, Thomas Huxley, and Herbert Spencer, increasingly portrayed humans as subject to forces beyond their control, queer Victorian aesthetes realized that becoming self-aware of one's same-sex desires was both personally liberating and an affirmation of what philosophers have called, after Kant, subjective autonomy.[11] Kant defined the modern individual by her ability to determine and pursue a course of action for herself, rather than relying on external authority for guidance. This capacity does not arise spontaneously but must be cultivated over time. As he states in his essay "What Is Enlightenment?" (1790), the modern era is defined by "man's emergence from his self-incurred immaturity," gained through having "the courage to use your own understanding."[12] The formation of the autonomous self is at the heart of the aesthetic theories of Kant and, especially, Hegel, who propose that artworks are the sensual expression of humanity's capacity to develop freedom, and that our responses to art cultivate our individuality. What the Victorians referred to as *Bildung* (borrowing the German term) named the process of self-cultivation that was central to the nineteenth century's understanding of independent selfhood.[13] Yet while *Bildung* supposes the eventual reconciliation of the individual with society, queer aesthetes instead defined autonomy as the individual's ability to develop her or his capacities of self through resistance to social norms.

Aestheticism is one of queer theory's unacknowledged ancestors. While this study does not purport to offer a comprehensive prehistory of or origin story for the complex and dynamic field of queer studies, it does claim that within the writings of one of the very first self-consciously queer literary collectives, there already existed an impulse toward reparation and utopianism that would later find theoretical articulation in the writings of figures such as Eve Kosofsky Sedgwick and José Esteban Muñoz. This lineage has been difficult to perceive, however, because the aesthetes' belief in humanity's capacity for subjective self-determination departs significantly from the poststructuralist models of subjectivity that have dominated queer theoretical discourse. I place Victorian aestheticism within an alternative genealogy of queer thought that links Hegel's aesthetics of subjective autonomy to Michel Foucault's rapprochement with the self-determining subject in his late writings. The aesthetes demonstrated that it is possible to have a radical theory of sexuality that assumes, in contrast to queer negativity, that the subject possesses a limited, yet meaningful, capacity for self-determination. Their aesthetic version of autonomy inheres in the individual's ability to reflect critically on his or her historical moment and test whether it is possible to envision new modes of seeing, forms of thinking, and ways of living.

In his essay "Coleridge's Writings" (1866), Pater describes the "modern spirit" as a "relative spirit" that embraces the fact that "nothing is, or can be rightly known, except relatively and under conditions," a temperament comfortable with the fact that apparently stable and unquestionable truths are actually socially and historically contingent. For Pater, the modern spirit's task is to break down the premodern "absolute spirit," which seeks "to arrest every object in an eternal outline, to fix thought in a necessary formula, and the varieties of life in a classification by 'kinds,' or genera."[14] The aesthetes realized that the aims of the modern spirit could be accomplished most effectively in and through the aesthetic, a realm where the commonsense logic that limits everyday thought is relaxed yet nevertheless still present. By extending and transforming Hegel's belief that art serves as the sensual reflection of transcendent human freedom, queer aestheticism defined the aesthetic *itself* as the realm where one's autonomy could be realized in an oppressive social world.

The present volume ultimately speaks to the vital role art can play in developing self-determining queer identities. To be sure, people who are not queer can have deeply transformative aesthetic experiences, as Victorian art writers such as John Ruskin and Matthew Arnold knew very well. Yet queer aesthetes recognized that the cultivation of an identity grounded in the aesthetic was a particularly effective bulwark against cultural discourses that oppressed those who possessed nonnormative desires through "classification by 'kinds,' or genera." Art provided an alternative to medical and legal discourses portraying queers as passive victims of their own degenerate desires. Queer aesthetes made the counterintuitive claim that queerness can be an advantage intellectually, creatively, and ethically, not in spite of but because of social opposition toward nonnormative desires, eliciting a sense of freedom perhaps unattainable by those who are never forced to confront their own social abjection.

Despite being more than a century old, this insight has yet to take hold in contemporary discussions of sexual identity. There are, of course, many hardships that come with being LGBT, including the insidious, life-threatening violence that occurs on both an individual and institutional level. This is a fact the aesthetes, most notably and spectacularly Wilde, knew all too well. Yet despite Sedgwick's plea more than two decades ago in her landmark essay "How to Bring Your Kids Up Gay" (1991) for a discourse that would present queerness as an unequivocally positive and desirable developmental outcome—not in some far off, tolerant future, but *right now*—neither critical theory, nor psychology, nor mainstream culture has responded to this call. Even in our presumably enlightened era, LGBT individuals continue to be defended within the paradigm of the Foucauldian reverse discourse.[15] Progressives assert that some people are biologically "born this way," implying that, if one had a choice, one would inevitably not want to possess desires that put one at odds with what society considers normal and natural. Yet Sedgwick reminds us that "the number of persons and institutions by whom the existence of gay people—never mind the existence of *more gay people*—is treated as a precious desideratum, a needed condition of life, is small."[16] The chapters that follow argue that Victorian aesthetes created an important early version of this radically queer-affirmative discourse. In their writings, the aesthetes are largely agnostic regarding whether queer sexuality is innate to a minority or potentially available to anyone willing to cultivate their artistic sensibilities. Yet they powerfully and rigorously articulate a position rarely uttered in either Victorian or modern culture: that one might *want* to be queer, when being so provides the opportunity to be part of an emancipated artistic vanguard, charged with the self-appointed task of reimagining how life might be lived.

~

The aesthetes were far from orthodox in their artistic rendition of negativity. Their version anticipates, in some ways, Muñoz's discussion of the "potentiality in negative affects that can be reshaped by negation and made to work in the service of enacting a mode of critical possibility," which makes them a "resource for a certain mode of queer utopianism" seeking to imagine better alternatives to an inadequate present.[17] Yet Muñoz's utopian negativity is always merely potential, leaving it uncertain how, when, and where its conversion into critical energy can take place. For the aesthetes, however, it is precisely the realm of art where this transformation can occur. They pick up on a suggestion implicit within Hegel's description of the negative, which actually begins with something of a rejection of the aesthetic. He states that "a powerless beauty hates the understanding, because the understanding expects it to do what it cannot," that is, maintaining its existence in the face of the "colossal power of the negative."[18] Yet Yirmiyahu Yovel comments that Hegel means his phrase to distinguish "powerless beauty" from "a powerful beauty which admits negativity and death. Powerless beauty is shallow, pale, rosy, one-dimensional; it hates the understanding not only because it cannot stand analysis, but also because it abhors negativity. . . . Beauty, however, need not be powerless."[19] Powerful beauty elicits acts of looking of the sort Andrew Cole describes in his gloss of Hegelian negativity, which "converts the negative into being in that uniquely phenomenological way: there is delay so as to acquire vision, to see what is at first unseeable, to undergo a formative experience (*Bildungs-Erfahrung*) that . . . sharpens perception and establishes the phenomenological investigation of appearances. This is the 'eye that has not seen.'"[20] For queer aesthetes, this describes the fundamentally aesthetic process inaugurated when one gazes upon a beauty strong enough to embrace negativity's destructive force, which transforms pain and destruction into the creative energy needed to re-form the self and reimagine the world.[21]

By placing Hegelian negativity at the center of the aesthetes' accounts of how queer desire inspires the development of autonomous subjectivity, this study departs from conventional critical accounts of the aesthetes' preoccupation with perverse sexualities. Definitions of who or what exactly counts as aestheticism are famously contentious, since there were no self-identified adherents to an "Aesthetic Movement" during the nineteenth century. Some scholars claim that it stretches as far back as the late Romantic celebration of truth and beauty by Percy Bysshe Shelley and John Keats, and forward to early modernist attempts to separate artistic from social discourse.[22] Yet the general scholarly consensus is that a group of writers and artists espousing an "art for art's sake" philosophy coalesced around Algernon Charles Swinburne and Walter Pater, both of whom drew inspiration from the artistic radicalism of English Pre-Raphaelite painters and poets and French Romantic

writers.[23] They shared a general sense that works of art should be both produced and judged without immediate reference to any scientific, religious,
moral, or social purpose other than their artistic effects.

Representations of the bizarre and outré could thus be excused by the
claim that beauty alone was art's highest aim. This has made it easy for modern literary critics to understand the movement's appeal to those whose sexual interests fell outside the Victorian mainstream—so easy, in fact, that it has
been more of an unstated assumption than an explicitly articulated position.
The implication is that aestheticism opened a space for the representation
of immoral and unproductive desires by providing the readymade excuse
that artists were not portraying their own proclivities but simply realizing an
artistic ideal. Richard Dellamora, Linda Dowling, Thaïs Morgan, James Eli
Adams, and Stefano Evangelista have built on this insight to discuss how the
rhetoric of "art for art's sake" became a covert code for gay men to build a
nascent sense of identity and community in a hostile society.[24] More recently,
Christopher Reed has argued that the discourse surrounding aestheticism,
especially the Wilde trial and its aftermath, was a key moment in the development of the public's association of the figure of the artist with the homosexual. According to him, in aestheticism "sexologists' ideas of personality
types combined with" the Romantic ideal of the "artist-genius" who is "a
breed set apart . . . a personality type defined by ambition, adventurousness,
rebelliousness, and constant innovation."[25]

Reed identifies aestheticism as one of the late nineteenth century's "avant-
garde subcultures" that "experiment with provocative ideas and behaviors
on behalf of the middle class" and whose "claims to heroism and freedom
often mask conventional forms of authority."[26] Important works by Regenia
Gagnier, Jonathan Freedman, Kathy Alexis Psomiades, and Talia Schaffer
have focused on the Aesthetic Movement's subversion of gender and sexual
norms in the context of its place both inside and outside bourgeois Victorian
society, as part of the rise of commodity culture occurring in the nineteenth
century's closing decades.[27]

Yet Linda Dowling and Diana Maltz have established that characterizations of "art for art's sake" as a covert form of bourgeois aesthetics is an over-
simplification.[28] Both critics argue that aesthetes, rather than believing that
art had absolutely no connection to society or politics, instead sought to interrogate and reimagine reciprocal relations between art and the world with
the goal of reforming antagonisms between social classes. This book explores
an unexamined corollary to this insight: that aestheticism's vision of the sub-

ject is neither identical to the bourgeois notion of absolutely unfettered personal sovereignty, nor a wholehearted embrace of the socially constructed subject of poststructuralist thought, but instead an attempt to rethink entirely the relationship between artistic experience and the process of self-formation.

This encounter does not take place in the autonomous aesthetic sphere of bourgeois ideology, which supposes art to exist beyond the struggles of history and politics, which many critics have mistakenly ascribed both to Kantian-Hegelian aesthetics and Victorian aestheticism's "art for art's sake" philosophy.[29] Neither is it located in the nineteenth century's dominant notion of beauty as a playful sense of equilibrium between contending human drives, articulated in Friedrich Schiller's influential *Letters on the Aesthetic Education of Man* (1795).[30] Aestheticism's vision of beauty is neither a symbol nor an imitation of human freedom, as Kant and Schiller suggest, but *freedom itself* given sensuous form. Freedom inheres in the aesthetes' ability to leverage their desires into a critique of oppressive social discourses, an act of mental resistance that grounds their subjective sense of personal autonomy. As Robert Kaufman argues, this is the hallmark of the "quasi-conceptual quality" of Kantian-Hegelian aesthetic purposiveness. Kant states that "a judgment of taste is not a cognitive judgment and so is not a logical judgment but an aesthetic one, by which we mean a judgment whose determining basis cannot be other than subjective," yet it is nevertheless also universally communicable between subjects.[31] Kaufman calls attention to the fact that "although the aesthetic looks like conceptual, purposeful, rule-based thought or activity it *only* looks like the latter. . . . The aesthetic is 'free' (as concept-based thought cannot be) from preexistent concept, purpose, law, or object." Consequently, the aesthetic is the "engine for new, experimental—because previously non-existent (and therefore free of status quo determined)—concepts." Although the aesthetic exists beyond socially determined thought patterns, it is far from divorced from history and the social. Art instead "provides a prerequisite of critical thought when (if only by negation or in art's negative space) it offers formal means for allowing new (and not necessarily utopian) aspects of contemporary society to come into view."[32] For this reason, queer aesthetes believed that Kantian-Hegelian purposiveness could produce the powerful beauty capable of withstanding the power of the negative.

Aesthetes turned to the negative to imagine a version of individual freedom appropriate for a cultural moment when the Enlightenment ideal of the self-determining subject met with increasing skepticism. One of the most important "political transformations of nineteenth-century Europe," Heike Bauer argues, was the fusion of "Enlightenment theorisations of the human into legalistic and scientific definitions of the subject."[33] Paradoxically, this fusion challenged the autonomy that was supposed to be the hallmark of post-Enlightenment selfhood. For Kant, threats to self-determination were always external, in the forms of religious and political authority, yet advances in the sciences and social sciences increasingly showed how autonomy was compromised by physical impulses residing within the self. In 1859 John Stuart Mill could assert in *On Liberty* that "desires and impulses are as much a part of a perfect human being, as beliefs and restraints," but late Victorian philosopher-scientists were apprehensive about the biological origins of those desires and impulses, as Elisha Cohn has discussed.[34] She notes James Ward's assertion in 1883 that it would "be a mistake to seek to explain the individuality of the psychological subject by reference to the individuality of the organism," and Edmund Montgomery's comments in 1880 that, "in the free exercise of our thought and volition, we could laugh to scorn the intimation that not in our own undivided personality are lodged these sovereign powers, but that they originate outside of it, dispersedly, within the diminutive lives of a vast number of microscopial threads and dots. We would resign our autonomy to the five or six billions of corpuscles composing our bodies."[35] Actions that feel like they are done out of our own free will really arise out of biological necessities not chosen by us, and of which we are not consciously aware. In one sense, this account of human behavior was liberating for the aesthetes, insofar as it effectively freed one from the ethical obligation to aspire to the "absolute spirit" of religious or metaphysical ideals. For this reason, many aesthetes embraced evolutionary science as part of their progressive artistic and political visions.[36] At the same time, however, these insights presented a seemingly fatal challenge to the possibility of autonomous subjectivity that was central to the aesthetes. As Pater wrote in 1866, the modern "sciences of observation" revealed that "character merges into temperament; the nervous system refines itself into intellect."[37] Qualities once attributed to humankind's spiritual nature were now explained through empirical observation of material phenomena. According to Benjamin Morgan, this development led many Victorian aesthetic theorists to reject the idealist notion of *Bildung* in favor of more materialist and positivist accounts of the self. There is a "tendency within Victorian aesthetic thought," he writes, "in which the self is not painstakingly cultivated but is instead constantly revealed to be on the verge of dissolving outward into its material surroundings, or inward into individual nerves and organs. In this regard, it is sensitive to the antihumanist energies of humanist aesthetics, tracking a counternarrative in which the aesthetic denatured rather than recuperated the autonomy and distinctiveness of human beings."[38]

It was, ironically, the Enlightenment notion of sovereign subjectivity, the Kantian injunction to free oneself from dogma by using one's own understanding to investigate worldly phenomena, that by the late Victorian era seemed to undermine the very possibility of self-determination. Foucault, in his study of the rise of the nineteenth-century social sciences, *The Order of Things* (1966), identifies this trajectory as the inevitable consequence of the modern episteme's contradictory vision of the human as what he calls a "strange empirico-transcendental doublet."[39] The Enlightenment subject, in its attempt to become free from "self-incurred immaturity," endeavors to know itself on its own terms through recourse to its innate capacity for reasoned deliberation, rather than deferring to an external authority. This gave rise to empirical investigations of the human body and human culture: biology, economics, philology, et cetera. These fields of study rendered human beings as figures of finitude, fundamentally no different from any other objects in nature and thus, it was assumed, completely knowable through scientific inquiry.

According to Foucault, for nineteenth-century intellectuals finitude held the possibility that human life might be fully known through observation of its concrete, external conditions, such as the physiology of the human body and the history of human culture, the labor, life, and language shaping an individual's perception of the world before he is even born. As Pater wrote, nineteenth-century social sciences revealed that "the mind of the race, the character of the age, sway him this way or that through the medium of language and ideas."[40] At the same time, however, researches into human biology and culture presuppose that the humans doing the investigating have access to a transcendental reason that cannot be grasped through empirical observation alone. José Guilherme Merquior explains in his summarization of Foucault that, "in order to sever truth from error, science from ideology, knowledge needs a critical standard of some external bearing," one that is possessed by the same humans who are the objects of scientific investigation.[41] This leads Foucault to claim that the nineteenth-century's rendering of the human was "a being such that knowledge will be attained in him of what renders all knowledge possible."[42] For him, modernity's understanding of the subject is incoherent: it is expected to be the sovereign originator of all the empirical knowledge it gains about the world, including itself. Yet the subject's ability to know itself thoroughly through the methods of empirical investigation compromises the very sovereignty that makes empirical ways of knowing possible.

Foucault presents this as one of the insurmountable contradictions besetting modernity, a definitive rebuke to humanist ideology. Yet I claim that the aesthetes, rather than embodying the anti-humanist, anti-autonomy positivism Morgan identifies with Victorian scientific aesthetics, instead promoted an attenuated idealism, one that attempted to solve the problem of the empirico-transcendental doublet by presenting autonomy as an aesthetic experience. They demonstrated that a measure of self-determination, arising from the ability to critique and resist dominant discourses, could be exercised in a realm where the subject was relatively free from the logical rules of noncontradiction and identity that govern scientific, medical, and legal discourse. Jonathan Loesberg has argued that the intellectual appeal of Kantian-Hegelian aesthetics lies in its ability to stand outside the rationalist discourses vaunted by post-Enlightenment culture, and it is usable for critiques that "show those concepts as contingent rather than universal."[43] For the aesthetes, human freedom belongs to neither the subject's empirical nor transcendental being, but instead to the quasi-conceptual realm of the aesthetic, where the innovative formal structures of art articulate new and controversial ideas undetermined by preexisting thought patterns. Their position is exemplified by the closing paragraph of Pater's 1867 "Winckelmann" essay, which is also the Aesthetic Movement's most explicit discussion of the relationship between art and homoerotic desire. He states that "the chief factor in the thoughts of the modern mind concerning itself is the intricacy, the universality of natural law, even in the moral order," and that what "modern art" must do in response is "rearrange the details of modern life, so to reflect it, that it may satisfy the spirit. And what does the spirit need in the face of modern life? The sense of freedom" (*R* 185). This statement returns in various guises throughout the writings of queer aesthetes, as they harnessed the "colossal power of the negative" in their art to create innovative visions of themselves and their world. These acts created a subjective sense of personal freedom outside the confines of the empirico-transcendental doublet.

Pater is careful to specify that this new version of subjective autonomy does not look very much like the old one. "That naïve, rough sense of freedom," he says, is something humankind "can never have again." The question, rather, is, will modern art be able to "represent men and women in these bewildering toils so as to give the spirit at least an equivalent for the sense of freedom?" (*R* 185). Key here is the notion of equivalence. Although the Kantian ideal of the sovereign subject may no longer be either scientifically or spiritually justified, art can still offer a viable alternative by providing a venue where the subject can feel free by resisting dominant cultural norms. In art, aesthetes can test whether the conceptual limits structuring their lives are absolute and uncontestable, or whether they can be challenged and reimagined. This is a humbler, but more tenable, version of autonomous subjectivity.

The need for queer aesthetes to find a version of personal freedom compatible with modern intellectual conditions did not arise solely from abstract philosophical commitments. Although art's transformative potential is available for everyone, Victorian queers faced particularly dire consequences from the loss of an older understanding of subjective autonomy. In the latter half of the nineteenth century, medical doctors, psychologists, and sexologists deployed the power and prestige of science to diagnose, regulate, and punish those whose desires transgressed cultural norms. According to Foucault's well-known argument, this was the era when sexual difference stopped being a religious or social transgression and became instead an innate biological deviation affecting the very core of selfhood. "The sodomite had been a temporary aberration," he famously states, "the homosexual was now a species." As scientific authorities consolidated their power to define the subject, they took away queers' ability to define themselves, delimiting them to the pathological, criminal body of the sexual pervert. They made "his sexuality . . . the root of all his actions, because it was their insidious and indefinitely active principle."[44] To have perverse desires meant that one was, by definition, incapable of personal self-determination. As Sonja Ruehl writes, for Foucault sexual "categories have a rigidifying effect, imprisoning individuals whose lives are administered under them."[45] I ask that we take seriously Victorian aesthetes' attenuated idealism as an attempt to maintain a sense of autonomy in the face of discourses intent on reducing queers to mere bodies, passively in thrall to diseased impulses beyond their control.

My account of queer aestheticism differs significantly from dominant accounts of the sexuality of the Aesthetic Movement. Dellamora argues that Victorian aestheticism should be considered part of what Foucault calls the "'reverse' discourse" arising in response to the medicalization of same-sex desire in the late nineteenth century, "when homosexuality began to speak on its own behalf, to demand its legitimacy or 'naturality' be acknowledged, often in the same vocabulary, using the same categories by which it was medically disqualified."[46] This suggests that the aesthetes, despite their radical pretentions, were locked within the same discourses that presented queer people as incapable of attaining personal independence. Defending one's nonnormative sexuality through recourse to the "born this way" argument inevitably affirms that one's freedom is bounded by the materiality of the body. This is precisely the seemingly self-evident, natural, and absolute limit to self-determination that aestheticism sought to challenge.

This study shows that the aesthetes consciously departed from the essentialist understandings of sexual identity promoted by the sexologists.[47] They realized that the aesthetic, as a space located within the social yet not strictly bound by its rules, was a realm where sexual difference could be embraced without being pathologized. Dellamora, who focuses exclusively on male homosexuality in Victorian aestheticism, suggests that "the interplay of discourses of masculine self-identification is even richer than Foucault anticipates," including aesthetics. Yet queer aesthetes deliberately chose flexible terms drawn from artistic and humanistic discourses to describe their sexuality, to the pointed exclusion of scientific vocabularies.[48] In a letter Wilde wrote to his publisher Leonard Smithers after his release from prison, he laments, "I am now simply a pauper of a rather low order: the fact that I am also a pathological problem in the eyes of German scientists: and even in their works I am tabulated, and come under the law of averages! *Quantum mutatus!*"[49] Heather Love has shown that Pater's writings express his despair at the advent of modern gay identity through the Foucauldian reverse discourse.[50] And although Vernon Lee, Katharine Bradley, and Edith Cooper were friends and readers of the sexologist Havelock Ellis, the author of the first English-language medical textbook on homosexuality, none of them used a sexological vocabulary to describe either themselves or their relationships with other women.[51]

Instead, queer aesthetes installed erotic difference at the very heart of their new philosophical account of aesthetically cultivated personal freedom. By portraying aestheticism as a serious intervention in the history of aesthetic philosophy, I build upon Morgan's affirmation that Victorian art writing, despite its frequently informal character, was not intellectually derivative. "Victorian aesthetic thought," he says, participated "in a tradition of philosophical aesthetics despite the fact that its practitioners often avoided a philosophical idiom."[52] This was especially true of the aesthetes, who stood at the intersection of academic philosophy, popular essayistic writing on art and literature, and the traditional genres of the novel, short story, and poetry.

Their outlook owed much to ideas initially encountered by Pater while he was a student and teacher at Oxford during Hegelianism's reign in the latter half of the nineteenth century. Hegel first became known in Britain through early nineteenth-century efforts to promote German literature and culture, beginning with the publication of Samuel Taylor Coleridge's *Biographia Literaria* in 1817.[53] As Kirk Willis states, by the 1830s "propagandists for the serious study of German literature" such as Thomas Carlyle, J. H. Stirling, J. G. Lockhart, John Mitchell Kemble, J. S. Blackie, and George Moir began making scattered references to Hegel in their reviews, though the first article to address any aspect of Hegelian thought in depth was George Henry Lewes's review of "Hegel's Aesthetics: Philosophy of Art," in the *British and Foreign Review* in 1842. Willis notes that "Lewes's choice of the *Asthetik* as the means of introducing Hegelian thought into Britain was carefully calculated" because "it complemented the growing British fascination with German culture and might therefore have been expected to provoke the serious study of a wide range of Hegelian thought." For the next half century, discussions of Hegel in general-interest periodicals were mostly limited to his aesthetic doctrines and theories.[54] Many of these discussions appeared in the *Westminster Review*, a periodical known for its progressive literary, philosophical, and political views that also, significantly, published Pater's earliest essays.

It was academic philosophy, however, that proved to be the most thorough and influential source for the dissemination of Hegelian thought in nineteenth-century Britain. Beginning in the late 1820s and continuing through the 1840s, Hegel began being mentioned in the writings of philosophers such as Robert Ferguson, William Hamilton, and J. D. Morrell.[55] Although these allusions were generally less than comprehensive and often quite critical of idealism, interest in Hegel among professional philosophers grew steadily throughout the 1850s and early 1860s, with more sympathetic accounts appearing in works by H. L. Mansel, Edward Dowden, Shadworth Hodgson, J. F. Ferrier, and Benjamin Jowett. Yet, according to Willis, "the most important contribution to the popularization and understanding of Hegelian thought in mid-Victorian Britain" was John Hutchison Stirling's *The Secret of Hegel* (1865), an extended explication and polemical defense of his philosophical system. From then until the early years of the twentieth century, academic philosophy in Britain was dominated by the British Idealist school, which turned to German idealism to both adapt to and push back against scientific positivism and the concomitant growth of reactionary religious movements.

The British Idealists believed that idealism, and Hegel's dialectic especially, provided tools for synthesizing Darwinian evolution with liberal Christianity, insofar as they both seemed to support the notion that all aspects of existence develop gradually toward perfection over time. This is, of course, something of a misrepresentation of Darwin's ideas, and the British Idealists' religious and moral concerns led them to emphasize the harmonious and reconciliatory aspects of Hegel's thought, generally to the minimization or exclusion of negativity's destructive role in the dialectic.[56] In the words of Stirling, "The true result of the latest philosophy—the true result of Kant and Hegel—is, that knowledge and belief coalesce in a lucid union, that to reason as to faith there is but one religion, one God, and One Redeemer."[57] It was during this time when the first English-language history of aesthetic philosophy appeared, Bernard Bosanquet's *A History of Aesthetic* (1892).

Although the depth of queer aesthetes' knowledge of Hegel varied, their discussions of queer sexuality were informed both by the philosophical idealism coloring discussions of art and literature during the period and, especially, the (homo)eroticized version of negativity offered by Pater. His works synthesized two important strands of Hegelianism in Victorian intellectual life: the period's general literary interest in Hegel's aesthetic theories, and professional philosophy's concern with his dialectical system. He learned German for the purpose of reading the *Phenomenology of Spirit* in the original, before it was translated into English. He owed his fellowship at Brasenose to his knowledge of German Idealism, and, as Kit Andrews notes, "He regularly lectured on philosophy from the early 1860s till near his death in 1894, precisely the decades when the Oxford Hegelians came to dominate the teaching of philosophy in Great Britain."[58] Wilde's aesthetic philosophy also engages with the idealist tradition, as William Wimsatt, Cleanth Brooks, and René Wellek recognized long ago. More recently, Philip E. Smith and Michael Helfand's edition of his Oxford "Commonplace Book" has established Wilde's detailed knowledge of many of Hegel's works.[59] While Vernon Lee, Katharine Bradley, and Edith Cooper lacked the credentials of their university-trained male peers, their writings offer versions of negativity that likely derived at least partially from their readings of Hegel, but primarily through their engagements with Pater, the central figure with and against whom they articulated their versions of aestheticism.

This study establishes that queer aesthetes were deeply engaged in a complex and nuanced philosophical conversation with each other about the nature of artistic experience, its relationship to sexual desire, and the cultivation of subjective autonomy. Although they were far from programmatic or homogenous in their views, their writings express a shared set of questions and references that defined them as part of a coherent intellectual project. In this capacity, queer aestheticism was an important forerunner to modern queer theoretical discourse, insofar as the aesthetes anticipated and addressed similar concerns about desire, identity, and the nature of representation. Unlike the Lacanian negativity that currently dominates queer theory, however, Victorian aestheticism's Hegelian coordinates affirm the possibility of an autonomous, self-directed queer self.

~

Victorian aestheticism's anticipation of queer theory has not played a prominent role in discussions of either movement. This is partially because queer aesthetes' philosophical investigations of aesthetic experience are inextricable from their concern with the nature of erotic desire: two discourses that have traditionally been opposed to one another in post-Kantian art philosophy. One of this study's aims is to demonstrate how queer aesthetes deployed negativity to transcend this opposition between sexuality and aesthetics. "Queer theory has always been shaped by an investment in the aesthetic," Glavey states, "but has not always made the limitations of this investment explicit."[60] And although the Aesthetic Movement has often been analyzed in visual and cultural studies scholarship informed by queer theory, it has rarely been thought to offer a coherent theory of sexual subjectivity in its own right.[61]

Critics have long noted the association between aestheticism and the homoerotic, as discussed earlier in this introduction, but the connection has not often been theorized. Art philosophy from Plato through the eighteenth-century writings of Johann Joachim Winckelmann portrayed sexual desire as a key element of artistic experience. Yet, despite Dowling's powerful analysis of the influence of the *Symposium*'s Socratic eros on Pater's "Conclusion," scholars of aestheticism have tended to repeat a discursive opposition between the erotic and the aesthetic that, according to Whitney Davis, has existed in Western philosophy since Kant's attempt to "straighten" Winckelmann in the *Critique of Judgment* (1790).[62] In these modern accounts, sexuality is sublimated into an idealized appreciation of artistic form, or the language of aesthetics is merely a code to express otherwise unspeakable desires, as I discuss in detail in chapter 1. Because of this divide, aestheticism's innovative combination of a radical theory of sexuality with an investment in autonomous subjectivity has gone unrecognized. Queer theorists have assumed that individual self-determination is inevitably identical to the Enlightenment notion of sovereign subjectivity and thus anathema to their political project, but aestheticism makes queerness central to the achievement of the "equivalent for the sense of freedom" Pater identifies as the goal of modern art. Richard Kaye notes that queer readings of literary texts often portray subjectivity as a mere "refraction or residue of history," because they rely on Foucault's precept that the discourse of sexuality is "not inherent or otherwise attached to the individual but . . . the product of a system of knowledges that regulate individual bodies and pleasure and in so doing construct the subject in different ways."[63] Selfhood is always and inevitably socially constructed as an effect of discourse and power. Foucault's thought is presumed to form part of the "death of the subject" that is the hallmark of poststructuralism's inheritance from Friedrich Nietzsche's imperative to expose individualism as a bourgeois myth.[64] This intellectual genealogy has led to one of the most provocative claims in recent critical theory, discussed earlier in this introduction: the queer "turn to the negative" or "anti-social thesis," which advocates queers to forego attempts to cobble together a workable version of selfhood, embrace their misery, and abandon futile attempts to join an oppressive social order that is constituted through the abjection of queerness.[65]

Yet, in response to these bracing provocations, recent works of queer theory such as Michael Snediker's *Queer Optimism* (2009), Muñoz's *Cruising Utopia* (2009), and Glavey's *Wallflower Avant-Garde* (2016) have defended concepts traditionally dismissed by poststructuralist theory, such as optimism, utopianism, and aesthetic formalism.[66] This text joins their company by placing Victorian aestheticism's defense of autonomous subjectivity within the genealogy of modern queer discourse. Mari Ruti has recently argued that "queer negativity" risks making the rejection of normativity a new norm.[67] Major figures such as Judith Butler promote, she says, "a form of poststructuralist 'essentialism' that forecloses certain conceptual possibilities, such as the idea that autonomy might sometimes be a desirable part of human life." This rejection of the very possibility of subjective autonomy is a position Butler shares with many other queer poststructuralists who, as Ruti claims, "seem obsessively fixated on the idea that the subject must be ground to dust." Although "we are not fully autonomous creatures," Ruti says that this does not mean "we have no capacity for autonomy whatever. . . . [I]n the same way that having an unconscious does not erase the conscious mind but merely complicates its functioning, our lack of seamless autonomy does not render us entirely devoid of it."[68] The fantasy that there exists a completely sovereign, unified, and ahistorical core of self has been definitively exploded by poststructuralism, but an underexplored queer response to this could be, as Snediker writes, the "cultivation of a vocabulary of coherence that more precisely does justice to the ways in which coherence isn't expansively, unilaterally destructive, reductive, or ideological."[69] Although the historical and intellectual conditions Victorian aestheticism responded to are, obviously, different from those modern queer theory addresses, the writings of the aesthetes nevertheless show that it is possible to imagine a sexually nonnormative subject who gains some measure of genuine self-determination through engagement with art.

For the authors discussed in this book, the aesthete is in the perfect position to develop this disposition. To understand how their version of autonomy differs from more traditional renderings of Kant and Hegel, one can look to none other than Foucault and his reassessment of Kantian thought in his late writings. Earlier studies such as *The Order of Things* and *The History of Sexuality* are major statements of poststructuralist anti-humanism, but many critics have asserted that Foucault was never as committed to the death-of-the-subject proposition as both his detractors and supporters believed him to be.[70] This is nowhere more apparent than in his essay "What Is Enlightenment?" (1984), which responds to Kant's essay of the same title. Foucault reaffirms his commitment to the critique of bourgeois humanist ideology but also indicates that Kant's notion of subjective autonomy must be redefined rather than rejected outright. In his three critiques, Kant's project is to determine the absolute limits of the human faculties, yet Foucault says the project of critique must instead be reimagined as the testing of those limits, an attempt to see whether and how they may, in our current historical moment, be extended beyond their supposedly absolute thresholds. He says critique must be "oriented toward the 'contemporary limits of the necessary,' that is, toward what is not or is no longer indispensable for the constitution of ourselves as autonomous subjects."[71] Autonomy, for Foucault and for the queer aesthetes, means nothing more or less than the ability to question what we presently define as the indisputable and natural limits of what we can do and who we can be. The subjective sense of freedom inheres in an individual's ability to carry out this activity, what Foucault calls the "permanent critique of ourselves," which is the "work carried out by ourselves upon ourselves as free beings."[72]

He turns to the writings of another nineteenth-century aesthete, Charles

Baudelaire, to describe the form this permanent critique can take. The "modernity" Baudelaire famously describes does not, he says, "'liberate man in his own being'; it compels him to face the task of producing himself." The autonomous subject does not preexist the act of social critique but is instead constituted through and within the act itself. This work of self-creation does not "have place in society itself, or the body politic." It "can only be produced in another, a different place, which Baudelaire calls art."[73] Rather than transcending society and history, this version of the autonomous subject remains within the matrix of repressive social structures and cultural norms. She can use art and aesthetic experience, however, to reflect critically on her historical moment, to test whether it is possible to envision new modes of seeing, forms of thinking, and ways of living that would expand, rather than totally reject, the contingent limits that define present social conditions. James Muldoon has identified "What Is Enlightenment?" as the clearest expression of the Hegelian legacy in Foucault's thought, despite his emphatic rejection of Hegel in his anti-humanist writings. Although he often explicitly disavowed the connection, Foucault was deeply learned in Hegel's philosophy, and they both engaged with "the Kantian definition of autonomy in order to extend and transform it, rather than rejecting it outright," which led to them both becoming "anti-utopian anti-revolutionaries who support a version of radical reformism."[74]

Queer aesthetes share these qualities and, I argue, inhabit a central but overlooked place in a genealogy of aesthetic theory that leads from Kant and Hegel through Foucault to modern queer theory. Queer aesthetes turned to art, rather than science or politics, to create themselves as free subjects. They did so not to escape into the autonomous aesthetic sphere of bourgeois ideology. Instead, they allowed artistic experience to transform their abject desires into a feeling of liberation that would be efficacious, even for the intellectual conditions of a modern life hostile to notions of sovereign subjectivity. They understood art to be a realm where the commonsense rules of logic are suspended and where the supposedly absolute limits of real-world structures of oppression can be imagined along different lines. In his essay "Poems by William Morris" (1868), Pater says that Greek, medieval, and modern poetry "projects above the realities of its time a world in which the forms of things are transfigured," but the new aesthetic poetry "takes possession" of that transfigured world "and sublimates beyond it another fainter and still more spectral, which is literally an artificial or 'earthly paradise.'" It aims to satisfy "that incurable thirst for the sense of escape, which no actual form of life satisfies, no poetry even, if it be merely simple and spontaneous."[75] Aestheticism does not suppose the existence of an aesthetic sphere totally separate from the world. Instead, they understood that art tests how far the imagination can stretch reality's limits without drifting into meaninglessness. It remains tied to the real world, no matter how faint or spectral that world becomes through art's transformations. It is motivated by the "thirst for escape," the desire to transcend the oppressions of one's time and place, but does not suppose that it is actually possible to untether oneself entirely from one's historical conditions. Such desires are always and inevitably "incurable."

Yet this does not mean the attempt to do so is worthless. The queer aesthete, like the Baudelairean artist, "transfigures the world. His transfiguration does not entail an annulling of reality, but a difficult interplay between the truth of what is real and the exercise of freedom."[76] Art is the realm where one can explore the possibilities of a sustainable queer life, defined not by the limits of immediate social and political reality (a practical impossibility, given the conditions of late Victorian England) but instead within the limits of the human imagination as it exists at that moment in history. It attains the coherent, quasi-conceptual aesthetic form that is the first step toward the possibility of social transformation. Hegelian negativity describes the logic governing this complex interplay, the colossal power that reconfigures perceptions of reality to elicit a revised and renewed sense of individual freedom.

Despite living in a society that easily co-opts our efforts for change into self-discipline, aesthetic philosopher Anita Seppä claims that we exercise genuine personal autonomy when we commit "acts of affirming alternative identities" that perform "critical work on the limits imposed on individuals/ us. . . . The moment one ceases to do what one is expected to do, or transgresses the definitions and limits addressed to one, one starts to utilize power relations. So conceived, *resistance comes first* and remains superior to all other forces inherent in the struggle for power, *for it is resistance that forces power relations to change.*"[77] For the aesthetes, erotic negativity describes how acts of resistance ground a sense of personal coherence. Although subjectivity may become fragmented in the process of affirming one's queerness in a homophobic society, negativity rearranges those fragments into a new subjectivity that maintains unity through dynamic and sustained resistance to coercive power relations.

My highest ambition in this study is to use the vocabulary and concepts provided by the Victorian Aesthetic Movement to defend art as a place where queers can develop a defiant sense of self in a hostile world. Many of us, of course, long desperately for a world where nonnormative desires are no longer stigmatized. Yet the aesthetes demonstrated that even in a culture that defines itself by its rigid enforcement of sexual and gender norms, queerness can be an advantage, insofar as it places one in the vanguard of a form of intellectual and creative freedom not easily attainable by those who never have to question their place in the order of things. It makes one capable of envisioning and bringing into being a world that exists just beyond the horizon of what seems possible within one's historical moment.

～

This book is organized according to overlapping historical and conceptual trajectories. I begin with Pater's initial formulation of erotic negativity through his engagement with Hegel in his early writings. In each subsequent chapter I then pursue focused readings of texts by an author who was inspired by but also departed significantly from Pater's theory. Conceptually, I focus each chapter on an aesthete's revision of a key idea within queer studies: subjectivity, style, performativity, history, and the notion of "queering" itself.

In chapter 1, I show how erotic negativity emerged out of Pater's dissatisfaction with the tired dialectical stalemates he believed defined modern sociopolitical critique. Early essays such as "Diaphaneitè" (1864/95), and "Winckelmann" (1873) deploy Hegelian negativity to redeem queer subjects who have ostensibly failed in their attempts to challenge those paradigms. Recent queer theorists of the "antisocial thesis" have celebrated figures whose ambitions and aims at self-development are thwarted by a homophobic society, portraying failure as a form of resistance. Yet I demonstrate that, for Pater, the queer aesthete transforms a disabling sense of social alienation into a liberating sense of freedom from social strictures. When an artwork elicits the traumatic realization of one's same-sex desires, erotic negativity transforms that shattered self into a consciousness open to relativity, immanence, and conditionality, creating a disposition suited to the intellectual climate of a late Victorian modernity that embraced relative and immanent, rather than transcendent, forms of knowledge. Pater demonstrates how, for queers, artistic representations of same-sex desire break down static notions of the self to create a new vision of the autonomous subject. These early writings challenge moribund intellectual paradigms by exploding the post-Kantian opposition between sexuality and aesthetics that, in many ways, still holds sway in modern critical discourse.

In the next chapter, I explore the process through which Pater made himself into the queer aesthete anticipated by his earlier writings. He develops a version of queer literary style that gives open expression to the negativity structuring the queer aesthete's consciousness. Most theorists of "queer style" associate formal complexity with the closeting of the author. In these accounts, style is the revenant of a traumatic authorial biography that persists within the literary writing, a personal shame that can never quite be overcome by linguistic virtuosity. Yet Pater's late style, by contrast, insists that the subjective process by which the queer aesthete develops his autonomy can be communicated to and experienced by every reader, while at the same time remaining grounded in the specificities of queer experience. He develops this literary form in essays such as "On Wordsworth" (1874), "A Study of Dionysus" (1874), and his novel *Marius the Epicurean* (1885) by turning to the theory of "survivals" devised by the anthropologist Edward Burnett Tylor, his colleague at Oxford. Tylor defines "survivals" as cultural phenomena that have outlived the conditions under which they developed. His anthropological theory allowed Pater to develop a style of writing that draws on the structural homology between the survival's role in the development of human culture and homoerotic desire's role in cultivating the aesthete's subjectivity. By doing so, Pater does not attempt to present queerness in terms a broad readership might understand but instead makes a demand that was, and continues to be, radical: that all readers must aspire to live up to the intellectual and ethical ideals cultivated by queers.

Pater's most famous disciple, Oscar Wilde, is the subject of chapter 3. In contrast to queer theories of performative subjectivity, which celebrate the infinite creative potential of the non-essentialist subject, Wilde articulated a performative theory of lyric negativity, similar to that found in Hegel's account of poetic language. He did so to advance a homoerotic reading of William Shakespeare's sonnets in his novella "The Portrait of Mr. W.H." (1889/ 1921). I focus on Wilde's radical subjectivism, which celebrates the creative potential of anti-essentialist understandings of identity but also cautions against jettisoning notions of subjective autonomy altogether. His characters confront the very limits of their capacity for self-understanding when they attempt to express their sexual desire within language. By doing so, they dramatize the radical negativity of the lyric utterance, when the individual realizes there is no longer any guarantee that the language of self-analysis meaningfully interprets the self from which that language originates and proceeds. This inability to express their homoerotic desires throws Wilde's characters violently back upon their own existence, creating in them a fatal misrecognition: they believe that the inability to articulate their erotic desires indicates the irremediable failure of the self that a homophobic culture associates with queerness, rather than a failure of language. His unnamed narrator, who comes to realize that language can never fully capture the truth of the self, demonstrates how a specifically aesthetic attitude toward erotic desire's resistance to linguistic articulation can provide the ground for a limited yet perdurable form of autonomous subjectivity.

In chapter 4 I turn to another disciple of Pater, the historian, aesthetic theorist, and fiction writer Vernon Lee (Violet Paget). This chapter differs from others in this study by using Hegelian negativity as an interpretive framework for understanding the development of Lee's early career, rather than an explicit topos in her writings. Although Lee, a late Victorian proto-lesbian avant la lettre, was one of Pater's most ardent admirers, she realized his aesthetic philosophy was definitively masculine, insofar as it presupposed the existence of unambiguous historical representations of same-sex desire in art that lesbians could not—and to this day, still cannot—access. Lee's supernatural writings harness the force of erotic negativity to transform a damaging absence of explicit desire between women in the history of art into the material for constructing of a new historical sensibility, one that does not rely on empirical evidence to ground the historicity of lesbian identity. Recent attempts to "queer history" have dismissed coherent chronological accounts of sexual identities as inherently normalizing. Yet in this chapter I argue that Lee used her supernatural tales to construct histories of lesbianism that articulate an autonomous, but not essentialist, sense of queer selfhood for women. In writings from the 1880s and 1890s, such as "Faustus and Helena" (1880), "Oke of Okehurst" (1887), and "Prince Alberic and the Snake Lady" (1896), she develops an aesthetics of ghostliness that, she states, represents "what is beyond and outside the limits of the possible, the rational, the explicable" to demonstrate how queer women could gain a sense of historicity and, thereby, autonomy through their resistance to pathological discourses of same-sex desire. She does so without resorting to a historical empiricism that would affirm an essentialist, transhistorical vision of lesbian identity. Ultimately, though, Lee's supernatural tales look not just back toward the lesbian past but also forward toward the queer future, providing a theory of historical consciousness applicable even to nonnormative sexual identities that have yet be imagined.

Finally, in chapter 5 I discuss Katharine Bradley and Edith Cooper, the two women who wrote poetry under the pseudonym Michael Field. In addition to being aunt and niece, Bradley and Cooper were lesbian lovers, though that did not stop them from developing many erotic attachments throughout their lives that crossed lines of gender and sexuality. The ekphrastic poems in their collection *Sight and Song* (1892) show how aesthetic disinterest enables one to inhabit multiple erotic dispositions that are different from one's own. Departing from Pater's impressionism by focusing on the negativity embodied by the art object itself, rather than the viewing subject, Bradley and Cooper explore how negativity allows one to conceive of an erotized version of Kantian aesthetic indifference. This is the root of their interest in painting, which Hegel characterized as the artistic form par excellence for giving material form to the negative. Modern critics are often tasked to "queer" artworks by revealing their erotically interested subversion of normativity, but Bradley and Cooper show that it is precisely the normativity of disinterested aesthetic judgments that allows viewers to enter nonnormative subject positions. By enabling one to experience what it is like to possess sexual interests foreign to one's own appetites, aesthetic disinterest allows one to regain a sense of subjective autonomy by demonstrating that it is possible to transcend the limitations of one's merely personal desires. It also demonstrates that the aesthetic, as a realm located within the heart of normative social life yet not governed by its predetermined forms of thought, is the venue most suited for queers to imagine how their culture might be radically reformed along practically realizable, nonutopian lines.

For queer Victorian aesthetes, art was the most effective site for resistance to a hostile social world. By restoring aestheticism to the genealogy of queer thought, I seek to demonstrate how the intellectual climate of the late nineteenth century was, like our own, beset by claims seeking to place absolute limits on self-determination by portraying humanity as subject to material forces beyond its control. Yet, by looking back to the aesthetes' portrayal of the singular role art can play in developing one's sense of sexual identity, we can understand that aesthetic experience continues to have value as both a venue for the realization of personal liberation and the affirmation of humanity's collective capacity for freedom.

CHAPTER ONE

Homoerotic Subjectivity in
Walter Pater's Early Essays

On March 17, 1873, Walter Pater received what must have been an unwelcome letter. John Wordsworth, his colleague at Brasenose College, Oxford, was not enthusiastic about the recently published *Studies in the History of the Renaissance* (1873, hereafter *The Renaissance*). Wordsworth stated that Pater's "Conclusion" to that volume, which later readers have taken to be the manifesto of the Victorian Aesthetic Movement, espoused a "philosophy ... that no fixed principles either of religion or morality can be regarded as certain, that the only thing worth living for is momentary enjoyment and that probably or certainly the soul dissolves at death into elements which are destined to never reunite." He warns Pater of the "dangers" into which he is "likely to lead minds weaker than [his] own" and closes declaring, "The difference of opinion which you must be well aware has for some time existed between us must, I fear, become public and avowed, and it may be my duty to oppose you, I hope within the limits of courtesy and moderation, yet openly and without reserve."[1] There is no response to the letter on record, but Pater could not have been entirely surprised that Wordsworth, Brasenose's chaplain, would have found the irreligiousness of the "Conclusion" objectionable. Yet to have this opposition expressed so emphatically by an intimate associate, a man who used to be his private pupil as an undergraduate and a fellow member of the Old Mortality Society (a discussion group formed at Balliol College in 1856) must have been particularly stinging.[2]

Wordsworth was just one of the many members of the intellectual establishment who castigated *The Renaissance*. Despite promises of "courtesy and moderation," he soon became an instigating figure in behind-the-scenes efforts to sideline Pater for a routine promotion to a university proctorship.

College authorities had acquired letters suggesting a dalliance with an undergraduate named William Money Hardinge, an incident that has come to be known among scholars as the "Pater-Hardinge Affair."[3] Although he would remain associated with Oxford until his death in 1894, this event began his lifelong internal exile from the university's intellectual community.[4] The relative ease with which this scandal routed Pater's academic career suggests his colleagues were easily convinced that the "dangers" presented by his unorthodox aesthetic philosophy could be associated with an equally unorthodox sexual disposition.[5]

Intellectually, however, readers and critics of Pater have long struggled to unite the aesthetic and the sexual aspects of his writings. This inability arises from assumptions underlying post-Kantian aesthetic thought about the relationship between aesthetic indifference and sexual desire, assumptions that, I argue in this chapter, Pater's early writings actively sought to undermine. Recent critics have characterized Pater's aestheticism as a principled escape from the explicitly political aesthetics of his major forerunners and influences in Victorian art criticism, such as John Ruskin and Matthew Arnold. Heather Love, for instance, has discussed Pater's exemplification of queer modernism's characteristic rejection of the political, "forged in the image of exile, of refusal, even of failure."[6] Yet I argue that in the daring and iconoclastic essays Pater wrote early in his career, before the damaging attacks on his reputation, he develops an aestheticism that intertwines sexuality and aesthetics to envision a new type of queer subject capable of articulating innovative forms of sociopolitical critique.

Pater's early writings illustrate the difference between Victorian aestheticism's understanding of queer subjectivity and that of modern-day queer theory. Recent queer theorists, like Love, celebrate figures who appear to be failures when judged against normative social standards, the sad creatures who have had their ambitions for self-development thwarted by a homophobic society. Such scholars present failure as a form of social critique, "a way of refusing to acquiesce to dominant logics of power and discipline," in the words of Jack Halberstam.[7] Yet for aesthetes like Pater, queer subjects transform their abjection and alienation into a liberating sense of autonomy from the social strictures causing those feelings. This process brings into being a consciousness compatible with late Victorian culture's increasing skepticism of claims to absolute truth and fixed definitions of the subject. As Pater says at the end of his essay "Winckelmann" (1867), modern science has made it so "that naïve, rough sense of freedom, which supposes man's will to be limited, if at all, only by a will stronger than his, he can never have again." Yet it is nevertheless art's duty "to give the spirit at least an equivalent for the sense of freedom" to replace one's lost sense of self-determination. Although queer aestheticism anticipates queer theory's preoccupation with "failed" subjects, Pater shows that failure by itself is not resistance until it is transformed, through the labor of the negative, into an affirmation of the subject's desires against the coercive forces of normativity. This creates a feeling of personal coherence that is grounded in sustained resistance to social norms.

Pater's theory of erotic negativity was inspired by his readings in Hegel, perhaps the most influential philosophical influence on his early aestheticism. Pater's relationship to Oxford Idealism has been traced extensively by literary historians.[8] In addition to the numerous explicit references to Hegel throughout his writings, we know that he began his education as a star pupil of Benjamin Jowett, the dominant intellectual figure in mid-Victorian Oxford and a champion of German idealism in Britain, who would have almost certainly introduced Hegel's writings to one of his most promising students.[9] Ingram Bywater states that Pater read the *Phenomenology of Spirit* (1807) in the original German during the long vacation of 1862, and his library records indicate that he borrowed Hegel's *Lectures on the History of Philosophy* (1825–26), *Science of Logic* (1817), *Lectures on Aesthetics* (1835), and *Logic* (1830) between the spring of 1862 and winter of 1864.[10] Pater's biographer Thomas Ward says that, after losing his star status and gaining a disappointing second-class degree in the "Literae Humaniores" course, he owed his fellowship at Brasenose to his knowledge of German philosophy.[11]

Hegelianism, and German idealism more generally, was de rigueur at Oxford during the second half of the nineteenth century. As Kirk Willis claims, it appeared to "provide either a doctrine of religious consolation or an ethic of social duty" for liberal intellectuals convinced by Darwin's theory of evolution and Strauss's Higher Criticism of the Bible, "offering its own brand of secular transcendentalism and spirituality as well as its unique mechanism of intellectual and historical evolution."[12] For Hegel, ideas, individuals, and cultures are not static entities but develop over time, moving progressively from states of incompleteness toward increasing freedom and self-sufficiency, culminating in a state he calls "the Absolute" where, as Yirmiyahu Yovel explains, "an autonomous—that is, truly free—individual" finds herself "at home in society and the universe" that provide "self-sustaining ('absolute') meaning to human life and the world's existence."[13] Because Pater's Oxford Idealist contemporaries were drawn to Hegel for the spiritual solace they believed his philosophy to offer, they gave a positive spin to the dialectic that emphasized its harmonious and reconciliatory aspects.[14]

Pater's interest in sexuality as a disruptive and transformative force drew him to an element of Hegel's dialectic that his more optimistic colleagues neglected: what the *Phenomenology* refers to as "the colossal power of the negative."[15] Negativity drives Hegel's dialectic, breaking down anything that threatens to become static and imbuing it with the movement it needs to develop toward the Absolute. Despite the creative energy it unleashes, the negative is also, by necessity, damaging and painful. Hegel says that "the life of the spirit is not a life that shuns death and bewares destruction, keeping clean of it; it is a life that bears and maintains itself in it. Spirit only gains its truth by finding itself in absolute rupture. Spirit is that power . . . only in so far as it looks the negative in the face and dwells in it. This dwelling is the magic force which converts the negative into being."[16] Negativity includes not only the intellectual process of critique, where concepts are broken down by the analytical intelligence to create new ideas, but material and historical forces such as "suffering, passion, war, destruction, falsehood, violence," Yovel states, which Hegel conceives of as "organic constituents of truth and spirit's growth and actuality."[17] The "spirit" of individuals and societies cannot develop by positive means alone. The negative must be embraced in its full destructive energy, "looked at in the face" as a necessary constituent of spirit's growth. This is not done for the sake of cultivating stoic indifference to human suffering. Instead, negativity must be followed to its very endpoint, because it ultimately creates the dynamic energy necessary for individual and cultural change.

To imagine an immanent form of subjective autonomy that does not require the Absolute, Pater's early writings reconceived Hegelian negativity outside of his metaphysical system. These essays inaugurate Victorian aestheticism's interpretation of negativity as a fundamentally aesthetic phenomenon. It is through this reimagining that the negative becomes, in Robert Kaufman's words, the "engine for new, experimental—because previously non-existent (and therefore free of status quo determined)—concepts," one that "offers formal means for allowing new (and not necessarily utopian) aspects of contemporary society to come into view."[18] Similarly, Pater's aesthetic impressionism, his injunction to develop "a certain kind of temperament, the power of being deeply moved by the presence of beautiful objects," entails "active as well as passive receptivity: it suggests a constructive, or reconstructive, faculty in relation to the objects to whose impact oneself susceptible," as Adam Parkes asserts.[19] Pater reimagines negativity as the process by which a powerful beauty transforms the queer subject's passive endurance of pain and suffering into the active construction of radically new visions of the self and the world. By eliminating Hegel's metaphysical ideal, Pater also redefines subjective autonomy not as a goal only to be achieved when one reaches the Absolute but as a state that can be achieved immanently, within artistic experience itself. Pater, and the queer aesthetes who followed him, defined this new version of subjective autonomy as the ability to persist in new ways of seeing and being elicited by the encounter with the negative, and to resist the coercive force of normative social structures. In his essays written during the 1860s, Pater shows his readers that, when "failed" queer subjects are looked at through the lens of aesthetic negativity, it becomes clear their alienation from society is what allowed them to pioneer a new vision of artistically inspired personal freedom.

In early essays such as "Diaphaneitè" (1864/95) and "Winckelmann" (1867), Pater examines subjects who superficially appear not to have realized their ambitions. In the former, he describes a general type of human being defined by "impotence" and "ineffectual wholeness of nature," and in the latter, he focuses on the eighteenth-century German art historian Johann Joachim Winckelmann, who was murdered before he could see in person the original Greek statues that were the objects of his scholarly and erotic attachment, and before meeting Johann Wolfgang von Goethe, whose writings on Winckelmann were the reason the art historian was still remembered in the late nineteenth century. Pater uses these figures to demonstrate the role eroticism plays in the cultivation of new aesthetic perceptions and, in turn, how artistic experience facilitates the development of sexual self-awareness in a homophobic culture. The traumatic realization of one's same-sex desire is cancelled yet reconstituted in the dialectical process of crafting a definitively modern intellectual disposition, one that transforms negativity's destructiveness into a consciousness open to relativity, immanence, and conditionality. This creates a critical disposition suited to the intellectual climate of the late nineteenth century that embraces what Pater calls the "relative spirit," where "nothing can be rightly known, except relatively and under conditions."[20] In "Diaphaneitè," he provides a figure for this powerful beauty in the "diaphanous being," the embodiment of negativity in the form of what Hegel refers to as "contradiction." The diaphanous being's most direct challenge to the definition of the universal human subject is expressed by its "moral sexlessness," a phrase he repeats in his later essay on Winckelmann to describe the late eighteenth-century art historian's same-sex desires. In "Winckelmann," he finds in this central figure in modern aesthetic philosophy a model for homophobic cultural conditions of modernity, where the newly emergent identity of the "homosexual" rendered desire between men a source of alienation, rupture, and terror. Yovel describes Hegel's account of the self's development as "a series of negations which do not return the process to its point of departure, but rather each negation constitutes a new state of affairs, and a new state of consciousness."[21] Winckelmann's life is an example of how discovering one's homoerotic desires elicits the negativity driving the development of consciousness through self-shattering encounters that break down static notions of selfhood, with the aim of creating a new vision of the autonomous subject.

Pater between Aesthetics and Sexuality

Despite Pater's commitment to a vision of powerful beauty capable of tarrying with the negative, critics have continued to associate his aestheticism with the powerless beauty of bourgeois aesthetic autonomy. Even his defenders have ascribed to him and his followers what Kaufman calls the "essentialist or transcendental ideology of literary-cultural value" that seeks to escape entirely "the material, the social, and the historical."[22] The result has been that, whenever Pater discusses sexuality in his writings, critics present these moments as unrelated to his interest in the aesthetic and vice versa.

His critics reproduce the divide between sexuality and aesthetics that has haunted the post-Kantian philosophy of art. According to Whitney Davis, the development of modern aesthetic theory is characterized by the division between aesthetic judgment and sexual attraction, with the former associated with "a person's mature judgments of taste in the context of his or her immediate present-day encounters with objects in nature and in works of art," and the latter "defined as merely a preliminary stage in the canonical teleology of such judgments, especially in relation to the 'perfected ideals' supposedly projected in normatively beautiful works of art."[23] The rise of aesthetics as a field of philosophical inquiry in the eighteenth century featured an insistence on the conceptual distinction between these two realms, under the assumption that sexual desire was merely personal and must be transcended in order to attain a properly "disinterested" experience of beauty. This theory was given its most influential expression by Kant, who argued that disinterested aesthetic judgments testify to humanity's capacity for true freedom and autonomy, insofar as they evidence her or his ability to make judgments that are not reducible to mere practical usefulness or biological appetite.

The split between aesthetics and sexuality has meant that the political vision of Pater's work has been misrepresented throughout the history of his reception. The intermingling of art and sex has long been a source of consternation both for his detractors and his admirers. Although details of the Hardinge affair did not become public until nearly one hundred years after Pater's death, the homoerotic suggestiveness of his writings meant that rumors about his sexuality were not limited to backroom university chatter but were part of his public reputation, influencing his posthumous reception.[24] Former Oxford undergraduate W. H. Mallock's parodic novel *The New Republic* (1876/77) presented a thinly veiled caricature of Pater as the hedonist Mr. Rose, who makes grandiose proclamations about the nature of art while receiving homoerotic poems from young men.[25] The thrust of Mallock's satire is that Pater's aesthetic theories are a mask for his disordered sexual desires. *The New Republic* only exacerbated the damage the Hardinge affair did to Pater's image, causing him to withdraw his name as a candidate for the Slade Professorship of Poetry in 1876.[26] His reputation continued to decline after his death in 1894, especially in the wake of the trials for "gross indecency" of his most famous student, Oscar Wilde, in 1895. Although a handful of early twentieth-century gay authors continued to hold him in high esteem, Lesley Higgins notes that male modernists rejected Victorian aestheticism as a precursor "to protect modernist discourse (and most especially its enunciators) from the doubly-tainted undertones of effeminacy and homosexuality so often associated with Pater."[27] Homophobic dismissal continued to be the dominant attitude toward him until as late as 1965, when René Wellek claimed in the authoritative *History of Modern Criticism* that "today Pater is under a cloud."[28]

Beginning in the final third of the twentieth century, however, Pater's critical fortunes rose precipitously, largely because of the gradual waning of anti-Victorian modernist attitudes in literary studies. Yet his scholarly recovery has been strongly bifurcated between those who emphasize his philosophical bona fides and those who emphasize his participation in the homoerotic culture of Victorian aestheticism. This critical split can partially be attributed to changing attitudes toward homosexuality in the twentieth century. Pater's early champions during the recovery phase, such as U. C. Knoepflmacher, David DeLaura, and Gerald Monsman, were part of a culture whose homophobia was not terribly far removed from that of the Victorians.[29] They saw intellectual history as a safe foundation from which to rebuild his reputation as a champion of Victorian religious humanism, a much more respectable context than Wildean decadence. These studies characterized the seriousness of Pater's intellectual engagements as occurring despite, rather than because of, his affiliations with the Aesthetic Movement. Although they say nothing explicitly homophobic, Monsman's brief nod toward claims about Pater's sexuality, followed by the hasty conclusion that "there is no biographical evidence to indicate abnormal behavior," is characteristic of the defensive attitude these studies took.[30] The religious-humanist approach established intellectual historicism as the dominant approach to his writings and gave rise to accomplished studies by Billie Andrew Inman, F. C. McGrath, Carolyn Williams, and William F. Shuter, among others.[31] Although these were some of the first works of scholarship to make explicit and unapologetic reference to homoerotic themes in Pater's writings, they do not place his sexuality in relation to the development of his aesthetic philosophy: sex seemed implicitly beyond the purview of aesthetic-intellectual concerns.

This has remained the case even in studies that take Pater's sexuality as their explicit focus. With the advent of LGBT studies beginning in the 1970s and 1980s and queer theory in the 1990s, "it is no longer necessary to argue that same-sex desire is a relevant or worthwhile topic in Pater studies," as Love has stated.[32] Stefano Evangelista says that his writings represent "one of the earliest attempts to define a modern gay sensibility" in literature, and Michael F. Davis has gone as far as to call Pater perhaps the "first queer theorist."[33] The guiding assumption is that Paterian aestheticism freed its practitioners from Victorian sexual strictures by releasing art from its obligation to be moral. As discussed in the introduction, the dominant approach of critics interested in the sexuality of aestheticism has been to analyze the complexities of Pater's prose as aiding in the development of a "code," "aesthetic minoritizing discourse," or "mask" for the expression of same-sex desire.[34] They argue that his writings prefigured the Foucauldian reverse discourse of homosexuality, its veiled language a clandestine first attempt to defend desire between men and establish a nascent gay community in the face of social stigma.

It is undoubtedly true that Pater's notable, yet still less than explicit, invocations of homoerotic desire were a response to a culture that insisted on discretion in public speech surrounding sex between men. However, the problem with "homosexual code" readings is that, as Sara Lyons aptly notes, they "reduce" aestheticism "to a mask discourse, and make its preoccupation with art seem incidental to other, more important ends—arguably, the very instrumentalist logic that aestheticism aimed to circumvent."[35] Reading the language of aesthetics as an encryption of same-sex desire repeats the same binary opposition between sexuality and aesthetics that has structured homophobic interpretations of Pater from the nineteenth century onward.

A previous generation of critics sought to redeem Pater by suggesting that he appealed to a sense of beauty divorced from his merely personal sexual interests, but those who champion his "coding" imply that the political relevance of his work lies in hiding its transgressions within merely superficial gestures toward aesthetic disinterestedness.[36] This divide persists in recent studies that aim to revive the intellectual-historical approach to Pater, in the suggestion that taking his aesthetics seriously requires a willingness to bracket issues of sexuality: Benjamin Morgan insists that Pater's "interest in aesthetic freedom" along Kantian and Hegelian lines "grounds the politics of his work in a way that does not depend on its subversive queerness," and although Kate Hext acknowledges "the connection between homoerotic desire and aesthetic appreciation" in Pater's writings, she nevertheless states that, for him, "desire is ultimately superseded by the aesthetic realm."[37]

Yet Pater's writings demand that readers think beyond this either/or logic. In a notable exception to coded readings of Pater's sexuality, Jesse Matz presents his aesthetics as a fusion of "intellect and sense" that "could move in and out of consciousness, that could find an object's fixity in the veracity of subjective flux." Figuring this union "as a homosexual relationship," allows him to justify same-sex desire and place "social intersubjectivity," rather than the isolated bourgeois subject, at the heart of aesthetic experience.[38] When the process Matz describes is understood to be part of Pater's concerted effort to overturn recent Western philosophy's history of de-eroticizing the aesthetic, it becomes clear that the relationship between aesthetics and sexuality is dialectical in nature. His writings show how what looks like the "failure" of queer subjects can be reframed as their refusal to adhere strictly to the laws governing everyday life and logic. Instead, they use their faculty of aesthetic perception to facilitate the acquisition of sexual self-knowledge and, in turn, allow their erotic desire to catalyze the development of a new mode of seeing themselves and their relationship to the world. This insight was inspired by his deep knowledge of Hegel's dialectical negativity.

"The History of a Certain Failure"

One of the central principles of the queer antisocial thesis, derived from Leo Bersani's powerful critique of the "culture of redemption" associated with art's transformative powers, is that attempts to redeem queer suffering and turn it to positive account arrogate these experiences into (hetero)normative narratives of development.[39] This notion is at the heart of Love's insistence "on the importance of clinging to ruined identities and to histories of injury" and Halberstam's vaunting of "counterhegemonic modes of common sense" that "lead to the association of failure with nonconformity, anticapitalist practices, nonreproductive life styles, negativity, and critique."[40] Queer critiques of redemptive ideology echo one of the standard criticisms of Hegel's dialectic that has persisted from the nineteenth century onward. Many have claimed that his concept of negation-as-development subsumes difference into the dominant master narrative of the Absolute. For his critics, Hegel's dialectic is a steamroller: it flattens all differences into a spurious unity and forces individual and cultural trauma into the facile, bourgeois optimism characteristic of progress narratives.[41]

Despite Pater's youthful training in Hegelian philosophy, his firm stances against claims to absolute truth might suggest that he shares this critique. Inman states that Pater had "the peculiar habit of assuming that a hard, re-nunciatory attitude accompanied the tendency to seek Absolute truth."[42] This has led William Shuter and Kate Hext to argue that Pater dismissed Hegelian thought when he began writing seriously about art, embracing a position epitomized by his statement in the "Conclusion" that we must never acquiesce "to a facile orthodoxy of Comte, or of Hegel, or our own."[43] Although it is true Pater was uninterested in Hegel's metaphysical system, classing it as one of the "metaphysical questions, as unprofitable as metaphysical questions elsewhere" he famously eschews in the preface to *The Renaissance*, he never stopped being interested in Hegel's dialectic as a *method* of understanding the world (*R* 189).[44] His deployment of Hegel in his own writings treats the reality of the Absolute as a matter of indifference. Although Pater is famous for taking something of a grab-bag approach to his intellectual sources, which has led to accusations of inconsistent or facile thinking, there is an internal logic to his creative and sometimes unorthodox revisioning of Hegelian insights to his own queer ends.

In contrast to queer theorists who celebrate failure itself as a sufficient critique of a culture of redemption, Pater found in Hegel's dialectic a method for conceiving of negativity not simply as failure but as a necessary component in the history of human development. In an unpublished manuscript written during the 1880s, he attempts to write a history of philosophy in the spirit of negativity, echoing Hegel's rhetoric in his stated intention to compose a history of philosophy not "constructively," as it is usually written, but instead in "a destructive spirit," as "the history of a certain failure." Pater indicates his investment in negativity as a form of historical understanding most strongly in his description of Hegel himself, whom he characterizes as an essentially skeptical thinker, rather than the optimistic theorist of the Absolute embraced by his British Idealists colleagues:

> Hegel, who brings to its highest level of completeness the metaphysical reconstruction of all experience as a realisation of the creative Logic, must yet rank in his actual though indirect influence of many minds, as an essentially sceptical writer, though <by> the impression he leaves upon them, of a very imperfect reciprocity between the exacting reasonableness of the ideal he supposes, and the confused, imperfect, haphazard character of man's actual experience in nature and history—a radical dualism in his system, as to the extent of which he was perhaps not always quite candid, even with himself.[45]

Critics have taken this passage to indicate that Pater rejected Hegel later in his life, but his comments can be more properly understood as a critique of dominant Victorian readings of the dialectic that overemphasize "the exacting reasonableness of the ideal he supposes" over the "essentially sceptical" quality of his thought, the fact that Hegel's philosophy makes us all the more aware of the gap between daily existence and the autonomy and freedom promised by the Absolute.[46]

Despite the "radical dualism" he finds in Hegel's system, Pater knows that, as a method, the dialectic is "influential" because it calls attention to "the imperfect reciprocity" between the ideal and "the confused, imperfect, haphazard character of man's actual experience." In fact, as James Muldoon remarks, the growing consensus in present-day Hegel scholarship is that "it would be unsympathetic to characterise Hegel as having an overly idealised or fully progressive understanding of history . . . [, n]or is Hegel's phenomenology a description of the progress of a rational inevitability." Instead, his phenomenological method "can be viewed as a meticulous search through the historical past for problems, conflicts and moments of contradiction that illuminate key moments in the gradual struggle and development of humanity." These are not to be found "in ideal or heroic deeds" but rather, to use

Pater's words, in "the history of a certain failure."[47] Rather than rejecting Hegel, it would be more accurate to say that Pater asks for a reinterpretation of his dialectic, one that actually hews more closely to negativity's radical implications than his philosophical colleagues (or, occasionally, Hegel himself) wanted to admit.

Unlike his contemporaries, Pater valued the dialectical method not because it offered a theory of historical progress but because negativity provided a way of understanding how meaningful transformations occur in consciousness over time, despite the self's existence in a continuous state of flux. Yovel explains that, for Hegel, until the Absolute is achieved the subject is never stable but instead "in the process of becoming, a selfhood which will not actually exist until it reaches the end of the road. In other words, as long as the process is still ongoing there is no *actual* subject."[48] Because Hegel recognizes that the Absolute cannot be achieved in the current moment but must be deferred to some future time, he provided Pater a model for understanding how consciousness undergoes meaningful transformations without ever solidifying into static complacency. The trick would be to show how this constant process of aesthetic transformation-within-flux could be a viable replacement for the Absolute itself, now reconceived as the means to maintain one's freedom from preordained systems of thought. In his essay "Diaphaneitè," Pater represents this powerful beauty as the diaphanous being, an individual whose apparent failure to achieve anything of practical import in the world embodies the transformative force of negativity that Hegel refers to as "contradiction."

Embodying Contradiction: "Diaphaneitè"

Despite its brevity (only eight pages in the printed version), the enigmatic and densely written "Diaphaneitè" is "a kind of manifesto for Pater's subsequent work," as Anne Varty states, but one that "does not easily yield its meaning."[49] According to Monsman, it met with considerable controversy when first delivered to the Old Mortality Society despite the "avowedly 'radical'" outlook shared by members such as the art historian and defender of homosexuality John Addington Symonds, British Idealist philosophers T. H. Green and Edward Caird, and the soon-to-be-infamous poet A. C. Swinburne.[50]

Although "Diaphaneitè" is not explicitly homoerotic, its subtly transgressive nature is suggested by the fact that it was not published until after Pater's death more than thirty years after its composition. His literary executor, Charles Shadwell, whose physical attractions allegedly inspired the composition, included it with, in his words, "some hesitation" in the posthumous collection *Miscellaneous Studies* (1895).[51] In this piece, Pater describes a "basement," or fundamental "type" whose "divine beauty," he says, could "be the regeneration of the world" (*MS* 222).

Part of the essay's difficulty lies in Pater's contradictory claims for what I will refer to as the "diaphanous being" (Pater never gives this type a name). Although its capacity for cultural regeneration has suggested to Monsman and Williams a revolutionary "aesthetic hero" come to save Victorian society from its philistine materialism, Pater refuses to associate the diaphanous being's transformative beauty with the hero's characteristic ability to impose his will successfully upon the world, what Thomas Carlyle famously refers to in his essay "On Heroes, Hero-Worship, and the Heroic in History" (1841) as "Courage and the Faculty to do."[52] It is closer in spirit to John Stuart Mill's description of the "genius" who claims nothing but the "freedom to point out the way" to others. Unlike Mill's genius, however, diaphanous beings do not ground their freedom in "strong character" and the ability to "break their fetters" to social custom.[53] The diaphanous being's version of autonomy is paradoxically recessive: it "is the spirit that sees external circumstances as they are, its own power and tendencies as they are, and realises the given conditions of its life, not disquieted by the desire for change, or the preference of one part in life rather than another, or passion, or opinion" (*MS* 216). Yet such beings inspire a unique kind of "revolutionism," one that abjures "violence" and is instead "softened, harmonised, subdued as by distance. It is the revolutionism of one who has slept a hundred years" (*MS* 219–20). The diaphanous being embodies a form of active passivity, which Pater expresses figuratively as an "entire transparency of nature"—the diaphanous quality referred to in the essay's title (*MS* 219).

For many critics attuned to the erotic implications of Pater's essay, the diaphanous being he describes has seemed paradigmatic of the failed queer subject, felled by the machinations of a punitive society. Despite the notably abstract nature of the diaphanous being's desires, Dowling and Dellamora claim that Pater's essay indicates his anxieties about representing homosexuality in a homophobic environment, while other readers, such as Morgan and Hext, argue that he expresses the essentially apolitical nature of his aestheticism, giving a "swansong to society" and affirming the value of personal artistic experience over social engagement.[54] Jacques Khalip and Heather Love ascribe Pater's rejection of the social to his resigned acceptance of Victorian culture's intractable homophobia, with the essay recording his dejected retreat from a society he imagines will never have a place for people like him.[55]

Yet "Diaphaneitè" does not dismiss queer aestheticism as a force for cultural transformation. Pater's essay is difficult not because it accedes to homophobia but because it provides a new set of conceptual procedures for effecting social change. These were inspired both by his homoerotic desire and his readings in Hegelian idealism. The diaphanous being embodies negativity in the form Hegel calls "contradiction." In the *Science of Logic*, which Pater read the year before he wrote the essay, Hegel describes contradiction as the form negativity takes within philosophical logic. Contradictions, such as the diaphanous being's passive heroism, are not intellectual impasses but instead the "root of all movement and vitality" in thought. "It is only in so far as something has a contradiction within it," Hegel states, that it "moves, has an urge and activity."[56] Everyday life and language are limited by their commitment to an Aristotelian law of noncontradiction, the commonsense notion that something cannot be both *x* and not-*x* at the same time. This rule works well enough in situations that call for practical deliberation, but it stymies the speculative forms of thought necessary for intellectual and social progress. Because common sense can understand oppositions only as what he calls in the *Phenomenology* "lifeless and inert determination," it cannot imagine the new constellations of concepts that might exist beyond seemingly intractable differences.[57] For Hegel, philosophical innovation requires embracing contradiction: holding two apparently opposed ideas together at the same time inaugurates new patterns of thought that push against dialectical stalemates.

The diaphanous being transforms contradiction into a way of life. Rather than fitting into preexisting categories, which Pater says "work . . . in and by means of the main current of the world's energy," diaphanous beings "fill up the blanks between contrasted types of characters" (*MS* 215). They are individuals whom the world cannot transform into instruments to realize its own ends, as either a "service" or an "ideal" (*MS* 215). They do not depend on the perceptions of others to constitute their identities. The diaphanous being's paradoxically heroic passivity pushes beyond the dialectical opposition between passive and active, showing how it is possible to live not only beyond this conceptual contradiction but beyond all socially recognized identity categories.

Yet these revolutionary individuals often go unnoticed by the world, Pater states, because it has "no place ready in its affections" for them (*MS* 216). He suggests to his audience that they perceive the diaphanous being's contradictions aesthetically, rather than through the limiting and distorting lens of everyday logic. Williams observes that "the fact that [the diaphanous being] remains 'unclassified' testifies to its aesthetic value, for the world cannot 'use' it, even for contemplation."[58] It takes the "disinterestedness" of aesthetic perception—Kant's notion that the experience of beauty is defined by the absence of the viewer's merely personal desires and appetites—and embodies it as a way of being in the world, much as if it were an art object come to life: "The spirit which it forms is the very opposite of that which regards life as a game of skill," Pater states, "and values things and persons as marks or counters of something to be gained, or achieved, beyond them. It seeks to value everything at its eternal worth, not adding to it, or taking from it, the amount of influence it may have for or against its own special scheme of life" (*MS* 216). Pater presents the diaphanous being as an aesthetic object to emphasize that it is not, as Diana Coole says of Hegelian contradiction, "some alien force (a hidden god or essence), but . . . the unrepresentable process of becoming in which reason is itself caught and which aesthetics perhaps captures more successfully."[59] It is only when the diaphanous being is perceived aesthetically that it can be understood not as an abject figure existing beyond the pale of respectable society but instead as what Pater calls "a kind of prophecy of repose and simplicity" that it "is indeed within the limits of man's destiny" to live beyond socially recognized types and categories (*MS* 217).

Diaphanous beings are, in this way, similar to ancient Greek sculptures. Pater states, "The beauty of the Greek statues was a sexless beauty; the statues of the gods had the least traces of sex. Here there is a kind of moral sexlessness, a kind of impotence, and ineffectual wholeness of nature, yet with a divine beauty and significance of its own" (*MS* 220). Dellamora notes that the quality Pater refers to here is "the tendency in Greek statuary . . . to conflate aspects of male and female body-types in single forms whether male, female, or literally hermaphroditic. In this way Greek sculptors refrained from sexualizing sculptural form."[60] What Pater most wants his audience to recognize, however, is that diaphanous beings are living embodiments of this aesthetic form existing in the present, "like a relic from a classical age, laid open by accident to our alien modern atmosphere" (*MS* 219). Rather than actively militating against cultural norms, diaphanous beings passively demonstrate the ability to exist beyond the contemporary world's binary definitions of the self, the paradigm of which is the splitting of humanity into two complementary genders, the so-called opposite sexes. Stefani Engelstein argues that sex-

ual "complementarity—the idea that men and women have distinct but re-
ciprocally attuned bodies, attributes, and dispositions, so that they together,
as a heterosexual couple, create a single, functional unit" remains at the center of notions of the autonomous liberal subject, a holdover from eighteenth-
century theories of the organism mediated by the German romantic idealist
tradition of Kant, Johann Gottlieb Fichte, and Friedrich Schlegel. Complementarity is "manifested both physically, in sexual union, and morally, in the
newly validated affect of love, thus conforming to the dual nature of the
human."[61] Conversely, Pater draws upon the same idealist intellectual tradition to show how the morally sexless diaphanous being militates against
this by synthesizing a premodern physical ideal of hermaphroditism with the
modern ideal of the emancipated human subject. For Pater, opposition to the
gender binary is the most profound distinction the diaphanous being abjures,
showing that it is possible to live beyond the primordial categorical distinction that supposedly encompasses all of humanity.

"Diaphaneitè" registers Pater's hope that morally sexless outsiders might
be perceived aesthetically rather than logically, as proof that there are viable
ways of existing beyond social constraints and alternative ways of imagining
the self. By embodying the aesthetic's ability to introduce new concepts to
the world through its detachment from socially predetermined ways of thinking, the diaphanous being's "clear crystal nature" acts as a prism, refracting
and scattering cultural homophobia into an emancipatory version of queer
identity (*MS* 220). To challenge social norms directly by affirming a concrete
alternative course of action or system of values is, as he states in the "Conclusion," simply to replace one "facile orthodoxy" with another (*R* 189). Instead,
the diaphanous being persists in its own sexual singularity, allowing its continued existence within an indifferent society to present an aesthetic challenge to prevailing definitions of the subject.

Though Pater is careful to indicate that moral sexlessness can manifest
itself in either sex—he states that Dante's Beatrice and Charlotte Corday both
display diaphanous qualities—he obviously considers the diaphanous being
to be indicatively male. The quality of diaphanousness can, he says, be "felt
like a sweet aroma in early manhood," and his primary historical example
of the type is Raphael (*MS* 220). Unlike the more combative and socially engaged "Luther and Spinoza," Pater says of the painter that "in the midst of the
Reformation and the Renaissance, himself lighted up by them, yielded himself to neither, but stood still to live upon himself, even in outward form a
youth, almost an infant, yet surprising all the world" (*MS* 220). "Diaphaneitè"

presents morally sexless masculinity as one of the diaphanous being's definitive qualities, but Pater would soon suggest that submerged under this apparent asexuality was the presence of male homoerotic desire. This is most apparent in the essay on Winckelmann he wrote three years later. Just as Pater recounts how the eighteenth-century art historian discovered the homoeroticism underlying the apparently disinterested aesthetic ideal of ancient Greek sculpture, so too does Pater himself discover the potent, yet socially condemned, sexuality hidden within his diaphanous ideal.

Winckelmann's Erotic Negativity

In "Winckelmann," Pater describes a diaphanous being brought to life in concrete historical circumstances. He finds this figure in Johann Joachim Winckelmann, the eighteenth-century German art historian and archeologist. This essay spurred the project that would eventually become *The Renaissance*, the theoretical foundation of the Aesthetic Movement. Although "Winckelmann" is the only essay in that collection that does not focus on early modern France or Italy, it is the longest and, by many accounts, most substantial study in terms of research and intellectual content. Although today it is less well known than the widely anthologized "Conclusion," it received the most care and attention of any of the essays and is the central text for understanding the relationship between sexual and artistic experience in Pater's aestheticism and its legacy in the writings of later queer aesthetes.

Alex Potts notes that "Pater, as a British writer, was making in Winckelmann a very unusual choice of intellectual hero" in contrast to the more iconic Goethe, whose Hellenism was inspired by Winckelmann's writings.[62] At the time, Winckelmann was a decidedly secondary figure in cultural history compared to his more famous disciple, a man whose life was cut short before he could fully realize his intellectual and artistic ambitions. Although Pater's essay is ostensibly a review of Henry Lodge's 1850 translation of Winckelmann's *History of Ancient Art among the Greeks* and Otto Hahn's *Biographische Aufsätze*, Evangelista notes that "it is also a biographical study of Winckelmann in its own right; it is a critique of ancient Greek art and a critique of Winckelmann's critique of ancient Greek art, [and] it is itself written in the style of Winckelmann's *History of Ancient Art among the Greeks*, using the study of aesthetic questions to offer a total characterisation of the culture a past age."[63] Pater finds in Winckelmann a kindred spirit, someone who, like him, aspired to introduce to humankind a new way of perceiving the world through the erotics of aesthetic experience. It has long been a critical commonplace to see Pater's writing as an indirect form of autobiography.[64] He uses Winckelmann to think about how his own writings about aesthetics can be a new form of social critique, a portrait of the art critic as diaphanous being.[65] Pater directly inserts the passage from "Diaphaneitè" on the moral sexlessness of Greek statues to describe Winckelmann's historical insights into ancient Greek sculpture.[66] If that earlier essay is Pater's attempt to train an audience to perceive diaphanous beings as aesthetic harbingers of a new form of subjective autonomy, then "Winckelmann" is about how a diaphanous being can himself inspire this new vision. It is also in this essay that Pater identifies the manifestation of Winckelmann's moral sexlessness as the expression of homosexual desire in a homophobic culture.

"Winckelmann" fulfills the diaphanous being's promise to bring about the "regeneration of the world" by showing it is possible to lead a viable life beyond prevailing heteronormative definitions of human subjectivity. In addition to being the most explicitly homoerotic text in Pater's oeuvre, "Winckelmann" also shows him to be the Aesthetic Movement's most incisive philosophical thinker. The knowledge of German idealism that won Pater his academic position at Brasenose is nowhere more spectacularly on display. He presents an account of Winckelmann's life that takes special care to emphasize his breathless descriptions of statues of beautiful young men. In addition to his decisive importance in the development of the discipline of art history, Winckelmann is also an important figure in the development of the philosophy of art: his writings directly inspired the aesthetics of Kant and Hegel and, through them, the modern Western tradition of aesthetic theory.[67]

Potts and Evangelista both see "Winckelmann" as Pater's attempt to explore "the new modern consciousness" of sexuality's "constitutive role in definitions of the self."[68] Yet I argue that Pater goes beyond this to conceive of how, in a homophobic culture, homosexuality can be turned to one's advantage, to articulate a new vision of subjective autonomy. His response to cultural homophobia is not to defend the dignity of desire between men as part of the Foucauldian reverse discourse. Instead, he presents art as the preeminent vehicle through which powerful yet socially proscribed desire can transform into something more than itself, a force eliciting a subjectivity that embraces the relative spirit of intellectual modernity. In "Winckelmann," Pater establishes that this modern form of selfhood belongs superlatively to the queer aesthete.

According to Pater, Winckelmann inaugurated an entirely new way of looking at art and, through that, pioneered a new mode of relating to the world.

Pater begins the essay with his own translation from Hegel's *Aesthetics* that portrays Winckelmann as the ideal aesthete: "Winckelmann, by contemplation of the ideal works of the ancients, received a sort of inspiration, through which he opened a new sense for the study of art. He is to be regarded as one of those who, in the sphere of art, have known how to initiate a new organ for the human spirit."[69] Winckelmann's art-historical writings provided the foundation for Hegel's own theoretical account of the historically evolving relationship between art and the culture that produces it. He achieved his distinctly modern perception of the world, his "new organ," by paradoxically turning to the classical past for inspiration, which in turn inspired his fresh insights into ancient Greek sculpture. To explain how this historical interchange was possible, Pater focuses on the homoerotic quality of Winckelmann's appreciation of ancient sculpture and its effect on his psychological development in his own eighteenth-century context.

He states that Winckelmann's writing exhibited a creative energy that broke down outworn intellectual commonplaces about ancient Greek art. This is most apparent in the art historian's attunement to the erotics of the male body, which allowed him to identify the sexual motivations that inspired the original creation of the artworks in ancient Greece. "He fingers those pagan marbles," Pater suggestively states, "with unsinged hands" ("W" 89). More than any previous biographer of Winckelmann, Pater places special emphasis on the homoerotic quality, what he calls the "temperament," of his critical writings, a feature that had been, in Davis's words, "straightened out" by Kant's de-eroticized account of aesthetic disinterest.[70] Conversely, that Winckelmann's "affinity with Hellenism was not merely intellectual, that the subtler threads of temperament were inwoven in it, is proved by his romantic, fervent friendships with young men. He has known, he says, many young men more beautiful than Guido's archangel. These friendships, bringing him in contact with the pride of human form, and staining his thoughts with its bloom, perfected his reconciliation with the spirit of Greek sculpture" ("W" 87). Pater asserts that Winckelmann's insights into classical art were not arrived at merely through abstract cogitation but from his sexual desires. These feelings enabled his instinctual understanding of ancient Greece, his subintellectual understanding of its animating "spirit." Because Winckelmann's sexual orientation was the same as that of the artist who created the sculpture, Pater suggests, he was "reconciled" with it, despite its historical and cultural distance.

Pater follows this assertion with a translated quote from Winckelmann's impassioned letter to a "young nobleman," Friedrich von Berg, which states, "As it is confessedly the beauty of *man* which is to be conceived under our general idea, so I have noticed that those who are observant of beauty only in women, and are moved little or not at all by the beauty of men, seldom have an impartial, vital, inborn instinct for beauty in art. To such persons the beauty of Greek art will ever seem wanting, because its supreme beauty is rather male than female" ("W" 87–88). Pater's focus on the role Winckelmann's homoerotic temperament played in his acquisition of ostensibly disinterested aesthetic insights is revolutionary in the history of post-Kantian art philosophy. This is not because he refers to same-sex desire per se: discussions of ancient Greek homosexuality were commonplace in Victorian classical scholarship, though few shared Pater's unabashed candor.[71] Pater's references to homoerotic desire were not scandalous in and of themselves, but "Winckelmann" is remarkable in both its lack of embarrassment regarding the art historian's responsiveness to "the beauty of *man*" and Pater's presentation of sexual desire as compatible with aesthetic indifference: having an "impartial" view of art does not mean transcending bodily desires; instead, it requires that one be willing to depart from the normative heterosexual desire endorsed by modern culture and embrace the same-sex eroticism that inspired the sculptors of ancient Greece.

Yet, in a startling move, Pater associates Winckelmann's sexually inspired aesthetics not only with artistic inspiration but also with the pain and loss associated with Hegelian negativity. "Certainly of that beauty of living form which regulated Winckelmann's friendships," he states, "it could not be said that it gave no pain," and the "troubled colouring" of his letters form "an instructive but bizarre addition to the history of Art" ("W" 88). This labor of the negative reached its apex with Winckelmann's violent death. Potts argues that Pater's essay replaces the "free sovereign subjectivity" associated with Winckelmann's proto-Kantian Enlightenment aesthetics with proto-postmodern "fantasies of the dissolution of the self," arising from his anxieties about Victorian society's anathematization of sex between men, which culminates in Pater's wholesale rejection of "the idea of self as political agent" in this essay.[72] Yet the language Pater uses to recount Winckelmann's death shows that the danger presented by same-sex desire could actually generate the destructive yet artistically creative energy of Hegelian negativity that *enables* the development of autonomous subjectivity. Pater describes how a thief named Archangeli entered the art historian's private chambers under the sexually suggestive pretense of wanting to look at his private collection of "gold medals." Pater recounts that when Winckelmann "stooped down" to retrieve those medals, "a cord was thrown round his neck" by the thief as he snuck up behind him, leaving him "dangerously wounded" and eventually killing him. Yet, despite the gruesome and sordid nature of Winckelmann's demise, Pater nevertheless says that "it seemed as if the gods, in reward for his devotion to them, had given him a death which, for its swiftness and its opportunity, he might well have desired" ("W" 89–90). Instead of portraying this incident as a tragic consequence of cultural homophobia, an instance of violent exploitation or a prototypical form of gay panic, Pater renders Winckelmann's death in an oddly positive fashion, such that it seems a price well worth paying for a life lived among pagan deities in art. He lends the episode an erotic, sadomasochistic frisson that suggests this was the inevitable and, ultimately, desirable culmination of the art historian's Hellenic attitude toward life.

Pater shows that Winckelmann's homoerotic negativity is risky but also crucial for the development of his new aesthetic vision. Dellamora reads his account of Winckelmann's death in light of his relationship to Goethe as "the greatest living exponent of *Bildung*, of 'self-development' and 'self-cultivation,' to use Victorian terms" and Hegel's argument "that an individual needed to undergo an experience of personal disintegration if he or she were to overcome the limits of their prescripted existence."[73] Pater presents Winckelmann's same-sex desire as a force that destroys consciousness to rebuild it into a new way of being, one that does not seek stability and consolidation but is instead open to relativity, conditionality, and contingency—even at the expense of risking death itself. As an astute reader of the latest discoveries of epistemological philosophy and the physical sciences, Pater recognized that late Victorian intellectual culture was becoming increasingly skeptical of the stability and persistence of the individual subject.[74] He refers to this in the "Conclusion" as the "increasing tendency in modern thought" to "regard all things and principles of things as inconstant modes or fashions" and to understand subjectivity as, in his words, a "continual vanishing away, that strange, perpetual, weaving and unweaving of ourselves" (*R* 188). His investment in a model of consciousness that continually unmakes and remakes itself is what led him to embrace the Hegelian version of subjectivity, just as "Diaphaneitè" marked his embrace of Hegelian contradiction. Yovel describes the Hegelian subject as "a series of negations which do not return the process to its point of departure, but rather each negation constitutes a new state of affairs, and a new state of consciousness."[75] Similarly, Winckelmann's homoerotic self-knowledge does not result in the consolidated, static sense of identity being invented by the sexologists, as the Foucauldian reverse discourse would suggest, but rather embodies the negative force driving the self's development within its continual state of flux.

Pater shows that homoerotic art is the preeminent vehicle through which a dangerous and socially proscribed sexuality transforms into something more than itself, creating a dynamic form of consciousness that achieves autonomy without aspiring to stability. As the emergent identity of the "homosexual" rendered desire between men a source of alienation, rupture, and terror, he realized that the homophobia of modern European culture prevents the same-sex-attracted individual from having untroubled self-awareness of his desires. Yet he also realized that such feelings could be harnessed to bring into being an emancipated critical consciousness suited to the nineteenth century's increasing skepticism of the fully self-determining subject.

Negativity's transformative force depends upon the existence of knowledge that is *withheld* from the mind—present within consciousness but not recognized as such and thus, in a sense, "hidden" from the self so as to be subsequently revealed to it, thereby inaugurating the encounter with the negative. This revelation creates a situation where what had once been mere absence retrospectively transforms into a meaningful or significant elision, such as Winckelmann's discovery of the "hidden" presence of same-sex eroticism that had existed all along in ancient Greek sculpture or Pater's own recognition of the homoerotic subject in his formerly sexless vision of the diaphanous being. Michael Taussig uses Hegelian negativity to describe the revelation of culturally hidden knowledge to the individual as entailing "truly complex and yet marvelous notions of time compression and time expansion . . . involved in the events and material objects that occupy the memory as the past careens into the shocked present-time, such that time itself is suspended out of time." This "shock" is at once both intellectual and visceral, creating a "new reality" for consciousness—in other words, enabling the evolution of individual *Bildung*.[76]

The homophobia of Winckelmann's surroundings, which put obstacles in the way of becoming self-aware of his desires, paradoxically created the conditions making him capable of transcending the limits imposed upon him by his historical and cultural context. Pater describes the anguish felt by the young Winckelmann in the "tarnished" and "colourless intellectual world of Germany in the early half of the eighteenth century" that had forgotten the spiritual and physical freedoms of the ancient world. "He enacted in early youth an obscure struggle," he states, "the memory of which ever remained in him as a fitful cause of dejection" ("W" 80). Though he does not explicitly say that Winckelmann struggled with his same-sex desires, the freedom the art historian experienced upon encountering the classical past is rooted in the desiring body just as much as it is in the reflective mind: "passing out of [his German education] into the happy light of the antique he had a sense of exhilaration almost physical" ("W" 80).

Pater adapts elements of Plato's *Phaedrus* to describe how Winckelmann's critical insights into ancient Greek sculpture arose at the same moment he realized that his same-sex attractions had been hidden yet nevertheless always present within his mind: "This repression, removed at last, gave force and glow to Winckelmann's native affinity to the Hellenic spirit" ("W" 86). Pater states that, as a result, the

> world in which others had moved with so much embarrassment, seems to call out in Winckelmann new senses fitted to deal with it. He is *en rapport* with it; it penetrates him, and becomes part of his temperament. He remodels his writings with constant renewal of insight; he catches the thread of a whole sequence of laws in some hollowing of the hand, or dividing of the hair; he seems to realize the fancy of the reminiscence of a forgotten knowledge hidden for a time in the mind itself, as if the mind of one, lover and philosopher at once in some phase of pre-existence [. . .], fallen into a new cycle, were beginning its intellectual culture over again, yet with a certain power of anticipating its results. ("W" 89)

Winckelmann's encounter with ancient art uncovered sexual knowledge sequestered within his own consciousness. This revelation was the origin of his insights into the aesthetic form of the sculptures, rather than the acquisition of historical information about Hellenic culture. Although some might be "embarrassed" by this kind of desire, the homoerotic sculptures instead "call out new senses" from within Winckelmann that are "fitted to deal with" the sensuality of Greek art, they "penetrate" his mind. The "constant renewals of insight" Winckelmann gleaned from sculptural details seem not to come from the external world at all but rather from *inside* him as "the reminiscence of a forgotten knowledge hidden for a time in the mind itself," present within his consciousness yet withheld from his self-aware understanding. Winckelmann's unique version of *Bildung* therefore manifested as a mind "fallen into a new cycle, . . . beginning its intellectual culture over again, yet with a certain power of anticipating its results."

James Eli Adams identifies this passage as a version of Plato's theory of anamnesis, the notion that learning is actually a kind of recollection, the remembering of the transcendent Ideas we once knew in a previous incarnation.[77] For Pater, however, this sexualized version of anamnesis results not in the recovery of a stable, eternal truth hiding behind the fluctuating appearances of things but in the historically and socially contingent realization of one's homoerotic desire in a culture where such desires happen to be condemned. Rather than creating a stable sense of identity, this process instead creates critical self-awareness of one's historical moment. This new way of perceiving the self and the world is closer to the "relative spirit" Pater identifies with modernity. He characterizes this "hidden" knowledge as at once both intellectual and erotic in character. Pater states that "enthusiasm, in the broad Platonic sense of the *Phaedrus*, was the secret of [Winckelmann's] divinatory power over the Hellenic world. This enthusiasm, dependent as it is to a great degree on bodily temperament, gathering into itself the stress of the nerves and the heat of the blood, has a power of reinforcing the purer motions of the intellect with an almost physical excitement" ("W" 87). Winckelmann's insights into ancient Greek sculpture, founded as they are upon the recovery of hidden erotic self-knowledge, can "call out new senses" because they infuse the analytical power of his intellect with the visceral force of sexual desire, creating the "almost physical excitement" that reconfigures subjectivity, making him aware that his desire for other men had heretofore been "hidden" within his mind. This revelation, which is only possible in a cultural context where heterosexual desire is normative, transforms Winckelmann's consciousness and inaugurates his revolutionary new "organ of perception" for seeing the world.

In a homophobic culture, same-sex desire exists as a determinate absence in the mind because of its social invisibility and stigmatization. When it is finally revealed to the subject for what it is, that embodied experience of desire ruptures and radically transforms consciousness, such that one begins to question not only the sexual norms of one's culture but all stable definitions of the subject that have pretensions to universality. Once one realizes it is possible to embrace desires that society has declared verboten, it becomes possible for one to question all the truths society presents as absolute and unquestionable.

This experience created Winkelmann's emphatically autonomous subjectivity, what Pater calls (again, citing Goethe) his "wholeness, unity with one's self, intellectual integrity" despite his "narrow, exclusive" interest in ancient Greek sculpture (*R* 147). Negativity explains how this independence is achieved, paradoxically, through submission to the power of art. The erotic self-knowledge elicited through his encounter with art from the past enables him to affirm his dissident sexuality. Winckelmann's indirect, "diaphanous" challenge to the coercive power of social norms guarantees a personal coherence, "unity with one's self," that inheres in his continually renewed capacity for resistance, arising out of the fragmentation and subsequent re-formation of the self.

Pater's ambitions in "Winckelmann" go beyond offering an innovating intellectual biography of a major art historian and aesthetic theorist. Rather, his goal is to describe the inauguration of a historically momentous form of consciousness, one adequate to the task of being an aesthetic critic within a modernity that rejects attempts to find absolute truth or a transcendental grounding for subjectivity. According to Pater, Winckelmann repudiated an older model of criticism, what he refers to in "Coleridge" as the attempt "to arrest every object in an eternal outline."[78] He states, "It is easy to indulge the common-place metaphysical instinct, but a taste for metaphysics may be one of those things which we must renounce if we mean to mould our lives to artistic perfection. Philosophy serves culture not by the fancied gifts of absolute or transcendental knowledge, but by suggesting questions which help one to detect the passion and strangeness and dramatic contrasts of life" ("W" 109). Pater presents Winckelmann as a forerunner of his own vision of the queer Victorian aesthete, someone who challenges pretentions to universal truth and normative definitions of the subject by embracing whatever is singular and contingent within him. Pater recognized that in his own late Victorian era, which was experiencing a nascent homophobia arising in reaction to the development of homosexual identity, this ability would belong superlatively to one who is viscerally aroused by homoeroticism in art and whose *Bildung* is characterized by the revelation of sexual self-knowledge through the encounter with the negative.

The erotic negativity Pater describes in "Diaphaneitè" and, especially, "Winckelmann" was a decisive influence on the writings of later queer aesthetes, as they each in their own way attempted not just to describe but embody in their writing this open and dynamic form of selfhood. As he asserts of Winckelmann (quoting Goethe), the nature of his "secret . . . influence" is that "one learns nothing from him, but one becomes something" ("W" 84). This essay is the closest Pater comes to offering an account of how one can develop the disposition capable of jettisoning normative ways of perceiving reality, what he calls in the "Preface" to *The Renaissance* the possession of "a certain kind of temperament, the power of being deeply moved by beautiful objects" (*R* xxi). In "Winckelmann," he shows that that power belongs superlatively to the queer aesthete who can harness homophobic oppression into personal transformation through the labor of the negative.

These essays show that Pater shares a concern with modern queer theorists: that attempts to make a positive social change cause one to acquiesce to "punishing norms that discipline behavior," in Halberstam's words, and undercut efforts at radical change before they have even begun.[79] Yet, rather than suggesting that queer subjectivity be reoriented around failure as a form of resistance, Pater indicates that we alter our modes of perception to view these "failed subjects" in a different light. Through the labor of the negative, the failure a homophobic culture associates with queer desire is transformed into the realization that one need not be confined by social norms. Resistance can take the form of persisting in one's difference and gaining a sense of "wholeness" and "unity" that cannot be achieved by those who fulfill society's standards.

Fittingly, then, Pater refrains from offering a prescriptive set of directions for how to cultivate this disposition. Instead, he ends his essay by looking toward the future, expressing the hope that later writers will be able to cultivate the same renewed sense of autonomy from contemporary culture that Winckelmann derived from his devotion to the classical world. The art historian attained his modern critical disposition only by focusing squarely on the past, where he found inspiration in an older version of subjective autonomy as "that naïve, rough sense of freedom, which supposes man's will to be limited, if at all, only by a will stronger than his," a belief that modern humanity "can never have again." By contrast, the "modern mind" must concern itself with "the intricacy, the universality of natural law, even in the moral order," the knowledge that even in the moments when we feel like we are acting of our own free will, we are obeying laws of heredity, genetics, and biological systems lying beyond the purview of our conscious mind ("W" 110). According to Pater, then, it falls to "poetry" to reconstruct for its readers some sense of subjective autonomy appropriate for modernity's skepticism toward the individual's capacity for absolute freedom. It is to Pater's own attempts to craft a modern poetics of subjective autonomy in his later writings that the next chapter turns.

CHAPTER TWO

Styles of Survival in Pater's Later Writings

Walter Pater's writings of the 1860s described how the aesthetic critic's sexual desires transform his subjectivity, eliciting in him a distinctly modern disposition toward his culture, one that finds its autonomy in the embrace of the "relative spirit." In the previous chapter, I explored how these early works express the phenomenon I call "erotic negativity": when the encounter with homoerotic art elicits the traumatizing recognition of one's same-sex desires yet converts it into a positive, consciousness-transforming experience. In these visionary writings, Pater anticipates the coming of queer aesthetes who will become modern-day Winckelmanns, diaphanous beings creating new forms and procedures of artistic and social critique for late Victorian modernity. Yet the scandal that greeted the publication of *The Renaissance* in 1873, combined with the fallout from the Hardinge Affair in 1874, made Pater wary in his later writings of continuing to discuss this type most suited to the vocation of aesthetic criticism. Pater's discussion of the aesthete's nonnormative erotic desires and indifference toward bourgeois morality made him dangerously close to the figure just coming to be known as the "homosexual" in sexological discourse, which had deleterious consequences for Pater's career and reputation.

Although Pater would continue to be a guiding light for later queer aesthetes, his contemporaries often saw these post-*Renaissance* writings as capitulations to cultural conservatism, altogether more tentative, more closeted, and more accommodating to traditional morality than the radical and subversive early essays. As Katharine Bradley, one of the two Michael Field poets, commented in her journal in 1890, "He has struck out the Essay on Aesthetic Poetry in 'Appreciations' because it gave offence to some pious person—he is growing hopelessly prudish in literature, & defers to the moral

weaknesses of everybody. Deplorable!"[1] Modern critics have often agreed
with this basic sentiment, seeing the excision of the "Conclusion" from the
second edition of *The Renaissance* and the tentative embrace of Christianity
by the eponymous hero of his novel *Marius the Epicurean* (1885) as evidence
of retrenchment into a more socially acceptable position.[2]

While these later writings are certainly more reticent in their discussions
of homoeroticism, I claim in this chapter that they nevertheless continue to
elaborate the theory of erotic negativity introduced in his early essays. The
damage done to Pater personally and professionally by the events of 1873–74
undoubtedly made it prudent for him to be less explicit about his unconventional philosophies and desires. Yet he soon made a virtue of this necessity.
His post-*Renaissance* writings explore how the negativity that structured the
queer aesthetes' consciousness could be expressed externally, in the formal
structure of his writing and the aesthetic response elicited by that form, and
thereby communicated to a broad, not necessarily queer audience. For Pater,
the aesthetic is the venue most suited to communicate erotic negativity between subjects because it allows for the intersubjective communication of
feelings and experiences that cannot be explained using reason and logic. As
Kant states, aesthetic judgments are "universally communicable" despite not
being grounded in preexistent, socially determined concepts because they
appeal to what he calls the "*sensus communis*," our sense of a commonly held
experience of beauty.[3] Similarly, in his late essay "Style" (1889), Pater states
that the goal of the prose writer should be to offer "the transcript of his sense
of fact rather than the fact." Rather than presenting objectively verifiable concepts, the author should show the truth "modified by human preference in
all of its infinitely varied forms," which can be expressed only stylistically,
rather than discursively. For Pater, this is what makes even a nonfiction author's style a "*fine* art" rather than a science.[4] In this chapter, I argue that the
universally communicable subjectivity that is the hallmark of Paterian style
relies on the aesthetic sensus communis to communicate to all readers, queer
and non-queer alike, the critical consciousness, historical self-awareness, and
subjective autonomy characteristic of erotic negativity.

This shift to a concern with form put Pater in a safer position, making it
more difficult for readers to infer his own inclinations from the sexual interests he ascribed to other exemplary critics. Yet these later writings also inten-
sified a line of inquiry already begun in the 1860s. As discussed in the previous chapter, Pater ends "Winckelmann" affirming that "what modern art has
to do in the service of culture is so to rearrange the details of modern life, so

to reflect it, that it may satisfy the spirit. And what does the spirit need in the face of modern life? The sense of freedom."[5] Yet he wonders whether art is up to the task, if it can "give the spirit at least an equivalent for the sense of freedom" (*R* 110). He says the only genre that might provide this reasonable facsimile of subjective autonomy for the modern world is "poetry," which he defines broadly as "all literary production which attains the power of giving pleasure by its form, as distinct from its matter," a definition he must have thought included his own meticulously crafted prose. "Only in this varied literary form," he says, "can art demand that width, variety, delicacy of resources, which will enable it to deal with the conditions of modern life" (*R* 110). For Pater, modern science and philosophy have so blurred the lines between what is done of one's own free will and what is merely a response to a biological impulse or internalized social norm that literary language is the only genre complex enough to recuperate a version of human freedom by redefining its parameters.

The queer aesthete is in a privileged position to craft this new literary language of subjective autonomy. Through the process of negativity, he circumvents the contradictions of the "strange empirico-transcendental doublet" that is the modern subject, identified by Foucault, by finding his freedom in aesthetic experience itself and its characteristic ability to critique and expand the limits of cultural norms, including normative definitions of personal freedom. In his later writings, Pater attempts to transform himself into the queer aesthete anticipated by his earlier works by crafting literary forms capable of eliciting in all readers this aesthetic equivalent for the lost sense of freedom. He theorizes and puts into practice a poetics of erotic negativity to provide a workable modern replacement for the experience of unfettered human agency—even if it is not grounded in either empirical fact or transcendent spirituality—by crafting an aesthetic equivalent for the feeling that our actions are meaningfully self-determined by reasoned ethical deliberations. Art can make us feel this way, despite our knowledge that "the universality of natural law, even in the moral order" is a force "subtler than our subtlest nerves," that the origins of actions are neither fully transparent to ourselves nor entirely under our control (*R* 110). This form of writing would elicit in a wide range of readers the same ability to transcend tired dialectical stalemates that occur in the mind of the queer aesthete when he encounters homoeroticism in art.

Pater develops a form of writing that might be designated a "queer style," a term that describes the effect an author's nonnormative desires has on his or her techniques of literary expression. Yet he does so in a very different sense than the one in which the concept has been used by queer theorists, who understand style to be a way for authors to cope with the traumas associated with queer sexuality in a homophobic culture. Heather Love has compared Pater's style to the "queer performativity" Eve Kosofsky Sedgwick identifies in Henry James's writing, which combines "reticence and virtuosic stylistic performance" as an expression of the queer subject's "shame," which she defines, after the psychoanalyst Silvan Tompkins, as a "combination of alienation [and] extreme self-consciousness."[6] Love and Sedgwick's definition forms part of larger body of work on queer style that portrays a writer's formal ambiguities and obliquities as covert expressions of closeted desires that cannot be articulated explicitly in the text and which inevitably exist in tension with the explicit content of the writer's prose. This rendering has its origins in Roland Barthes's theory of style as "a self-sufficient language . . . which has its roots only in the depths of the author's personal and secret mythology."[7] It has been most notably articulated in D. A. Miller's rereading of Barthes's definition of style as the expression of the "intensity and inventiveness of a desire to circumvent the socio-intellectual doom" of being publicly and explicitly identified as a homosexual "that, but for this intervention, they would otherwise spell for its author."[8] Kevin Ohi has recently adapted the theory of queer style to the queer antisocial thesis in his definition of Jamesian style as "a radical antisociality, that seeks to unyoke sexuality from communities and identities—gay and straight—that would tame it."[9] In all these accounts, queer style marks the revenant of a painful authorial biography that persists within the form of literary writing, a personal shame that can never quite be overcome by linguistic virtuosity.

Yet Pater's version of queer style is rooted in a very different vision of self and world from the Barthesian autobiography that has inspired queer theorists. Far from advocating a radical antisociality stemming from the intractable social alienation of the queer subject, Pater believed erotic negativity had important implications for the culture at large. Although he was, and for many readers continues to be, infamous for telling his audience to reject the obligations of social duty in favor of enthrallment to one's private aesthetic sensations, this impulse always contended with his desire to communicate this message as widely as possible. Diana Maltz notes that in 1888 Pater gave a talk on Wordsworth's poetry at Toynbee Hall, the university settlement house in London's East End dedicated to disseminating academic knowledge to working people and narrowing the gap between social classes. Although she notes that "the lecture was less than a success, mostly because the shy Pater did not look up from his manuscript," his later writings use literary style to bridge the gap between subjective experience and intersubjective communication he struggled to transcend in person.[10]

Pater's version of queer style insists that the sense of alienation that accompanies the recognition of one's same-sex desire in a homophobic culture can be turned to positive social account, and it insists that insights derived from queer experience can be generalized without losing their grounding in the specificities of nonnormative sexual desire. Despite Sedgwick's assertion "that there are important senses in which the word 'queer' can signify *only when attached to the first person*," Pater shows that it is possible to use literary form to communicate a version of subjective experience of queerness to broad audiences.[11] This poetics bears closer affinities to the dialectic Theodor Adorno has famously called "late style," as Carolyn Williams notes. Although Pater might be considered rather young to be developing this style in his immediate post-*Renaissance* writings—he was only thirty-five years old in 1874—in Williams's words, "*all* Pater is 'late' Pater," insofar as he self-consciously positions his writings as a belated addition to the canon of British literary prose.[12] In contrast to Barthesian queer style, which is grounded in the author's ineluctable personal traumas, Adorno says that the "formal law of late style brings about an *evacuation* of the personal, of biographical experience, from the late work." Williams argues that one of the goals of Pater's writings is to effect this shift from the personal to the impersonal, creating moments where the "'mind and soul' of a text of an author . . . suddenly gives way to the mind and 'soul of humanity.'"[13] Andrew Goldstone explains that, in Adorno's theory, "the autonomy of lateness is not mere . . . untrammeled personal expression. Rather, late style is an *objective* liberation, through form, from the limits of biographical contingency"—in other words, late style embraces the autonomy of aesthetic form to express the artist's sense of distance and alienation from his or her culture. Yet, in this very process, it necessarily "takes a dialectical turn back toward the constraints of personal existence from which it strives to be autonomous," because the artist's investment in the autonomy of form derives from a personal sense of estrangement from the established social order.[14] Yet in Pater's queer version of late style, he insists that the personal and subjective process by which the queer aesthete develops his partial autonomy from a homophobic culture can be reproduced in every reader through the aesthetic experience inspired by the form of his prose, yet also remain grounded in the specificities of queer experience.

To craft his poetics, Pater turned to the unlikely resource of Victorian anthropology. Although anthropology would appear to promote a vision of the human as a finite object of empirical investigation, Pater embraced the methods and concepts of the nascent discipline from the beginning of his professional literary career as a tool for aesthetic criticism. He was especially inspired by the writings of his Oxford colleague Edward Burnett Tylor, a key figure in establishing anthropology as a modern academic discipline.[15] His seminal work, *Primitive Culture: Researches into the Development of Mythology, Philosophy, Religion, Art, and Custom* (1871), built upon evolutionary thought to develop a methodological breakthrough he calls the "doctrine of survivals" to explain the persistence of supernatural religious belief in modern Western culture.[16] According to this theory, practices that today seem irrational are, in fact, holdovers from earlier stages of cultural development. When we look to the practices of past civilizations or "primitive" people in the present, we can find reasons for these phenomena that are entirely logical, provided we account for the low level of scientific knowledge achieved by those cultures. Practices that look meaningless to us today only do so because scientific advances have caused us to forget the reasons why they made sense in the first place.

Pater's late writings show that potent survivals of premodern forces underlie even the most advanced elements of cultural modernity. These include, most notably, elements of sexual impulsiveness and animalistic violence. Stefano Evangelista and Giles Whiteley both note that Pater's late writings are preoccupied with what Evangelista calls the "'dark' possibilities of the erotic which include violence, self-destruction, and death," despite his discretion regarding male same-sex desire, an interest they construe as expressing resentment toward the homophobic responses that greeted *The Renaissance* and the Hardinge affair.[17] Yet Pater interprets these seemingly sinister impulses as survivals of primitive human existence that continue to underlie modern cultural practices. Rather than being antithetical to modern life, Pater construes these dark survivals dialectically, as forces of negativity that persist within and contribute to the development of cultural life, the "suffering, passion, war, destruction, falsehood, violence" that are, according to Hegel, the "organic constituents of truth and spirit's growth and actuality."[18] Once one recognizes those elements, it becomes apparent that modern culture has not transcended primitive behavior so much as harnessed those energies for new purposes.

Pater draws on Tylor's theory of survivals to craft a poetics that provides an "equivalent for the sense of freedom" developed by and for queer aesthetes, but works for everybody.[19] He accomplishes this by exploiting the structural homology between survivals' roles in the development of human culture and homoerotic desire's role in cultivating the autonomy of the queer aesthete. Survivals are, in a sense, the "coming out" of primitivism within modern culture. Just as the queer aesthete's fearful confrontation with his homoerotic desires both shatters and radically reconfigures his subjectivity, so too does the recognition that primitive practices survive in modern social life radically reconfigure one's understanding of one's own cultural context. One realizes that features of modern life originated in premodern practices that now appear unsavory and disturbing to modern sensibilities, which elicits critical reflection on one's historical moment and reveals seemingly absolute timeless cultural norms as relative and subject to processes of historical change. For Pater, queers' recognition of homoerotic content and general readers' recognition of cultural survivals elicit similar aesthetic experiences in the reader. Both Hegelian erotic negativity and Tylorian anthropology create the conditions necessary for the development of a renewed, reworked sense of autonomous subjectivity.

Pater found the aesthetically mediated, intersubjective expressiveness of this style useful for transmitting different sorts of nondiscursive content—especially, in the case of *Marius the Epicurean*, religious belief, as Sebastian Lecourt has discussed in detail.[20] Yet in this chapter, I show late Paterian style to be indicatively queer, arising as it does from the homoerotically inclined aesthete's self-conscious distance from cultural norms of gender and sexuality. The lingering elements of dark eroticism in modern culture, which become perceptible only once one is aware of the contingency of contemporary mores, are not hidden in the closeted rhetorical feints typically associated with queer style. Instead, they are expressed in both the explicit subject matter and structure of his writing. As Hegel says in the *Encyclopaedia Logic* (1817), "The only genuine works of art are precisely the ones whose content and form show themselves to be completely identical."[21] Readers are not simply told about the persistence of the primitive within the modern, they experience it as an aesthetic response to the words on the page. The queer aesthete transmits his experience, and his "equivalent for the sense of freedom," to the general reader in and through the aesthetic effects of his writing.

In two works composed in the immediate wake of *The Renaissance* and Hardinge controversies, "On Wordsworth" (1874) and "A Study of Dionysus" (1876), Pater explores how poetic language draws upon the survivals of primitive impulses to create singular artistic effects. This includes, most notably, his realization that he could use the structure of the critical essay to allow his readers to hold in their minds simultaneously a contradictory understanding of the human subject as capable of self-determination yet also in thrall to dark and destructive sexual desires. Pater enlists the style he develops in these essays for the composition of *Marius the Epicurean*, a bildungsroman narrating the psychological development of an aesthetically inclined young man in the last days of the Roman Empire. In a chapter-long excurse on the ultrarefined, self-aware prose style he refers to as "Euphuism," he draws on the ideas of Edward Tylor and Matthew Arnold to articulate a version of what Rebecca Walkowitz calls "cosmopolitan style." By disrupting the logic underlying cultural categories that threaten to become static and essentialized, Pater's euphuistic style becomes a vehicle for his anthropological critique of Victorian culture's imbrication of its ideals of masculinity, violence, and British national identity in the chapter pointedly titled "Manly Amusements." Through the development of this literary style, Pater's novel attempts to grant all readers a qualified form of autonomy by encouraging them to reflect critically on their own historical moment, giving them a limited yet meaningful sense of intellectual distance, and thus reflective freedom, from the givens of their culture. In this capacity, Pater's novel makes a demand on his readers that was, and continues to be, radical. Rather than attempting to present queerness in terms a broad readership might understand, he asks his readers to aspire to the advanced form of ethical consciousness developed by queers.

Wordsworth, Dionysus, and the Art of Survival

Given Pater's avowed interest in applying the "sciences of observation" to human culture, it is no surprise he began incorporating insights from anthropology into his aesthetic criticism as early as the 1870s. These were the years immediately preceding anthropology's formal installation as an academic discipline, with Tylor's appointment first as keeper of the University Museum at Oxford in 1883, then as reader in anthropology in 1884. Lecourt asserts that the 1871 publication of *Primitive Culture* was a decisive intervention in the discourse of evolutionary anthropology. He proposes that "only the postulate of long-term historical evolution could fully explain the chain of resemblances between animals, primitive humans, and modern subjects."[22] Previously, anthropologists devoted to the theory of monogenesis, the notion that all of humanity shared a single origin, asserted that racial differences were the result of certain populations having "fallen farther away from the original human type."[23] Tylor instead introduced the notion of "Culture, or Civilisation" as a "complex whole which includes knowledge, belief, art, morals, law, custom, and any other capabilities and habits acquired by man" that advances through the same stages of development across all human societies but at different rates.[24] He proposed that present-day "primitive cultures" were moving slowly, but inexorably, toward the conditions of the modern West. The existence of "survivals," his term for the "processes, customs, opinions, and so forth, which have been carried on by force of habit into a new stage of society different from that in which they had their original home . . . remain as proofs and examples of an older condition of culture out of which a newer has been evolved."[25] For example, from a Tylorian perspective the modern American practice of children trick-or-treating at Halloween would be not simply a cultural quirk but the "survival" of a pagan religious practice that, although meaningful many centuries ago, is now customary. Survivals are the evidence proving that civilizations evolve over time.

Pater innovates on Tylor's theory by aestheticizing it: he explores the extent to which works of art contain survivals from earlier stages of cultural development and assesses the artistic effects and value they continue to have for the present. William F. Shuter, Steven Connor, and Robert Crawford have established that concepts derived from Tylor's anthropology can be found sprinkled throughout *The Renaissance*.[26] Yet Pater's first systematic application of anthropological methods to aesthetic criticism did not occur until immediately after the controversies of 1873–74, when he began to consider whether most culturally persistent forms could be considered survivals. His essay "On Wordsworth," from the April 1874 issue of the *Fortnightly Review*, presents the Romantic poet as what David DeLaura calls the epitome of Pater's "view of the ideal aesthetic observer which he had been developing since the essay on Winckelmann."[27] Yet while the Winckelmann essay focuses on the queer aesthete's *Bildung* through the process of Hegelian erotic negativity, "On Wordsworth" provides an anthropological analysis of the poet's attitude toward external objects in the natural world. Pater's decision to write about the by-then canonical British poet might seem (and perhaps actually was) a retreat to a safer, more staid topic than Winckelmann's same-sex enthusiasms. However, the essay is also his first attempt to use anthropological concepts to determine how poetic form could elicit in its readers the aesthetic equivalent of a queer sense of freedom.

In "Winckelmann" Pater claims the art historian could enter the ancient Greek worldview through his aesthetic appreciation of their statues, which derived from his attunement to the erotic desires that inspired the creation of those works. Yet he says the "attempt to" recreate that premodern world-view in modern "art would have so little verisimilitude as to be flat and un-interesting" (*W* 110). In "Wordsworth," however, Pater claims that the poet successfully fused in his writings premodern and modern attitudes toward the natural world through his ability to create in readers an aesthetic experi-ence that accesses the surviving traces of the animistic nature worship that persists within modern culture. He describes Wordsworth's innate intimacy with the natural world as aligning him with premodern forms of animistic nature worship on an intuitive, sub-intellectual level, in much the same way Winckelmann's homoerotic desires inspired his understanding of Greek sculpture. He saw a world, Pater says, where "every natural object seemed to possess more or less of a moral or spiritual life," which "was like a 'survival' in him of that primitive condition, which some philosophers have traced in the history of human culture, in which all outward objects alike, even the works of men's hands, were believed to be endowed with life and animation, and the world was full of souls; that mood in which the old Greek gods were first begotten, and which had many strange aftergrowths."[28] The "philoso-phers" of "the history of human culture" Pater refers to here are contempo-rary cultural anthropologists who study comparative mythology, and Craw-ford has noted that Pater's quoted use of "survival" in the singular is a direct reference to Tylor's unique use of the term in *Primitive Culture*.[29]

Pater's reference to "animation" also recalls Tylor's theory of animism as the historical origin and essential core of mythological and, ultimately, of mod-ern religious beliefs. According to Tylor, the animism of "primitive" people was an attempt to make sense of the biological difference between living and dead bodies, as well as the nature of the illusory human figures who appear to them in dreams and hallucinatory visions, by drawing the "the obvious inference" that individuals have a "ghost-soul" that exists apart from the physical body as "the cause of life or thought in the individual it animates," one capable "of leaving the body far behind" and "continuing to exist and appear to men after the death of that body."[30] Tylor claims these animistic beliefs survive in modern culture through the medium of religious rites and ceremonies, which have evolved "upwards from the simplest theory which attributes life and personality to animal, vegetable, and mineral alike ... up to that which sees in each department of the world the protecting and foster-ing care of an appropriate divinity, and at last of one Supreme Being ordering and controlling the lower hierarchy."[31] Yet even as Tylor defends the essential "rationality" of primitive spiritual belief as a first attempt to make logical sense of phenomena that appear otherwise inexplicable, he takes a dim view of their modern survival in the form of supernatural religious belief, believing them to be doomed by the inevitable march toward secularization and supplanted by "a slowly-growing natural science."[32]

For Pater, though, it is precisely Wordsworth's ability to use poetic form to access survivals of earlier, pagan forms of consciousness that persist within the modern imagination, to recreate "that mood in which the old Greek gods were first begotten," that gives his poetry its distinct artistic value: "In Wordsworth this power of seeing life, this perception of soul, in inanimate things, came of an exceptional susceptibility to the impressions of eye and ear," he says, "and was at bottom a kind of sensuousness. At least it is only in a temperament exceptionally susceptible on the sensuous side that this sense of the expressiveness of outward things comes to be so large a part of life."[33] One may think of, for example, Wordsworth's famous image of the "ten thousand" daffodils he saw "at a glance / Tossing their heads in sprightly dance."[34] Pater emphasizes the poet's embodied experience of the materiality of nature for the development of the animistic consciousness displayed in his poetry. The "sensuality" that makes his poems artistically compelling derives from his "temperament," which is a particularly potent manifestation of what he calls "pagan" forms of consciousness that subtly persist in culture, one whose characteristic feature is its intuitive and instinctual animistic belief that objects in the natural world have a sentient consciousness like our own.

Although Pater recognizes that Wordsworth's animism is an unscientific fiction, the "survival" of a premodern religious belief that is actually just a projection of the poet's psychic operations onto the external world, he says that his poetry is nevertheless aesthetically valuable to modern readers. It has a singular power to "awaken" what Pater calls, quoting Percy Shelley, "a sort of thought in sense."[35] Its supreme value is the ability to use language to revive the subjective sense of the embodied "sensuousness" of animistic thought, to impress upon his modern readers how it might feel to live in a spiritually vivified natural world, despite their possession of the knowledge that this is not literally, empirically true. Wordsworth's poetry is not a flat and uninteresting nostalgia for premodern paganism but an attempt to harness and revivify a superannuated animistic belief system to create the distinctly modern artistic effect of feeling as if one has momentarily left one's own historical moment and entered the psychological conditions of the past. For Pater, the poet accesses the residual traces of animistic belief that persist in modern culture and transforms this survival into an artistic strategy for simultaneously experiencing modern and premodern relationships to nature.

The Wordsworth essay marked the beginning of Pater's systematic thinking about the relations among anthropological survivals, literary form, and queer desire that would inflect his late style. These writings were to be collected in a never-realized volume called *Dionysus and Other Studies*, which would have included "On Wordsworth" along with two pieces that also appeared in the *Fortnightly* the same year: "The Myth of Demeter and Persephone" and "A Study of Dionysus: The Spiritual Form of Fire and Dew" (1874). Evangelista suggests that Pater withdrew the project because of a growing homophobia among conservative critics that manifested as anti-Greek sentiment.[36] Both mythological articles, which would eventually be collected in the posthumous *Greek Studies* (1895), examine the origins of the figures referenced in their titles in preclassical Greek culture and, as Williams notes, offer "both evolutionary and aesthetic explanations of the process" by which mythological stories "form and transform themselves" over time.[37] In the Dionysus essay, Pater deploys his aestheticized version of Tylor's evolutionary anthropology to create an aesthetic effect for his readers similar to that created by Wordsworth's poetic use of the survival.

Rather than turning to poetry, however, he puts these strategies into play using the characteristic features of his own preferred literary genre: the critical essay.[38] Pater's piece is not merely a scholarly investigation, but also a polemical tract.[39] It raises the stakes of the Wordsworth essay by exploring the implications of the theory of survivals for the entirety of Western culture, rather than for an individual poet. Pater shows that one of the foundational myths of the ancient Greek culture that Matthew Arnold celebrated as the fount of autonomous liberal selfhood was but the survival of a violent preclassical cult. If, as Arnold asserts, aspects of Hellenic culture's "spontaneity of conscience" needed to be revived to rejuvenate English culture by emancipating it from the Hebraic "strictness of conscience," then Pater implies Victorian liberalism must necessarily reconcile itself with the surviving elements of eroticism and violence underlying the classical tradition.[40]

Most of the essay recounts the development of the figure of Dionysus in classical Greek culture. In its closing pages, however, Pater shifts abruptly to the more sinister "minor" tradition that portrays the god as "the white and wintry deity who gives birth to tragedy," a figure he portrays as a survival, hidden yet immanent within the sunnier major tradition. This is the dark figure of the Dionysus Zagreus (literally "Dionysus torn apart"), the god dismembered in an erotic frenzy by female worshippers known as maenads, which originated in a preclassical Greek cult of tree worship. Pater uses the formal structure of his writing in these final pages to mimic the process of erotic negativity. By doing so, he attempts to elicit in his readers the capacity to perceive simultaneously two contradictory versions of Dionysus: the liberal Hellenic version that celebrates the consciousness emancipated from strict moral rules, and the animalistic, preclassical version where freedom only means succumbing to one's violent and irrational impulses. Just as Wordsworth's poetry simultaneously evoked both pagan and modern visions of nature, so too can the cultivation of this dual mode of perception, Pater suggests, elicit for readers a more inclusive and capacious experience of subjective autonomy, one rooted in the aesthetic's characteristic ability to harness the destructive forces of negativity and transform them into an energy that transcends the moribund dialectical opposition between freedom and unfreedom.

"Dionysus" implicitly responds to Arnold's harmonious and optimistic vision of classical Greek culture in *Culture and Anarchy* (1867/68–69). Here, he famously characterizes ancient Greece as the historical locus of the "Hellenic" spirit of "sweetness and light," embodied by practices of self-development, intellectual freedom, and the disinterested pursuit of knowledge for its own sake.[41] He opposes this to "Hebraism," the term he uses to refer to the externally enforced "repressive but morally rigorous Protestantism" that dominated Victorian culture, the overvaluing of which encouraged social conflict and prevented the development of a genuinely liberal culture of disinterested intellectual freedom.[42] Linda Dowling has discussed how Arnoldian Hellenism, and its influence on the reform of classics curriculum in late Victorian Oxford, enabled a "homosexual counterdiscourse able to justify male love in ideal or transcendental terms: the 'spiritual procreancy' associated . . . with ancient Greece itself," rendering it "the very fountain of civic health in an English polity imperatively in need, precisely as liberal theorists . . . had all along been insisting, of some authentic source of new ideas and intellectual power."[43]

However, in "Dionysus" Pater establishes that myriad forms of sexual perversity, including but not limited to male homosexuality, were survivals within a Hellenic tradition that had the exact opposite effect. According to Evangelista, Pater concludes "Dionysus" with the figure of Dionysus Zagreus to explode Arnold's "sanitised and bloodless idealisation of ancient Greece by focusing on the sidelined elements of primitivism, irrationality, fluidity, murkiness, the grotesque."[44] By doing so, Pater aligned himself with those anthropologists who, in the 1870s, were grappling with the implications of Tylor's evolutionary model of culture. Lecourt comments that during the 1870s, these anthropologists came to the uneasy realization that the "shared point of origin from which it derived all humankind was now indistinguishable from the animal kingdom broadly. The common ancestor in Tylorian monogenesis was not a spiritual, linguistic agent but rather a primitive creature who likely lacked the capacities for inward reflection." The process of cultural development was thus "collective rather than individual, and deterministic instead of voluntary."[45] Pater's essay suggests that he came to the same realization as these anthropologists but did not find it to be an unsettling rebuke of liberal humanism. Although one might expect a Tylorian reading of ancient Greek culture to contravene the qualities of Hellenism valued by Arnoldian liberals, such as its ability to cultivate rational self-determination in the individual, Pater shows that the animalistic violence embedded within the Dionysus myth paradoxically helped to cultivate these qualities.

He does this to dramatic effect through the essay's unconventional structure. The opening thirty-eight pages describe a version of Dionysus compatible with Arnoldian Hellenism, the god of the vine who is the "inherent cause of music and poetry," the embodiment of the playfulness and spontaneity Arnold wished would be embraced by English culture.[46] In the final nine pages of the essay, however, Pater shifts abruptly to the version of the Dionysus myth found in the preclassical Orphic hymns, where the god is the child of Zeus and Persephone and is torn apart by the Titans under the direction of Hera. This sudden switch from the classical version of the myth to its surviving preclassical core has been called a "structural disunity" by Wolfgang Iser.[47] Rather than a lapse in compositional rigor, however, I argue that this narrative break is Pater's deliberate attempt to dramatize in the essay's formal structure an objective equivalent to the subjective process of erotic negativity. Rather than occurring in the mind of the queer art critic, in "Dionysus" the shift occurs in the literary object itself.

Pater outlines the history that led from the preclassical tearing apart of an avatar of the god to its survival as part of the ritualized worship of Dionysus in classical Greece. Evangelista identifies the "dark possibilities" embodied by the Dionysus Zagreus as "the unconscious, the inadmissible, and the tabooed," which are expressed through rituals of "ecstasy, violence, extreme states of consciousness, and loss of self," especially in the practice of "the *sparagmos*, a ritual dismemberment of a live animal—sometimes, as in Eurip-ides's *Bacchae*, a human being."[48] Pater emphasizes the role of the maenads, whose name literally translates to "raving ones," female worshippers of Dio-nysus known for "mystical ceremonies" where they "ate . . . raw flesh and drank blood" in commemoration of "the actual sacrifice of a fair boy deliber-ately torn to pieces," as part of the reenactment of the god's death.[49] In Greek myth, the maenads combine this destructive frenzy with wild sexual abandon as well as acts of physical transmutation meant to signify the regeneration of the earth in spring.

Yet Pater discusses Dionysus Zagreus's association not only with primitive sexual impulsiveness but also with male homoerotic desire. He does so to highlight the structural homology between the recognition of the Dionysian survivals within Arnoldian liberalism and the recognition of one's homo-erotic desires in a homophobic culture. He refers to a painting of Dionysus made by "a young Hebrew painter" that visually embodies this violent, minor tradition of the Zagreus.[50] The unnamed painter is Simeon Solomon, a Jew-ish Pre-Raphaelite artist who had been publicly disgraced the year before Pater's essay was published when he was arrested and charged with attempt-ing to commit sodomy in a public urinal.[51] Pater says of this painting, which Solomon titled *Bacchus* after the god's Roman name, that it represents "a complete and very fascinating realisation of such a motive [that is, the 'mel-ancholy and sorrowing Dionysus' of the Orphic tradition]; the god of the bit-terness of wine, 'of things too sweet'; the sea-water of the Lesbian grape be-come somewhat brackish in the cup."[52] As Dellamora, Inman, and Hext have argued, this reference to Solomon's melancholy painting is Pater's attempt to cast the Dionysus Zagreus as a historical prefiguration of the plight of the late Victorian homosexual, doomed to destruction by desires beyond his control by a cruel and oppressive society.[53] Solomon's abandonment by his friends after his arrest, as well as Pater's own recent exile from Oxford in the wake of the Hardinge affair, would have made the association between sexual de-sire and the destruction of self, so aptly figured by Dionysus ripped limb from limb in an act of erotic frenzy, especially poignant.

By identifying the classical myth of Dionysus as, historically, the survival of the more radical and disturbing cult of Dionysus Zagreus, Pater uses the historical record to challenge the principles of Arnoldian liberalism by sug-gesting they willfully ignore the "dark" impulses that will necessarily be re-leased by the reintroduction of unfettered expressive freedom and "sponta-neity of conscience" into English cultural life.[54] Dennis Denisoff goes so far

Bacchus, 1867 (oil on paper laid down on canvas), Simeon Solomon
(1840–1905). Birmingham Museums and Art Gallery / Bridgeman Images.

as to read "Dionysus" as rejecting humanism altogether. He draws parallels
between Pater and his contemporary Friedrich Nietzsche to argue that "the
Apollonian self-conscious intelligence—that is, rational mental thought—is
juxtaposed explicitly [in 'Dionysus'] with an instinctual sense of being that
is not characterized by a humanist notion of the self or even necessarily of
the human species. . . . Pagan human sacrifice is, in this context, a symbolic
performance of the sacrifice of liberal humanism itself."[55] Yet Pater's intention in "Dionysus" is not to reject the liberal ideal of the emancipated, self-

determining subject entirely but instead to expand its definition. He shows that embracing Hellenism for its spirit of untrammeled personal freedom and self-development necessarily entails accepting Dionysian as well as Apollonian sides of human nature. The spontaneity of conscience vaunted by Arnold and his followers as central to the Hellenic spirit and liberal subjectivity has, historically, been accompanied by a willingness to acknowledge humanity's capacity for irrational violence and erotic mania as part of its freedom.[56]

Yet, despite its importance in the history of classical culture, Pater notes that the image of Dionysus Zagreus "has left, indeed, but little effect in Greek art and poetry, which criticism has to put patiently together, out of late, scattered hints in various writers."[57] Much like the body of Dionysus himself, the myth has been torn apart and "scattered" throughout various works of antiquity. For a modern mythographer-critic like Pater, however, it is possible to draw upon the theoretical resources of comparative anthropology to research and reconstruct the story of Dionysus Zagreus into a whole. Once this process has been completed, one recognizes that the survival of the torn-apart Dionysus has been a continuous yet hidden surviving presence in the story of Greek humanism all along, "as a tradition really primitive, and harmonious with the original motive of the idea of Dionysus."[58] The moment when this is recognized, the whole story of Hellenic liberalism changes: "You have no longer caught a glimpse of this image, than a certain perceptible shadow comes creeping over the whole story; for, in effect, we have seen glimpses of the sorrowing Dionysus, all along."[59] The sudden "glimpse" of Dionysus Zagreus's survival undermines the liberal-humanist version of the god from inside the myth itself, revealing what Pater calls a "phase" of the god's "own personality, in the true intention of the myth."[60]

The metaphors of vision Pater uses in this passage to describe Dionysus's sudden transformation when he is put under anthropological investigation—the "glimpse of the image," the "perceptible shadow"—also characterize the transformation of consciousness he attempts to elicit in his readers upon their encounter with the shift in his essay's conclusion from the classical Dionysus to the preclassical Dionysus Zagreus. Once one "sees" the violent and destructive aspect of myth, its fundamental character changes radically, transforming into a story about the erotic violence and destructiveness that is part and parcel of unbridled human freedom. After making this statement, Pater takes two paragraphs to retell briefly the history of the myth itself, focusing on the "melancholy" nature of Dionysus that persists as the myth develops over time. This is simply a highly condensed version of the exact same story Pater has narrated over the previous forty-four pages of the essay of the classical, humanist Dionysus. Now, however, Pater emphasizes the persistence of the figure of the Dionysus Zagreus that had really been hidden within the classical version of the myth all along. Both stories are, in fact, the same story, simply viewed from different angles. The abrupt shift in tone and focus forces the reader to reassess in an instant the entire preceding discussion and engage with what Connor calls the "palimpsestic" quality of the Dionysus myth.[61] The reader realizes in a moment that the narrative of the Arnoldian liberal-humanist Dionysus was also, simultaneously, the story of the persistence and survival of the violent and erotic impulses embodied by the Dionysus Zagreus. Pater does not justify queerness by showing how it conforms to socially acceptable liberal values but uses anthropological theory to force liberals to confront the radical queerness, the polymorphous sexual perversity, that survives within their highest ethical ideals.

I want to suggest that, at this moment of radical reassessment, the essay attempts to trigger in the mind of its reader an experience akin to that of erotic negativity. The sudden realization of Dionysus Zagreus's presence within the otherwise anodyne story of the god of the vine breaks down and rearranges one's previous perceptions of the classical myth. This is similar to the process by which homoerotic art converts the traumatizing recognition of one's same-sex desires into a positively consciousness-transforming experience. In case of Pater's essay, it enables in the reader, at least momentarily, the mental capacity to hold together simultaneously two visions of Dionysus and, by extension, two opposed ways of understanding human subjectivity. Neither the preclassical nor the classical version of the myth cancels the other out. Instead, the dialectical opposition is transcended as Pater forces his reader to understand how the single mythological figure holds in dynamic tension both a liberal-humanist understanding of autonomy with the knowledge that individuals are subject to forces beyond their control. Pater uses the essay's structure to elicit in the reader the equivalent of the sense of freedom he demands of modern art. The essay does so by recreating on the level of form the binary-transcending moment of insight invoked by the subjective experience of erotic negativity. In his next major work, the novel *Marius the Epicurean*, Pater builds upon this insight to craft a literary style that will create for readers a sense of autonomy from their ability to reflect critically on their historical context, a quality he explicitly and primarily associates with queer experience.

Euphuism and Cosmopolitanism in *Marius the Epicurean*

Like the Dionysus essay, the figures of Tylor and Arnold continue to loom large in *Marius the Epicurean*, Pater's novel about the intellectual and spiritual development of an artistically inclined young man during the last days of the Roman Empire under the reign of Marcus Aurelius. Short on external events, *Marius* narrates the eponymous hero's thoughts as he goes through the process of initially embracing, then rejecting as inadequate, each of the major philosophies on offer in his culture. Marius begins life as a believer in the ancient Etruscan faith, then falls under the sway of the Epicureanism, before finally becoming an ambivalent member of a Christian community and dying as a martyr.

Pater obviously wanted to draw parallels between this transitional moment in Western culture and his own Victorian moment, indicated by his anachronistic references to nineteenth-century ideas when describing Marius's cogitations.[62] As Marius himself says, he is "retracing in his individual mental pilgrimage the historic order of human thought."[63] References to Tylor's doctrine of survivals abound, as do references to Arnold's essays "Marcus Aurelius" (1863), "Pagan and Medieval Religious Sentiment" (1864), and "The Function of Criticism at the Present Time" (1864). Pater uses Marius's personal spiritual crisis to explore the historical logic underlying cultural transformation. This project was both inspired and enabled by the dominant Victorian definition of "culture" created by Tylor and Arnold. Despite their methodological differences and seemingly opposed understanding of the origins of human subjectivity, Peter Melville Logan notes that both authors "redefined *culture* from a term limited to individuals to one that encompassed society" and focused "on the problem of overcoming a narrow subjectivism and learning to comprehend the social body as a whole."[64] One of Pater's goals is to build upon the dialectical synthesis of Arnold and Tylor that he initially achieved in "Dionysus" to elicit in his readers a similar sense of historical self-consciousness. This will allow them to understand that their own subjectivities are constructed by their cultural and social context, that what they accept as normal, natural, and self-evident is actually historically contingent. Yet he also wants his readers to be able to transcend, at least partially, the limits of their historical moment, to interrogate those cultural norms and imagine them differently. He wants, in other words, for *all* of his readers to attain through their aesthetic response to his language the same sense of autonomous subjectivity that queer aesthetes gain through erotic negativity.

Tylor and Arnold are key interlocutors for Pater in his attempt to articulate for his readers the structural laws connecting large-scale historical change to transformations in individual consciousness. Their influences are nowhere more apparent than in Pater's extended discussion of literary form in the chapter titled "Euphuism." He updates the account of the highly ornamental and artificial prose style associated with the early modern English writer John Lyly, describing "euphuism" as "the always and increasingly artificial" style that is "manifested in every age in which the literary conscience has been awakened to forgotten duties towards language, towards the instruments of expression" (*ME* 88). Pater uses ideas from Tylor and Arnold to offer a theoretical account of how a literary style can disrupt the logic underlying any cultural category threatening to become static, essentialized, and seeming ahistorical, thereby creating what Rebecca Walkowitz calls a "cosmopolitan style." Pater's euphuistic cosmopolitanism becomes the vehicle for his queer critique of normative Victorian ideals of male gender and sexual expression that, by the late nineteenth century, had led to the association of plain literary style with normative masculinity and the martial health of the nation. By allowing his anthropologically informed literary style to perform the Hegelian labor of the negative on this discourse, Pater uses the aesthetic effects of his language to elicit a historical self-consciousness in his readers, a disposition granting them a limited, but nevertheless meaningful, sense of reflective freedom and autonomous ethical self-determination. Walkowitz identifies cosmopolitan style as a part of a theoretical project similar to Hegelian negativity, which seeks to "supplement and in some ways contest" the Kantian injunction to reflect upon and demystify the intellectual and social categories organizing human experience by "extend[ing] the investigation of categories that seem to be neutral to the affective conditions (rationality, purpose, coherence, detachment) that have seemed to make argument or engagement possible."[65] In this sense, cosmopolitan style is the literary form most appropriate for the Paterian queer aesthete.

The queer aesthete uses the aesthetic experience of Hegelian negativity to push against and expand the static categories and stale dialectical oppositions masquerading as absolute, transcendental limits to human thought and culture. Similarly, Walkowitz's cosmopolitan style "implies a new reflection on reflection," that seeks "to transform and to disable social categories."[66] Its descriptive self-consciousness calls attention to "the conventions of writing, which determine how arguments are made, how words can be used, and even which comparisons are relevant and which irrelevant or impertinent," all of which shape how the social order is understood both intellectually and affectively.[67] Cosmopolitan style denaturalizes the process of literary description, rendering the national and political investments of literary convention legible and, consequently, malleable. Walkowitz argues that literary forms of cosmopolitanism were influenced by "changes in the study of culture in the late nineteenth century," such as the advent of Tylor's comparative ethnography in modern anthropology, and with "the syncretic but less-than-national tradition of cosmopolitanism . . . which is often associated with aestheticism, dandyism, and *flânerie* at the fin de siècle."[68] She emphasizes the "association between cosmopolitanism and the late-Victorian tradition of aesthetic decadence, a repertoire of excessive and purposefully deviant cultural strategies whose values include pleasure, consumption, syncretism, and perversity."[69]

Cosmopolitan, perverse, and artificial were the qualities associated with euphuism in the mid-nineteenth century, before Pater redefined the term in *Marius*. As Lene Østermark-Johansen remarks, "Charges of foreignness, effeminacy, and of a false focus on manner rather than matter were frequently raised against such writers as Swinburne, Rossetti, and Pater, and the term 'Euphuism' was invoked to illustrate the ridiculous extremes to which such concern with verbal ornament could be taken."[70] The word "euphuism" derives from two popular early modern romances written by Lyly, *Euphues: The Anatomy of Wit* (1578) and *Euphues and His England* (1580). These tales made use of a highly ornate prose style partaking of literary devices associated with poetry (such an alliteration, simile, and antithesis) and were extremely popular during the Elizabethan era and into the early seventeenth century, before precipitously falling out of fashion for over two hundred years. Østermark-Johansen traces the Victorian revival of debates about literary style to John Morley's 1861 review of F. W. Fairhold's new edition of Lyly's dramatic works. She argues that "the hidden agenda of Morley's review was to launch a debate about prose style in general and thus to give a far wider meaning to the term 'Euphuism.'" Morley offered this as a conclusion: "By the fate, then, of the writers who have flattered fashion and are read no more, let modern Euphuists be warned. Nothing is lasting that is feigned."[71]

Euphuism soon became associated with the ornate, complex, and self-consciously artificial style of writers associated with the Aesthetic Movement. Østermark-Johansen cites John Addington Symonds's declaration that euphuism was "the English type of an all but universal disease. There would have been Euphuism, in some form or other, without Euphues; just as the so-called aesthetic movement of to-day might have dispensed with its Bunthorne [a character from Gilbert and Sullivan's operetta *Patience* (1881) parodying James McNeill Whistler and Oscar Wilde], and yet have flourished."[72] Østermark-Johansen also identifies an association between elaborate literary style and failed versions of masculinity. In the anonymous article "An Alexandrian Age," which appeared in *Macmillan's Magazine* in 1886, the author of this essay equates the elaborate, self-consciously literary language of contemporary writing with the inadequacy of contemporary masculinity, citing Thomas De Quincey's assertion "that our native disregard for the graces of style had its origin in the native manliness of our character, in the sincerity and directness of the British taste, in the principle of *esse quam videri*, which might be taken as the key to much in our manner, much in our philosophy of our lives."[73] The anonymous author goes on to explain that

> it is certain that manliness is not just at this moment the capital distinction of our literature either in prose or verse. In the general bulk of our original work this quality of manliness is certainly not conspicuous; in our criticism it is, one might say, entirely wanting; and in our more serious work, historical, philosophical, and the like, the general tendency is to a minute, dissecting, curious mood, more given to pulling down than to building up. And this tendency is inevitably reflected in the style. The modern style is, indeed, the modern man.[74]

When this essay was written in 1886, the words "manly" and "manliness" would have resonated in the popular imagination with the ideals of the "muscular Christianity" movement. Muscular Christianity, as articulated in the writings of Charles Kingsley and Thomas Hughes, called for a program of Christian activism combined with an ideal of disciplined, athletic, and eminently British form of masculinity. "An Alexandrian Age" exemplifies what James Eli Adams has identified as the nineteenth century's characteristic association between masculinity and literary style. According to him, muscular Christianity introduced into British literary discourse a particular style of masculinity, incarnated in the image of the healthy, ascetic, virile, robustly heterosexual male body as the epitome of the nation's moral virtue.[75] When the author of "An Alexandrian Age" contrasts the unmanliness of contemporary criticism's "minute, dissecting, curious mood, more given to pulling down than to building up," with the "pre-eminently robust, sincere, and direct—in a word, pre-eminently manly" English prose style that has gone out of fashion, he identifies euphuistic literary style not only as a signifier of modern masculinity's failure to live, but with the corruption of the English nation itself.[76]

When Pater gave the title "Euphuism" to *Marius*'s sixth chapter, he alluded to a cultural debate that not only focused on the nature of good literary style but also associated the revival of euphuistic style with the failure of British masculinity and consequent perversion of the English nation.[77] Pater's goal, though, is not simply to intervene in this debate but to examine the conceptual, social, and affective categories embodied by literary conventions that made the discursive association among style, gender, and nation possible. The euphuism chapter is both an intervention in the debate about literary style's relationship to gender and national politics and an investigation into how literary language, even on the level of the sentence, functions to naturalize hetero-patriarchal power relations within society.

As we will see, Pater makes use of these insights in his representation of Marcus Aurelius in the chapter of *Marius* titled "Manly Amusements." Initially, however, the narrator uses "euphuism" to describe the literary style of Flavian, the aloof and highly attractive Roman schoolboy with whom Marius develops an intense homoerotic bond, thereby insouciantly highlighting and confirming connection between a "perverse" literary style and a perverse form of desire asserted by mainstream culture. After the two boys discover the story of Cupid and Psyche in Apuleius's *Golden Ass*, Flavian decides his task in life is to revivify the literary language of the declining Roman Empire. Pater even goes so far as to ascribe an actual Latin poem, the anonymously written *Pervigilium veneris*, to Flavian's pen. The narrator anachronistically displaces euphuism from its Victorian and early modern contexts to the Rome of late antiquity and defines euphuistic style as that which "manifests in every age in which the literary conscience has been awakened to forgotten duties towards language" (*ME* 90). This definition recalls Tylor's definition of "survivals" as "processes, customs, and opinions, and so forth, which have been carried on . . . into a new state of society different from that in which they had their original home, and they thus remain as proofs and examples of an older condition of culture out of which a newer has been evolved."[78] Euphuistic style, like a Tylorian survival, is an aspect of culture that persists across time and is revived periodically to "awaken" literary language to its "forgotten duties," that is, to its vital relationship to "an older condition of culture," both in Marius's time and in Pater's own.

The narrator defines these duties in specifically masculine and nationalist terms when he compares Flavian's rhetorical ability to a form of military prowess, stating that "the secrets of utterance, of expression itself, of that through which alone any intellectual or spiritual power within one can actually take effect upon others, to over-awe or charm them to one's side, presented themselves to this ambitious lad in immediate connexion with that desire for predominance, for the satisfaction of which another might have relied on the acquisition and display of brilliant military qualities" (*ME* 88). In the first half of this sentence, until the appearance of the main verb "presented," the narrator uses a series of appositional clauses to realize a progressively more accurate definition of the "secrets" that "presented themselves" to Flavian. A close examination of each apposition reveals a gradual redefinition of what these "secrets" regard: "utterance" refers specifically to vocalized speech, which the narrator then redefines an "expression itself," referring to any method by which the individual makes his thoughts known by externalizing mental activity, a definition that includes but is not limited to spoken "utterance." In other words, the rhetorical form of this sentence mimics the effort of mind needed to express the true "intellectual or spiritual power within one."

This process of steady redefinition and expansion, which suggests a certain playful attitude towards language and its mimetic capacity, recalls Arnold's discussion of the "free play of mind upon all subjects" in his essay "The Function of Criticism at the Present Time." Arnold defines this free play as "a pleasure in itself, being an object of desire, being an essential provider of elements without which a nation's spirit, whatever compensations it may have for them, must, in the long run, die of inanition," a spirit that, Arnold claims, "hardly enters into an Englishman's thoughts" because of his overweening commitment to an external, Hebraic moral uprightness.[79] Taken together, the narrator's deployment of Tylor's and Arnold's ideas implicitly counters charges that euphuistic style is a symptom of the perversion and degradation of modern English nation. On the contrary, it represents an effort made toward restoring the nation's dignity, a revival of forgotten duties and food for the starved Roman and, by extension, English national spirit.

This seems, on the surface, to be a straightforward defense of euphuism against the muscular Christian men who would denigrate it. Upon closer examination of Pater's literary form, however, it becomes apparent that he critiques euphuism for being part of the same logic of appropriation and domination that defines the dominant Victorian ideal of masculinity. His style exposes the process by which literary language conceals its political work by naturalizing static and limiting ideological categories. Pater's narrator, through his own spectacularly euphuistic performance in this chapter, undermines euphuism from within, thereby rendering it a cosmopolitan style.

Returning to the sentence quoted above, one notices that the narrator, after he redefines "utterance" as "expression," then defines expression as "that through which alone intellectual or spiritual power within one can actually take effect upon others," placing less emphasis on the purely communicative function of language and more on language's capacity for rhetorical persuasiveness, defined as the transformation of one's subjective desires into a means of affecting the beliefs of others in order "to over-awe or charm them to one's side." Ultimately, the "secrets" the narrator describes sounds much more like the ability to exert control over others through rhetorical skill and much less like the ability to articulate clearly one's thoughts and feelings for the benefit of another. Flavian's intuition of an immediate "connexion" between "utterance" and "the acquisition and display of brilliant military qualities" indicates the process by which the relationship between rhetorical facility and the capacity to dominate others becomes sedimented and naturalized. The narrator performs this same process in the formal structure of the sentence itself, through the accretion of appositional phrases that rhetorically mimic the mental act of thinking through the implications of the concept of utterance. This complex process stands in marked contrast to Flavian's ostensible "immediate connexion" of rhetorical prowess "with the desire for predominance." The narrator thereby demonstrates the power of rhetorical artifice both to create and undermine the illusion of a natural "connexion" between language and dominance by performing the very rhetorical operation that normalizes the ideological assumption that the passage appears to represent as natural and intuitive.

A similar process is at work when the narrator relates that "the popular speech was gradually departing from the form and rule of literary language, a language always and increasingly artificial. While the learned dialect was yearly becoming more and more barbarously pedantic, the colloquial idiom, on the other hand, offered a thousand chance-tost gems of racy and picturesque expression" (*ME* 88–89). This passage associates aesthetic power with a "colloquial idiom" whose "chance-tost gems" offer a spiritually edifying alternative to the pedantry of learned literary language, which leads the reader to expect that the artistic value of colloquial speech might provide leverage for a certain democratizing impulse, in a manner similar to Wordsworth's famous injunction that a poet should be "a man speaking to men" by using "a selection of language really spoken by men."[80] Especially given contemporary fears regarding literary English's transformation into a self-referential "dead language" for scholarly elites, as Linda Dowling discusses, such an assertion would have suggested to a learned Victorian audience that euphuism had the capacity to revive literary language by opening that language to a broader and more diverse range of influences.[81] Thus, the narrator's description of Flavian's "literary programme" as "a work, then, partly conservative or reactionary, in its dealing with the instrument of the literary art; partly popular and revolutionary, asserting, so to term them, the rights of the *proletariate* of speech" would seem to refer to the political implications of euphuism insofar as it vindicates "the rights of the *proletariate* of speech."[82] Yet, upon closer examination of the formal structure of Pater's prose, it becomes apparent that the use of "popular" speech cannot be "revolutionary" specifically *because* Flavian uses it as part of his "literary art," thereby removing it from its dynamic existence as a spoken dialect. Flavian appropriates the language of the common people only so that his literary compositions may seem naturally "racy and picturesque," when really those compositions merely appropriate popular speech to achieve a desired rhetorical effect. The narrator calls attention to the markedly undemocratic impulse underlying Flavian's arrogation of popular speech by undermining the reader's assumptions regarding the political resonance of terms such as "colloquial idiom," "revolutionary," and "*proletariate*" to describe Flavian's selfish desire to use his rhetorical skills to dominate others.

Pater's style inaugurates a self-reflexive analytical process that uses euphuism against itself, rendering it the object of its own linguistic operations. It is a critique of the tendency, identified by Jason Camlot, for "late Victorian theories of style" to endow "the individual with the power to construct a desirable national character . . . by naturalizing in style the linguistically manifest, multitudinous forces of modernity."[83] Pater, by contrast, uses the resources of an "unnatural" literary style to expose the spuriously naturalizing function of literary language, thereby rendering euphuism a cosmopolitan style. Pater similarly deploys linguistic self-reflexivity as a critical method in the later chapter "Manly Amusements," which continues the critique of dominant ideals of Victorian masculinity begun in "Euphuism." Pater emphasizes the development of Marius's homoerotic desires as he shifts his attentions from Flavian's feverish paganism to the reserved Christian soldier Cornelius. It is this refinement of sexual sensibility that encourages Marius to reject the "grim acts of blood-shedding," the violent displays of ritualistic animal sacrifices presented in the Roman amphitheater authorized by the

Emperor Marcus Aurelius, a Victorian icon of muscular Christian masculinity before the fact (*ME* 167). The narrator provides a historical and anthropological account of the primitive impulses motivating such acts of violence, the "manly amusements" of the chapter title. His ability to make this queer critique becomes the cornerstone not only of Marius's own subjective autonomy but that of his novel's readers as well.

Marius, Marcus Aurelius, and "Manly Amusements"

In "Manly Amusements," Marius becomes the queer aesthete who, through the process of erotic negativity, transforms the shock of his sexual awakening into a sense of liberation from repressive social norms and a personal coherence grounded in the resistance to those norms. The chapter begins with his encounter with Cornelius, the beautiful Christian soldier who has, the narrator informs us, now become his intimate, "peculiar" friend after Flavian dies during a plague (*ME* 165). Marius's reflections on his relationship with Cornelius articulate an antithetical relationship between the two boys and the different intellectual systems they respectively embody, which he figures as two opposed versions of homoerotic desire: one he identifies with an unaware, lustful physical desire he felt for Flavian, and the other he identifies with his more self-conscious and "disinterested," yet still markedly erotic, attraction to the beauty of Cornelius. It is only after meeting him that Marius realizes the sexual qualities of his attraction to Flavian, associating his relationship with his deceased friend with the heat of his diseased body, a "feverish attachment, which had made [Marius] at times like an uneasy slave." He metaphorically connects this with the life he leads as the official scribe to the court of Marcus Aurelius in Rome, referring to his "fervid, corrupt life" (*ME* 165). Marius retrospectively understands his attraction to Flavian and his euphuism to be symptoms of a corrupted and diseased culture—what he refers to as the "world's disillusion," over which "people, at their best, seemed only to be brooding" (*ME* 165). Marius reinforces this connection when he asserts that Flavian would have "eagerly" and "with . . . a light heart . . . taken his place in the amphitheatre" to observe the ritualized slaughter of animals therein, the event he is about to attend with the emperor (*ME* 166).

In opposition to Flavian's feverish lust for violence, Cornelius represents the "clear, cold corrective, which the fever of [Marius's] present life demanded" (*ME* 165). He expresses this ethically charged form of difference in his very person, serving as "a kind of outwardly embodied conscience" for Marius (*ME* 165). Yet Marius acknowledges that the "charm" attracting him to Cornelius is "rather physical than moral," more sexual than spiritual. Marius is motivated to follow Cornelius's example not because his Christian worldview offers a superior moral philosophy but because he desires his body. For Marius, Cornelius's Christian morality, "the regular beauty of his exquisite correctness of spirit," depends upon "the regular beauty of his person." The narrator tells us that "it was still to the eye, through visible movement and aspect, that the character, or genius of Cornelius made itself felt by Marius." Matthew Burroughs Price notes the connection between Christianity and homoeroticism in Pater's novel, which "offers Christianity and its place in the Antonine world as an affirmation of the queer witness-observer's role in history." Just as "the Christian stands between the worlds of earth and heaven, witnessing (and witnessed to) the earthly world to promote its transfiguration; the modern queer historian, caught between the homophobic world and the world of queer subcultures, gazes at the world from the side, recording future pain for a present beyond its decadent decay."[84]

The historical consciousness Marius develops through his visual infatuation with Cornelius's body makes him now "wholly of the same mind" with Cornelius "when, alone of a whole company of brilliant youth, he had withdrawn from his appointed place in the amphitheatre," no longer able to condone its socially accepted embrace of violence (*ME* 165). The narrator intrudes to provide an explicitly Tylorian anthropological explanation of this violence, describing in grotesquely vivid detail what goes on in the Roman amphitheater, "the spectacle of animal suffering," of creatures "artificially stimulated and maddened to attack each other" and "escape of the young from their mother's torn bosoms" (*ME* 167–68). "Artemis or Diana," the narrator states,

> as she may be understood in the actual development of her worship, was, indeed, the symbolical expression of two allied yet contrasted elements of human temper and experience—man's amity, and also his enmity, towards the wild creatures, when they were still, in a certain sense, his brothers. She is the complete, and therefore highly complex, representative of a state, in which man was still much occupied with animals, not as his flock, or as his servants after the pastoral relationship of our later, orderly world, but rather as his equals, on friendly terms or the reverse,—a state full of primeval sympathies and antipathies, of rivalries and common wants—while he watched, and could enter into the humours of those "younger brothers," with an intimacy, the "survivals" of which in a later age seem often to have had a kind of madness about them. (*ME* 167–68)

In an explicit reference to Tylor, the narrator identifies the spectacle as a "survival" of ancient rituals associated with the worship of Artemis and Diana. Although the narrator is ostensibly presenting the natural history of the rituals of the ancient, preclassical cult of Artemis/Diana, goddess of the hunt, this analysis recalls Pater's discussion of the Dionysus Zagreus. Both figures represent the "symbolical expression" of a period before the development of a specifically human subjectivity, when animals and humans cohabitated as "brothers" and "equals," and both ancient cults hearken to a time when the boundary between humans and other animals was more porous, as implied by Tylor's theory of cultural evolution. Yet the narrator emphasizes that in the Roman amphitheater of late antiquity, this impulse toward the creation of an "ordered world" where animals are rendered the "servants" of humankind has transformed into a brutal celebration of mankind's own powers of domination, a violent physical act continuous with the will to domination through language expressed by Flavian's euphuism: "the humanities" of the ancient relationship between man and animal, the narrator asserts, "were all forgotten to-day in the excitement of a show, in which mere cruelty to animals, their useless suffering and death, formed the main point of interest" (*ME* 168).

The "manly amusement" to be found in the enjoyment of dominating others and causing them to suffer is the true perversion, not homoerotic desire. Marius, turning away from this violence in disgust, trains his eye on the Emperor Marcus Aurelius, who stares impassively at the spectacle, and declares him to be his "inferior now and forever on the question of righteousness," despite his superior social position, because of his ability to view the spectacle with passive indifference (*ME* 170). Marius suddenly realizes history will judge the emperor harshly for the ethical contradiction between his Stoic philosophy and his willingness to condone violence, despite its present-day acceptability. In many ways, the objects of Pater's scorn in this section could hardly be more overt. As discussed above, Pater's use of the word "manly" to describe the violence of the amphitheater registers his critique of the normative ideal of aggressive, athletic masculinity that muscular Christianity introduced into Victorian culture. Dellamora points out as much when he asserts that Pater uses the "scene of gladiatorial combat to attack ideas of masculine self-worth that depend on aggression and physical brutality."[85] It is also apparent that Pater is critical of the ideal of Stoic masculinity embodied in the figure of Marcus Aurelius.[86] Marius's disgust at the emperor's ability to endure the violence of the amphitheater passively—a spectacle it is well within his power to stop—would have carried marked significance to a Victorian readership. Many critics have attested to Marcus Aurelius's status as a towering figure in nineteenth-century intellectual discourse, serving as a touchstone for thinkers ranging from John Stuart Mill to Friedrich Nietzsche.[87]

The emperor's significance for Victorian literary culture is most characteristically and famously discussed in Arnold's essay "Marcus Aurelius." Arnold asserts that Aurelius "lived and acted in a state of society modern by its essential characteristics, in an epoch akin to our own, in a brilliant centre of civilization."[88] In addition to his status as "perhaps the most beautiful figure in history," Arnold asserts that Aurelius provides a model of behavior that can restore the English nation and English "race" to its former greatness, standing as "one of those consoling and hope-inspiring marks, which stand for ever to remind our weak and easily discouraged race how high human goodness and perseverance have once been carried, and may be carried again."[89] As Frank Turner states, for Arnold "the great charm of Marcus Aurelius was not that he was a Roman but rather that he might have been a Christian."[90] His *Meditations* (170–180 AD) provided Roman antiquity with a spiritual philosophy akin to muscular Christianity. Arnold presents the emperor as an exemplary figure from the historical past whose moral vision should be emulated by modern men. By necessity, Arnold must tiptoe around the well-known historical fact that Christians were persecuted during the reign of Marcus Aurelius, most famously in the killing of forty-eight Christians in Gaul in 177 AD. Arnold attempts to extenuate the emperor's actions by explaining, "Christianity appeared something anti-civil and anti-social, which the State had the faculty to judge and the duty to suppress," thereby explicitly using national and imperial concerns to justify Aurelius's permissive attitude toward violence.[91]

Pater almost certainly had Arnold's essay in mind when his narrator asserts, in reference to the emperor's indifference at the amphitheater, that "Marius remembered well [Marcus Aurelius's] very attitude and expression on this day, when, a few years later, certain things came to pass in Gaul, under his full authority; and that attitude and expression defined already, even thus early in this so friendly intercourse, and though he was still full of gratitude for his interest, a permanent point of difference between the emperor and himself" (*ME* 169). It is apparent in this passage that Pater believes Aurelius's Stoic philosophy to be morally inadequate, especially when faced with the world's violence and injustice. "Manly Amusements" all but explicitly criticizes the violence underlying Victorian culture's dominant understandings of normative masculinity and its relationship to ideals of national character.

More than simply criticizing the canonization of Marcus Aurelius as a moral model for the British nation, however, Pater uses the figure of the emperor to draw attention to the ways in which literary language enables facile understandings of the past, by emphasizing the fundamentally aesthetic nature of Marius's moral awakening. The narrator, after having described the violent acts of the amphitheater in lurid detail, informs us that a "weary and indignant" Marius "could not but observe that . . . Aurelius had sat impassibly through all the hours Marius himself had remained there" (*ME* 169). By gazing upon Marcus Aurelius, Marius realizes that the emperor's "indifferent attitude and expression" will serve as "a permanent point of difference between the emperor and himself. . . . There was something in a tolerance such as this, in the bare fact that he could sit patiently through a scene like this, which seemed to Marius to mark Aurelius as his inferior now and for ever on the question of righteousness; to set them apart on opposite sides, in some great conflict, of which that difference was but a single presentment" (*ME* 169–70). As Iser has noted, Marius's action and his realization at this moment are both negative: he turns away from the spectacle so that he may define his ethics against those of Marcus Aurelius.[92] This passivity was at heart of Wilde's critique of Pater's novel, when he says in *De Profundis* that "Marius is little more than a spectator . . . a spectator merely, and perhaps a little too much occupied with the comeliness of the benches of the sanctuary to notice that it is the sanctuary of sorrow that he is gazing at."[93]

Yet Marius's act is also a Hegelian labor of the negative that transforms him into the autonomous queer aesthete. What might have been merely a traumatic experience transforms into an occasion for Marius to develop his ethical consciousness, a process he conceives of as fundamentally aesthetic in nature, grounded as it is in his visual perception of the world. Rather than indicating Marius's moral quietism, as Wilde suggests, after his observation of the events in the amphitheater, Marius can assert that "his chosen philosophy had said,—Trust the eye: Strive to be right always in regard to the concrete experience: Beware of falsifying your impressions. And its sanction had at least been effective here, in protesting—'This, and this, is what you may not look upon!'" (*ME* 170). By affirming the singularity of his vision against social norms, Marius embodies the resistance to social discourses that is the first step in challenging dominant power relations, and thus the development of subjective autonomy, for the aesthetes.

The narrator, focalized through Marius's morally indignant conscience, articulates his realization that one need not have an ethical philosophy that can be discursively articulated. Instead, he realizes that morality can be founded upon the immediacy of one's aesthetic impressions. The immediate impulse to recoil from the ugliness of a representation of cruelty can, Pater suggests, be a more effective basis for autonomous ethical deliberation than attempting to adhere to an abstract and external moral formula, such as Kant's famously rationalist and formalist categorical imperative.

The narrator attempts to stage an encounter with the negative for his readers similar to Marius's erotic negativity, one created by the aesthetic effects produced by the style of his literary language. In a restaging of euphuistic linguistic self-reflexivity on the level of novelistic form, he says he seeks to avoid writing the sort of "novel" that merely provides help for "sluggish imaginations" by representing "grisly accidents, such as might happen to one's self; but with every facility for comfortable contemplation." Instead, he wants to encourage the reader's self-awareness of the position from which he or she casts ethical judgment upon the narrative. After presenting the awakening of Marius's conscience, he asserts:

> That long chapter of the cruelty of the Roman public shows may, perhaps, leave with the children of the modern world a feeling of self-complacency. Yet it might seem well to ask ourselves—it is always well to do so, when we read of the slave-trade, for instance, or of great religious persecutions on the side of this or that, or of anything else which raises in us the question, 'Is thy servant a dog, that he should do this thing?'—not merely, what germs of feeling we may entertain which, under fitting circumstances, would induce us to the like; but, even more practically, what thoughts, what sort of considerations, may be actually present to our minds such as might have furnished us, living in another age, and in the midst of those legal crimes, with plausible excuses for them: each age in turn, perhaps, having its own peculiar point of blindness, with is consequent peculiar sin—the touch-stone of an unfailing conscience in the select few. (*ME* 170)

The purpose of this paragraph is to prevent the reader from falling into "self-complacency" by identifying uncomplicatedly with Marius's own ethical awakening. As Stephen Arata has argued, Pater cultivates in his readers an "impersonal intimacy" that enables the novel to "block all avenues to readerly identification" by reminding them that the book they are reading is an aesthetic artifact, "an artful arrangement of words that indexes rather than reproduces a particular subjectivity."[94] At this moment in *Marius*, the shift from the personal to the formal is key for the production of both the sensus communis and the impersonality of late style. Pater realizes that readers, by sharing Marius's disgust at the useless slaughter of animals for the purposes of entertainment, may very well be tempted to gloss over the intellectual, emotional, and erotic conditions that led to his realization. Marius, in becoming what Price calls the "queer historian," also has to make himself into a queer anthropologist. He becomes capable of critically assessing his present moment from a sideways perspective. He extricates himself from his culture's normative ideals and conceptual categories to gain some measure of ethical awareness and thereby gain the capacity for self-directed action. Yet the reader, who already inhabits the ethical worldview predicted by Marius, is in danger of feeling the facile pleasures of moral self-satisfaction and complacency.

The narrator suggests a too-easy identification with Marius may leave readers in an attitude of Aurelian indifference toward his profound struggle to gain a sense of ethical autonomy through the aesthetic encounter with the negative. The purpose of the narrator's turn to the readers is to make them cognizant of the extent to which their affective responses to cruelty, such as "the slave-trade" and "religious persecution," are conditioned by their placement within a historical location in a culture that now condemns those things, rather than their own rigorously refined ethical sensibilities. The narrator suggests that understanding the moral failings of the past does not require an imaginative act of historical sympathy, which he describes as a consideration of the "germs of feeling we may entertain which, under fitting circumstances, would induce us to the like." Rather, it necessitates an intense self-examination that leads to the historical-anthropological insight that personal "morality" is dependent upon contingent social norms. This act of self-reflection will lead us to realize, the narrator states, that thoughts and conditions "actually present to our minds . . . might have furnished us, living in another age, and in the midst of those legal crimes, with plausible excuses for them." In other words, our consciousness as it exists *right now* would gladly participate in the cruelty we abjure if it were transferred to a different time and place, "each age in turn, perhaps, having its own peculiar point of blindness, with its consequent peculiar sin." One can only become aware of this ethical blind spot and begin to construct one's own subjective moral philosophy, the narrator implies, through a process similar to the anthropologically inspired ethical development Marius has undergone within the chapter itself.

The style and structure of *Marius*'s prose brings readers to the threshold of developing the critical consciousness that will make them capable of re-imagining the conceptual categories and ethical norms that govern their perception of the world. Yet the narrator stops before prescriptively offering a new, more refined set of moral principles. By ending the chapter at this moment, Pater leaves his readers pondering how their subjectivity has been shaped by their situation within their own historical moment. This provisional sense of distance from the givens of one's society, and the chain of reflections consequent upon that realization, provide for the reader an "equivalent for the sense of freedom" by eliciting the feeling that they, like Marius, might attain a sense of freedom and self-direction by transcending the ethical norms of their culture, despite the fact that this autonomy is not grounded in scientific truth or empirical evidence but is indexed through the aesthetic effect of Pater's prose style. This helps to produce the feeling of psychological alienation from the social present that produces the subjective autonomy that is, for Adorno, the goal of late style.

Pater grounds Marius's ethical development in the specificity of his homoerotic desires yet also expects his readers to be able to come to a similar conclusion through their engagement with the novel's literary form. This is in marked contrast to recent queer theorizations of style, which are defined by a logic of displacement. For Sedgwick, Love, and Ohi, style translates closeted desires into verbal extravagance. By refusing to name their identity, queer stylists create linguistic forms that covertly undermine the expectations of a homophobic society that insists on disciplining the subject through sexual categorization. The Paterian queer stylist, by contrast, expresses subjective autonomy through the positive affirmation of queer desire, which is expressed within the aesthetic sensus communis elicited by the texture and structure of the author's language. Through this process, Paterian style shows the reader that oppressive social discourses are mere historical contingencies. This is a form of writing that seeks to transmit the ethical advantages of queerness to others, rather than trying to hide it.

This does not mean that Pater merely translates queer experience into terms a broad readership will understand. His version of queer style is radical in its demand that his readers live up to the ethical insights Marius derives from his homoerotic desires. The idea that queer experience can be made relevant to a broad audience, yet without pandering to or accommodating heterosexual expectations, was not only revolutionary in the nineteenth century but continues to be so to this day. Far from hiding his desires within the confines of Barthesian queer style, Pater uses literary form to demand his readers to inhabit a queer "sense of fact" and learn from the perspectives it provides on the self and the world, irrespective of their own personal inclinations. The fact that this aspect of Pater's writing continues to be unacknowledged attests to the truth that, even among the most sympathetic readers, it is difficult to accept the possibility that the fruit of queer experience might stand as an ideal.

CHAPTER THREE

Oscar Wilde's Lyric Performativity

In the commonplace book he kept as a student at Oxford in the 1870s, Oscar Wilde recorded a skeptical response to Walter Pater's "Winckelmann." He copied out the passage where Pater states, "we must renounce metaphysics if we would mould our lives to artistic perfection" and use philosophy only to "detect the passion and strangeness and dramatic contrasts of Life." To this, Wilde responded, "Yet surely he who sees in colour no mere delightful quality of natural things but a spirit indwelling in things is in a way a metaphysician."[1] It is unclear to whom the pronoun "he" in this passage refers. Wilde could be claiming that Pater is more of a metaphysician than he believes himself to be, that his writings covertly engage with the transcendental qualities of aesthetic experience, despite his best efforts to live a life devoted solely to the physical enjoyment of beauty. Wilde could also be talking about himself and the philosophical profundity of his own responses to art, thus admitting his covert commitment to a Kantian vision of beauty as the external symbol of an internal, ineffable truth. Alternatively, "he" could refer to the universal human subject, Wilde's recognition that anyone's aesthetic experience always necessarily entails something more than mere "delight." In this last reading, Wilde would be insisting that, in the words of Linda Dowling, "metaphysics would somehow have to be reconciled with aesthetics at a higher level," despite Pater's claims to the contrary.[2] No matter which reading one prefers, these comments make clear that, despite the immense influence Pater had on Wilde's aestheticism, they parted ways when it came to the possibility that artistic experience could be entirely and only sensual.

That Wilde and Pater had close intellectual and personal ties is indisputable. Wilde became an enthusiastic reader of Pater when he entered Oxford in 1874 and struck up an acquaintance with him during his final year at the university in 1878.³ The two men would write favorable reviews of each other's work in later years, and they maintained an amicable correspondence until Pater's death in 1894, one year before Wilde's trials. Throughout his life, he continually referred to *The Renaissance* as his "golden book," and in *De Profundis*, the letter he wrote to Alfred Douglas while serving his prison sentence for "acts of gross indecency," he refers to it as the "book which has had such a strange influence over my life."⁴ Wilde cites him so often in *Intentions* (1891), the volume that includes most of his major philosophical statements on aesthetics, that many critics and reviewers accused him of coming dangerously close to plagiarism. Lawrence Danson even points out that the title *Intentions* recalled Pater's own recently published *Appreciations* (1889), which Wilde reviewed positively in 1890.⁵

Yet, as Wilde's remarks in his commonplace book indicate, his admiration did not preclude major disagreements, even if they were not stated publicly.⁶ In this chapter, I argue Wilde developed his own theory of erotic negativity that both derived and departed significantly from Pater's vision of the relationship between aesthetics and the metaphysics of the subject. Wilde responded to Pater's call for a new generation of queer aesthetes whose experience of art would develop a sense of autonomy that could persist in the face of the late nineteenth century's growing philosophical and scientific skepticism. Although Pater's later writings explore different strategies by which a sense of subjective autonomy can be cultivated through aesthetic responses to literary form, as discussed in chapter 2, Wilde insists that the truth of an individual's subjectivity can never definitively be expressed within language.

Modern critics have suggested that Wilde's vision of the subject has many affinities with queer theory's poststructuralist notion of performative subjectivity. Yet, even as Wilde celebrates the creative potential of abandoning essentialist understandings of identity, he cautions against jettisoning subjectivity altogether. He dramatizes the deleterious consequences of losing all sense of selfhood in his novella "The Portrait of Mr. W.H." (1889, rev. 1921). Many queer readings of Wilde focus on *The Picture of Dorian Gray* (1890/91) as the central text for understanding the relationship between homoeroticism and subjectivity in his writings. This is despite (or, perhaps, because of) the novel's suggestive yet ultimately ambiguous depiction of desire between men. Alan Sinfield writes that the novel "invokes the queer image . . . *despite at no point representing it.*"⁷ This has led to readings that suggest Wilde either

closeted his desires in a modernist language of empty signifiers, as Eve Kosofsky Sedgwick argues, or rejected all "humanist notions of the organic and
autonomous individual," as Stephen Arata states.[8]

Yet "Mr. W.H." shows that Wilde's homosexual representations are not
always teasingly suggestive. I argue in this chapter that his most overtly homoerotic work also contains the most thorough expression of his theory of
sexual subjectivity. Wilde's novella presents a version of negative homoerotics that strongly echoes Hegel's performative theory of the lyric. For Wilde,
the ability to multiply one's identity depends upon the existence of a core of
selfhood that, in contrast to Pater, he believes can never be captured within
language. If the notion of an ineffable personal subjectivity is abandoned entirely, Wilde suggests, then the queer subject becomes radically self-estranged,
and enacts upon himself the violent social homophobia that erotic negativity
is supposed to transform and transcend.

Wilde, like Pater, focuses on aesthetic *Bildung* and its role in the development of what he calls the art critic's "personality." According to Alison Pease,
this personality "is for Wilde never essential, but potential and multiple."[9]
Yet it is also apparent that, for him, the cultivation of self-knowledge does not
necessarily result in a vision of the self as singular, coherent, and consistent.
Instead, it reveals that the individual contains many selves that resist sedi-
mentation into a univocal, self-consistent subjectivity. One of his crucial insights, according to Bruce Bashford, is his realization that the humanist's call
to self-culture through *Bildung* will not necessarily lead to the discovery of
a unified self. Wilde imagines art as a realm where inconsistency is not just
accepted but encouraged, where one realizes, in Bashford's words, that "the
self is plural and that it develops through being the many disparate selves it
contains."[10]

Self-knowledge must then remain necessarily incomplete for Wilde, because the self is inexhaustibly creative. The language used by the self to interpret itself is never capable of capturing entirely the dynamic plurality of
subjectivity without falling into contradiction. As Vivian states in Wilde's
critical dialogue "The Decay of Lying" (1891), "Who wants to be consistent?
The dullard and the doctrinaire, the tedious people who carry out their principles to the bitter end of action, to the *reductio ad absurdum* of practice. Not
I. Like Emerson, I write over the door of my library the word 'Whim'" (*SMS*
164). It is for this reason that Wilde's writings have proven so appealing to
queer critics, who see his oeuvre anticipating their own anti-essentialist celebration of the self's contingency and multiplicity.

Queer theorists have attempted to understand this loss of essential self-hood as an opportunity to reimagine how social transformation and ethical agency might be achieved, most famously in Judith Butler's work on the per-formativity of gender identity. Wilde's writings, however, resist such a recu-peration. Butler has built on her notion of performativity to advocate for the replacement of subjectivity with "relationality," which she describes as "an ongoing normative dimension of our social and political lives, one in which we are compelled to take stock of our interdependence."[11] Wilde, however, invariably privileges individuality over the collective. Unlike both Pater and Butler, he is deeply skeptical of language's powers, believing that its capacity for the creation and destruction of individual subjectivity is severely limited. Yet, given the dialectical nature of his thought, Wilde does not simply affirm the notion of plural subjectivity. "The Portrait of Mr. W.H." offers a pessimis-tic, disturbing portrait of queer individuals who mistakenly come to believe that language's inability to capture their selfhood testifies to their damaged and incomplete subjectivity—precisely the accusation levied against them by their homophobic society. Wilde presents a dark vision of what happens when the individual loses any sense of the personal coherence that ultimately grounds the self's multiplicity, and he indicates that one must hold on to a core sense of selfhood, even if one's possession of it can never be definitively articulated or proven within language.

Poet and Actor, Forger and Fatalist: "The Portrait of Mr. W.H."

In discussions about the methods and aims of sexuality studies in literary criticism, perhaps no other writer has been more central, or more controver-sial, than Wilde. Richard Kaye notes that his writings have occasioned a "cre-ative dialectical rupture" between critical enterprises he refers to as "Gay Studies" and "Queer Theory." According to Kaye, gay studies authors have understood Wilde to be an uncomplicatedly self-aware homosexual man, while queer theorists have stressed Wilde's circulation within the culture "as [a] historical figure and cultural commodity."[12] Accordingly, popular writings by Stephen Gee, Richard Ellmann, and Byrne Fone have perpetuated a senti-mental account of Wilde as the tragic victim of Victorian sexual repression and an early martyr for gay rights, while studies by queer theorists such as Eve Kosofsky Sedgwick, Ed Cohen, Alan Sinfield, and Gary Schmidgall have examined how the mythos surrounding Wilde decisively influenced the dis-cursive invention of "the homosexual" in the late nineteenth century.[13] Con-sequently, there exist today two opposing critical accounts of Wilde: the one,

an emotionally powerful but naïve narrative constructed by gay studies scholars that can be considered humanist, and the other, a rigorously historicized,
anti-essentialist queer account of Wilde's subversive eroticism that can be
construed as anti-humanist. Kaye criticizes the universalizing and normative
impulses underlying gay studies, but he also faults queer critics for "treating
literary texts as simply another discourse." He argues that anti-humanist
queer theories minimize Wilde's specifically aesthetic and philosophical significance by construing the writer's subjectivity to be a mere "refraction or
residue of history."[14]

Wilde himself negotiates this dialectical opposition between humanist
and anti-humanist versions of sexual subjectivity in "Mr. W.H.," by telling a
complex story about the creation and circulation of a homoerotic interpretation of Shakespeare's sonnets. Wilde undoubtedly rejects the notion that
an individual has transparent, unmediated access to his sexual desires: an
assumption that humanist gay studies approaches take for granted in their
characterizations of him as a self-consciously gay writer. At the same time,
however, Wilde's story cautions against jettisoning all aspects of the humanist notion of selfhood. As Foucault cautions in "What Is Enlightenment?,"
while one must be skeptical of the heroically independent subject freed from
history and society, "we must not conclude that everything that has ever been
linked with humanism is to be rejected."[15] "Mr. W.H." paradoxically demonstrates how one's experience of homoerotic desire gestures toward subjectivity's self-grounded nature—its limited yet perdurable form of autonomy—by
revealing language's limited ability to articulate the truth of the subject.

Wilde describes the relationship between language and subjectivity in
terms that bear striking similarity to Hegel's theory of lyric, which he likely
would have encountered as a student of the British Idealist philosophers
during his Oxford years. Both Wilde's and Hegel's accounts of lyric utterance
offer a theory of the performative that is similar to, but also crucially different
from, the version of performativity offered by queer theorists. Queer critics,
following Butler, have argued that non-essentialist, performative notions of
selfhood enable the subversion of social norms through creative acts of citation and iteration, but Hegel suggests that linguistic self-expressions do not
necessarily have any meaningful relationship to the self from which those
expressions originate. Similarly, in "Mr. W.H." the estrangement between
language and the self becomes most apparent when an individual attempts to
articulate his homoerotic desires through an act of literary-critical judgment.

Wilde's narrative uses the transgressive power of the homoerotic to suggest that a coherent sense of self is gained, paradoxically, only when the individual accepts that the subjective experience of selfhood can never be objectively confirmed within language.

For Wilde, neither empirical evidence nor intersubjective recognition provides adequate proof that one really experiences the homoerotic desires one believes oneself to possess. His characters confront the very limits of their capacities for self-understanding when they attempt to express their sexual desire within language. By doing so, they dramatize the radical negativity of lyric utterance, the moment when the individual realizes there is no longer any guarantee that the language of self-analysis meaningfully interprets the self from which that language originates and proceeds. This inability to express their homoerotic desires throws Wilde's characters violently back upon their own existence, creating a fatal misrecognition: they believe that the inability to articulate their erotic desires indicates the irremediable failure of the self that a homophobic culture associates with queerness, rather than a failure of language. Instead, Wilde's unnamed narrator, who comes to realize that language can never capture the truth of the self, demonstrates how a specifically aesthetic attitude toward erotic desire's resistance to linguistic articulation can ground a limited yet perdurable form of autonomous subjectivity.

"Mr. W.H." presents a reading of Shakespeare's poetry purporting to reveal the identity of the famous "Onlie Begetter of These Insuing Sonnets" mentioned in Shakespeare's dedication to his collection.[16] Mr. W.H. is identified as a young actor named Willie Hughes, a member of Shakespeare's troupe who became the object of his erotic longing and the inspiration for his dramatic art. Rather than presenting this reading in the form of a literary-critical essay, however, Wilde embeds it within a narrative frame that recounts the origin and circulation of this theory among three men: the narrator of the story, his friend Erskine, and Erskine's deceased friend Cyril Graham, the supposed originator of this interpretation.

The controversial theory these characters find so strangely compelling did not originate with Wilde but was first proposed in 1766 by the literary critic Thomas Tyrwhitt and subsequently endorsed by Edmund Malone in his influential 1790 edition of the sonnets. In 1839 the Willie Hughes theory was accepted but severely condemned by the literary critic Henry Hallam, who admitted his personal regret that the poems had ever been written and maintained that "there is a weakness and folly in all excessive and misplaced affection, which is not redeemed by the touches of nobler sentiment that abound in this long series of sonnets."[17] Yet, by the time Wilde wrote "Mr. W.H." in the late nineteenth century, the theory had largely fallen out of fashion among Shakespeareans. As the narrator states, late Victorian scholars had concluded that "[Lord] Pembroke, Shakespeare, and Mary Fitton are the three personages of the Sonnets; there is no doubt at all about it" (*SMS* 35).

Wilde's story begins when the narrator learns of the Willie Hughes theory from Erskine, who, in turn, has received the theory from his Oxford friend Cyril, an "effeminate" acting enthusiast who supposedly discovered Willie Hughes's existence by "working [through the] purely internal evidence" provided by the poems themselves (*SMS* 37). Erskine tells of how Cyril presented him with a portrait of Willie Hughes to prove the veracity of the interpretation. Erskine goes on to tell of his discovery that the painting was a forgery commissioned by Cyril himself and of his subsequent suicide in the name of the Willie Hughes theory.

While Erskine finds the Willie Hughes theory untenable, the narrator is convinced by Cyril's interpretation and proceeds to narrate the process by which he goes through the sonnets in search of supporting evidence. In the process, he offers digressions on the history of boy actors on the Renaissance stage, the revival of Neoplatonic thought, and the significance of the "Dark Lady" mentioned in the later part of the sonnet sequence. After writing a letter to Erskine outlining the evidence in support of the Willie Hughes theory, however, the narrator discovers that he no longer believes in it himself. Yet he soon learns that his letter has reconvinced Erskine of the theory and inspired him to travel to the Continent to find evidence that will persuade the now-unbelieving narrator of the existence of Willie Hughes. Two years later, the narrator receives a letter from Erskine declaring his intent to commit suicide in the name of the Willie Hughes theory. The narrator also travels to the Continent in hopes of saving Erskine but finds that he is already dead. He soon discovers, however, that Erskine died after a long struggle with tuberculosis rather than by suicide. The story ends with the narrator ambiguously claiming that, whenever he looks at the forged painting of Mr. W.H. (his inheritance from Cyril by way of Erskine), he now believes that "there is really a great deal to be said for the Willie Hughes theory of Shakespeare's Sonnets" (*SMS* 101).

Although critics have paid less attention to "Mr. W.H." than the rest of Wilde's literary output, the consensus is that the novella represents, in fictional form, the psychological and linguistic complexities inherent to acts of aesthetic criticism. Some scholars have bracketed the tale's homoerotic aspects in their attempts to understand "Mr. W.H." as a paradigmatic example of the kind of art criticism Wilde describes in the dialogues "The Decay of Lying" and "The Critic as Artist."[18] Other commentators, however, have argued that the novella presents Wilde's struggle to articulate a language for desire between men that escapes the pathologizing sexological discourse surrounding homosexuality in the late nineteenth century.[19] Yet, as Joseph Bristow has argued, before the trials in 1895 that led to his imprisonment, "there is little evidence to suggest that Wilde had much or any interest in the ways in which sexual behavior had become a focus of fascination for [fin-de-siècle] thinkers. . . . Wilde, until the time of his prison sentence, had no perception of himself as either a 'homosexual' or an 'invert,' even though these almost interchangeable labels were gaining credibility within scientific circles in the mid-1890s."[20]

Queer theorists such as William A. Cohen and Richard Halpern have thus provocatively brought together poststructuralist and psychoanalytic theory to argue that "Mr. W.H." finds an alternative to sexological definitions of homosexual identity. They argue that Wilde foregrounds the linguistic indeterminacy lying at the heart of literary interpretation to reflect or repeat the psychic incoherence lying at the heart of sexual desire.[21] In turning to the poststructuralist notion of *différance* to explain Wilde's deployment of homoeroticism, however, Cohen and Halpern rely on the unstated assumption that linguistic structures can be mapped onto psychic structures. They deploy Lacan's poststructuralist version of Freudian psychoanalysis, which famously claims that "the unconscious is structured like a language."[22] Both posit at the heart of "Mr. W.H." a mise en abyme of linguistic representation.

Yet a cursory examination of Wilde's story reveals that acts of literary interpretation, rather than being absolutely foreclosed by *différance*, continue unabated. The problem, it seems, does not lie in linguistic interpretation in and of itself. Rather, in Wilde's story it becomes no longer evident that acts of interpretation have any necessary or significant relationship to the self from which they originate. I argue that, instead of representing a Lacanian version of subjectivity, Wilde's representation of the relationship between homoeroticism and the aesthetics of poetry maintains an investment in autonomous subjectivity shared by those in his Oxford Idealist milieu and bears marked similarity to Hegel's discussion of the performativity of poetic language.

"All Art Being in a Certain Degree a Mode of Acting"

The concept of performativity is key for analyzing the conjunction between homoeroticism and self-estrangement that is characteristic of the homosocial circulation of the Willie Hughes theory. Throughout "Mr. W.H." Wilde imbricates the act of articulating the theory with two other types of performative acts: the theatrical performances of the boy-actor Willie Hughes and the poetic performances that are Shakespeare's sonnets. Wilde's story presents literary interpretation itself as a kind of performance, one that stands alongside these other aesthetic acts in its creative relationship to the subject. The interpretive performance of the Willie Hughes theory offers characters the opportunity to express their unique sexual subjectivity through the articulation of their homoerotic desire. Yet these performances also demonstrate the process by which acts of self-interpretation collapse upon themselves to reveal the limitations of the subject from which those self-interpretive statements proceed.

Hegel is never mentioned explicitly in "Mr. W.H.," but Wilde's thinking about Shakespeare had long been influenced by idealist thought by the time he wrote this story. This is especially apparent in his essay on stage costume in contemporary productions of Shakespeare, "The Truth of Masks," which ends with the assertion that "it is only in art-criticism, and through it, that we can realize Hegel's system of contraries. The truths of metaphysics are the truths of masks" (*SMS* 304). During Wilde's years at Oxford from 1874 to 1878, Hegel dominated philosophical and religious discourse. Wilde was influenced during his university years by Pater's aestheticized version of Hegelian and Oxford Idealist philosophers such as Benjamin Jowett, T. H. Green, William Wallace, and F. H. Bradley. The idealist strain in Wilde's writing was recognized as early as 1892, when Max Nordau, in his infamous study *Degeneration*, classed Wilde with Friedrich Nietzsche as, in Smith's words, "egomaniacal individualists who had willfully distorted Hegel's idealism."[23] Major literary critics of the early twentieth century such as William K. Wimsatt, Cleanth Brooks, and René Wellek recognized Wilde's aesthetics to be part of the idealist tradition, and Rodney Shewan has discussed the Hegelian elements present within Wilde's notion of "soul."[24] More recently, Philip E. Smith and Michael Helfand's edition of his Oxford commonplace book has established once and for all Wilde's detailed and extensive knowledge of Hegel's works.[25]

While there is no conclusive evidence that "Mr. W.H." was directly inspired by Wilde's reading of Hegel's *Aesthetics*, it is clear that his story generates a version of erotic negativity marked strongly by Paterian aestheticism and Oxford Idealism, one which parallels Hegel's theory of lyric performativity. This can be seen in the novella's opening lines, which begin with a discussion between Erskine and the narrator regarding famous literary forgeries. When the topic of Thomas Chatterton's forgeries of medieval poems comes up, the narrator exonerates Chatterton by suggesting that the word "forgery" cannot apply to an act committed solely in the name of artistic perfection.[26] He claims that because "Art" is "to a certain degree a mode of acting," works of art do not make substantive claims about reality that can be adjudicated as either true or false, right or wrong. Instead, the narrator suggests that an aesthetic creation should be understood to be a type of performance in which the artist strives to actualize his "personality" as an ideal that transcends the "accidents and limitations of real life" (*SMS* 33). In other words, the narrator suggests that the forged art object is performative: it enacts the artist's ideal self for the benefit of an audience of interpreters. The artist, instead of erasing his personality to create an autonomous aesthetic object, uses the forgery's illusion of historical verisimilitude as part of a performance of selfhood that has been purified of accident and limitation—including, in the case of Chatterton, the accident of having been born in the eighteenth century instead of the Middle Ages. In the narrator's view, works of art can be evaluated only according to their effectiveness in presenting an idealized version of the artist's subjectivity, even (or especially) when the artist presents the work as the product of someone else's subjectivity.

The narrator thus also implies that all art is "a mode of acting" in the theatrical sense. He suggests that the artist's expression of selfhood, which is accomplished through an act of aesthetic creativity, is the expression of a self that is produced in and through that creative act, not the representation of a self that exists prior to or outside of the aesthetic performance. In a typically Wildean inversion, the deep subjectivity that supposedly precedes the creative act is, in fact, an ex post facto illusion created by the aesthetic performance. As Gilbert states in "The Critic as Artist," "When a great actor plays Shakespeare . . . [h]is own individuality becomes a vital part of the interpretation. . . . In point of fact, there is no such thing as Shakespeare's Hamlet. If Hamlet has something of the definiteness of a work of art, he has also all the obscurity that belongs to life. There are as many Hamlets as there are melancholics" (*SMS* 246). Gilbert asserts that the role of Hamlet, Western literature's representative of deep interiority and individuality par excellence, comes to its full fruition only through many individual interpretations by a multitude of actors and that no textual original of Hamlet exists outside of or prior to the many particular instantiations of that role. By interpreting the narrator's assessment of Chatterton's forgery in light of Gilbert's assertion, one can see that Wilde collapses the two possible definitions of the term "acting."

The narrator implies that works of art should be considered a form of *doing* on the part of the artist that cannot (or should not) be evaluated either as true or false, let alone right or wrong. In his reference to aesthetic creation as "a mode of acting," some critics might understand Wilde's narrator to anticipate queer theory's concept of performativity. This idea, which has its origins in the writings of philosopher J. L. Austin, and has subsequently been discussed in the writings of Jacques Derrida, Shoshana Felman, Judith Butler, and Eve Kosofsky Sedgwick, is a cornerstone of poststructuralist-influenced queer theory.[27] These thinkers use performativity to formulate non-essentializing theories of identity and to explore the role of language in the construction of subjectivity by referring to the various processes by which linguistic and bodily acts work to iterate or subvert normative social and sexual practices.

Wilde, however, was too shrewd a dialectician to celebrate performativity merely as an opportunity for the self-created subject to subvert social norms. He suggests that there exists some aspect of subjectivity that must be located outside of the performative act. Although there is no ideal Hamlet that exists apart from individual performances of the role, the fact that there are "as many Hamlets are there are melancholics" suggests that the unique selfhood of each individual actor inflects his particular performance of the role. These actors certainly do not embody the bounded selfhood beyond language typically associated with notions of subjective autonomy, insofar as the uniqueness they lend to Hamlet is given character within the dramatic performance itself. Yet the irreducible individuality of each performance hints at the existence of some perdurable form of selfhood that performative acts can neither contain nor efface.

Wilde surveys the contours of this perdurable aspect of the self by exploring how performative acts paradoxically gesture toward a qualified form of autonomy by casting doubt upon the subject's ability to acquire knowledge about itself through language. In this, "Mr. W.H." shares with Hegel's theory of lyric the belief that lyric poetry represents the simultaneous triumph and crisis of art in its relationship to subjectivity. According to Hegel, poetry stands as the preeminent artistic form of the modern era in its combination of the musical representation of spiritual interiority with the external, material, and phenomenal character of sculpture and painting. He asserts that poetry is the medium through which "the mind expresses all of its fantasies and art to the mind."[28] As Jan Mieszkowski explains, in Hegel's *Aesthetics*, "poetry's uniqueness stems from the fact that the subject and the object of poetry, the medium and the message, are one in the same. . . . [P]oetry can deal with any and every topic in any and every fashion because in the final analysis what poetry really expresses is the mind's apprehension of itself to itself in itself."[29] This is the likely inspiration for Pater's assertion at the end of "Winkelmann" that poetry is the only genre that can "demand that width, variety, delicacy of resources, which will enable it to deal with the conditions of modern life."[30] Hegel asserts that the human imagination, "that universal foundation of all the particular art-forms and the individual arts," is both the proper material and the proper medium of poetry.[31] Yet because poetry has no restrictions on either its form or its content, it "appear[s] as that particular art in which art itself begins . . . to dissolve. . . . [P]oetry destroys the fusion of spiritual in-wardness with external existence to an extent that begins to be incompatible with the original conception of art, with the result that poetry runs the risk of losing itself in a transition from the region of sense to that of spirit."[32] Even as poetry represents the ultimate conjunction between the inward and out-ward self and the purest expression of the subject's ability to interpret its expression of selfhood back to itself, its very "success leads it astray—in its autonomy, it threatens to abandon its mediating role and evacuate itself of any representational duties whatsoever."[33]

Lyric poetry exceeds drama and the epic in its capacity to express the self's ideas and feelings. Moreover, Hegel asserts that lyric utterances cannot "be so far continued as to display the subject's heart and passion in practical activity and action, that is, in the subject's return to himself in his actual deed."[34] According to Mieszkowski, "Hegel . . . insists that because lyric is the highpoint of artistic subjectivity, the expression of interiority as such, it must be grasped as an *act* of self in a way that epic and drama cannot be. The im-portant thing to realize is that a lyric act of self . . . must remain stillborn." For Mieszkowski, the expression of self through lyric occurs in a language "that acts in such a way that the action can never be grasped as the coordination of a self and an act. . . . Lyric acts without becoming someone's action."[35] The language of lyric poetry "does not present itself as a discourse that under-stands itself in and as its own acts of self understanding. This is a language that never offers a grammar or syntax that could serve as a model for relations between agents and their deeds or subjects and objects."[36]

Instead, according to Hegel, lyric is the place where the imagination "is essentially distinguished from thinking by reason of the fact that . . . it allows particular ideas to subsist alongside one another without being related, whereas thinking demands and produces dependence of things on one another."[37] Lyric poetry thus represents the violent negation of both art and thinking: "Lyric . . . becomes the outpouring of a soul, fighting and struggling with itself, which in its ferment does violence to both art and thought because it oversteps one sphere without being, or being able to be, at home in the other."[38] Mieszkowski concludes that, for Hegel,

> lyric poetry cannot self-clarify or self-interpret in the course of articulating itself as the product of its own articulations. Where lyric subjectivity is concerned, the self's expression of itself to itself is as destructive as it is creative. . . . Lyric fails to demonstrate that its own self-interpretation begins and ends with the acts by which it makes its own significance self-evidently meaningful to itself. On the most basic level, this means that the self-interest of self—the notion of the self as even minimally self-related or self-concerned— has lost its inevitability.[39]

Lyric poetry's expression of this loss of self-relatedness can be considered performative but in a very different sense from the way the term is used in poststructuralist queer theory. Critics such as Butler have argued that non-essentialist, performative notions of selfhood enable the queer subversion of social norms and the radical rethinking of ethics through creative or destructive acts of citation, iteration, and resistance, but Hegel states that lyric poetry reveals that linguistic self-expressions do not necessarily have any meaningful relationship to the self from which those expressions originate and proceed. Poetic language demonstrates that linguistic acts of self-interpretation need not lead to greater self-knowledge or self-consciousness.

Reading the Portrait

While Hegel's comments on performativity derive specifically from his analysis of lyric poetry, Wilde's novella shows us how the limitations of lyrical language have implications for the relationship between language and subjectivity more generally. Wilde demonstrates this by showing how the collapse of subject and object that seems characteristic of lyric poetry actually occurs in all self-reflexive linguistic acts, including the literary-critical assessments that Immanuel Kant refers to as acts of "subjective universal" aesthetic judgment.[40] Wilde shows how lyric performativity applies to all attempts to gain self-knowledge through language.

Cyril Graham's obsession with a homoerotic interpretation of a sonnet cycle is not only about a forgery committed to prove a literary theory. It is also about his attempts to attain self-knowledge through an aesthetic encounter with the homoeroticism found in Shakespeare's poetry. The portrait of Mr. W.H. itself stands as both the literal and metaphorical embodiment of Cyril's quixotic desire to attain erotic self-knowledge through a literary-critical interpretation of Shakespeare's sonnets. When Erskine presents the painting as a prelude to relating the story of Cyril Graham, the narrator sees "a full-length portrait of a young man in late sixteenth-century costume, standing by a table, with his right hand resting on an open book. He seemed about seventeen years of age, and was of quite extraordinary personal beauty, though evidently somewhat effeminate. Indeed, had it not been for the dress and the closely cropped hair, one would have said that the face, with its dreamy, wistful eyes and its delicate scarlet lips, was the face of a girl" (*SMS* 34). Mr. W.H. stands next to "the two masks of Comedy and Tragedy," which indicate his profession as an actor. Using a magnifying glass to take a closer look at the book, the narrator spells out the words "To the Onlie Begetter of These Insuing Sonnets" (*SMS* 35) and realizes that the Mr. W.H. referred to in the portrait's title is none other than Shakespeare's Mr. W.H.

We soon learn, however, that the painting is a forgery commissioned by Cyril to prove the veracity of the Willie Hughes theory to Erskine. The thematic connection between poetry and acting accentuated in both the painting and in the Willie Hughes theory suggests the complex motivations underlying the commission of the forgery. Erskine relates that the Willie Hughes interpretation began one day when Cyril summoned him to his rooms in London. Cyril tells Erskine "he had at last discovered the true secret of Shakespeare's sonnets; that all the scholars and critics had been entirely on the wrong track; and that he was the first who, working purely by internal evidence, had found out who Mr. W.H. really was" (*SMS* 37). Although Cyril's use of "purely internal evidence" initially indicates that he is prepared to offer a traditionally lyric interpretation of Shakespeare's sonnets as autotelic and hermetically self-sufficient, we soon learn that this evidence indicates "that the young man to whom Shakespeare addressed these strangely passionate poems must have been somebody who was a really vital factor in the development of his dramatic art" (*SMS* 38). By suggesting that the young man addressed *in* the sonnets is not the primary inspiration *of* the sonnets themselves but rather of Shakespeare's plays, Cyril roundly rejects common late-Victorian interpretations of the sonnets as an entirely idealized, self-referential edifice, "merely a philosophical allegory . . . in [which] . . . Shakespeare is addressing his Ideal Self, or Ideal Manhood, or the Spirit of Beauty, or the Reason, or the Divine Logos, or the Catholic Church" (*SMS* 40).

The philosophical-allegorical interpretations referenced by Cyril are, in fact, direct quotations from two major articles on Shakespeare's sonnets: the first, novelist and critic John A. Heraud's "A New View of Shakespeare's Sonnets: An Inductive Critique," published in *Temple Bar* in 1862, and the second, the anonymously authored "New Views of Shakespeare's Sonnets: The 'Other Poet' Identified," a two-part article published in *Blackwood's Edinburgh Magazine* in 1884 and 1885.[41] There is substantial external evidence indicating that Wilde was familiar with both of these essays. Cyril follows Heraud by mocking the "German commentator" who suggests "Mr. W.H." stands for "Mr. William Himself," and, according to Wilde's letter of inquiry to *Blackwood's*, the two-part article of 1884–85 provided the direct inspiration for the writing of "Mr. W.H." (*SMS* 40).[42] Both Heraud's essay and the *Blackwood's* article concur that the sonnets represent the high point of Shakespeare's artistic achievement as the precursor to a certain version of the transcendental, high Romantic lyric, and both also agree that the interpretive key to understanding the entire sonnet cycle is the infamous sonnet 20, "A woman's face with nature's own hand painted." Readers have long recognized this sonnet to be Shakespeare's most markedly homoerotic poem: its speaker refers to a young man as "the master mistress of my passion."[43]

Heraud asserts that, in this sonnet, Shakespeare finally "passes out of the dramatist into the poet," by apostrophizing his "*alter-ego,* in the ideal personality, in the universal humanity," through the image of "masculine beauty."[44] Heraud proceeds to offer this rhetorical question: "For does not the poet himself declare, that the Ideal Man, the Friend, who he has addressed, has all along been identified with himself—has simply been his Objective Self?" He asserts that the theme of the sonnets "is the love of the One for the Many; but the Many, how multitudinous soever, are yet properly but the reflex of the One, and the sum of both is the Universe. That Shakespeare saw this as clearly as any German sage of later times is to me manifest; but he had not theorized it."[45] In this idealist and explicitly Kantian-Hegelian interpretation, Heraud evacuates all individual specificity and erotic physicality from the figure of the young man. Instead, he suggests that the movement of the sonnet cycle from the praise of the object to the praise of the subject, and from praise of the subject to praise of the universal subject, recapitulates in its very form the operations of consciousness itself as it is conceptualized within philosophical idealism. Heraud understands the sonnets to be a completely self-referential and autotelic whole, the forerunner and epitome of lyric subjectivity in its high Romantic mode.

Similarly, the author of the *Blackwood's* articles maintains that the sonnets represent the culmination of Shakespeare's aesthetic achievement insofar as they represent the utmost embodiment of his subjective communion with the divine Logos: "He foretells, as with prophetic certainty, that his verse would be the permanent memorial of the life, name, and glory of the immortal beauty and love of which he sings."[46] By identifying the "other poet" referenced in the sonnets as none other than Dante Alighieri, the author suggests that, like Dante, Shakespeare's sonnets anticipate the Romantic sublime: "Though the thought, imagery, and style of both Dante and Shakespeare exhibit their great powers, . . . yet these two gifted and singularly able writers alike confess that the glory of their theme far exceeded the measure and the reach of their skill, even when taxed and stretched to the utmost possible extent."[47] According to the author, Shakespeare attempted to gesture toward this unrepresentable "Divine Wisdom" by giving it human form. Instead of making use of the ideal of feminine beauty, as Dante did with Beatrice, Shakespeare represents the divine in "the anonymous form of manly and youthful beauty."[48] The conjunction between masculine beauty and divine Logos is nowhere more apparent than in sonnet 20, where "for the full expression of his poetical invention, idea, or device, it was necessary to add to this form of manly beauty the figure of the woman." The author goes on to assert that "this complex figure, as pictured and described in the 20th sonnet, contains in it and expresses the poetical invention, idea, or device, on which all the sonnets depend. It is 'the master mistress' of Shakespeare's 'passion.' And the critic able to interpret and expound that 20th sonnet ought to be able to interpret every sentence, from first to last, in all the sonnets."[49] Much like Heraud, the author literally renders the young man of the poems anonymous and allegorical in the very process of placing this homoerotic celebration of masculine beauty at the center of Shakespeare's poetic vision.

These characteristic late Victorian readings attempt to present Shakespeare's sonnet cycle as his utmost poetic achievement, just the sort of self-referential, self-interpretive lyric whole theorized by Hegel in the *Aesthetics*. They do so by placing the figure of the beautiful young man at the heart of the sonnets yet evacuating him of any material, physical, or erotic specificity. Cyril Graham's championing of the Willie Hughes theory is a rebellion against these impulses, as he returns physical and erotic materiality to the figure of the young man by trying to "de-lyricize" Shakespeare's poems. Erskine asserts that Cyril "felt, as indeed I think we all must feel, that the Sonnets are addressed to an individual—to a particular young man whose personality for some reason seems to have filled the soul of Shakespeare with terrible joy and no less terrible despair" (*SMS* 40). Cyril's focus on the "individual," the "particular," and "personality" is an attempt to ground the sonnets in the physical and emotional reality of Shakespeare's lived experience.

Cyril's focus on Shakespeare's emotional life and the material reality of the young man is of a piece with Wilde's own youthful ideas about poetry. In his Oxford commonplace book, Wilde states:

> In proportion as poetry separates itself from human passions and feeling, so does it lose its own essence, and the quality of its power. Wordsworth's sonnet on the advantage of Compulsory Education is as unfit a subject for poetic art as are those flights of transcendent imagination to which Shelley sometimes soared. One flies too high: the other does not fly at all: So the pure intellect and the pure imagination are not themselves the right mainsprings of noble song which has [its] natural roots in the passionate side of nature.[50]

The young Wilde, like Cyril, believes that poetry's "essence" can be found only in "human passions and feeling," the subjective emotional responses to actual things, events, and people in the world. Both the youthful Wilde and Cyril position themselves against a certain version of the high Romantic lyric that vaunts the expression of the "transcendent imagination" above the "passionate side of nature." This lyricism was, for Wilde, embodied by Percy Bysshe Shelley's poetry and was, for Cyril, enshrined by those critics who try to understand Shakespeare's sonnets as a philosophical allegory written in praise of an abstract, imageless sublimity.

Cyril's wish to return the sonnets to the "passionate side of nature" requires him not only to insist on the material reality and erotic appeal of the young man but also to remove the sonnets from the ethereal realm of the autotelic lyric utterance. "Who was he," Cyril asks,

> whose physical beauty was such that it became the very cornerstone of Shakespeare's art; the very source of Shakespeare's inspiration; the very incarnation of Shakespeare's dreams? To look at him as simply the object of

certain love-poems was to miss the whole meaning of the poems: for the art of which Shakespeare talks in the Sonnets is not the art of the Sonnets themselves, which indeed were to him but slight and secret things—it is the art of the dramatist to which he is always alluding. (*SMS* 40)

By placing the young man as the "cornerstone," "source," and "incarnation" of Shakespeare's creativity, Cyril finds "a whole new meaning to the poems" hidden in the sonnets that, ironically, displaces their centrality in Shakespeare's oeuvre, where they had been situated by the late Victorian critical establishment. This emphasis on the embodied form of the young man renders the poems "slight and secret things" in comparison to "the art of the dramatist," which uses the materiality of the performing human body as its primary tool of expression.

By deemphasizing the aesthetic significance of Shakespeare's lyric in favor of his drama, Cyril discovers that the young man of the sonnets emphatically is not an allegorical embodiment of the "Objective Self" or "Divine Wisdom," but rather a very real erotic object, "none other than the boy-actor for whom he created Viola and Imogen, Juliet and Rosalind, Portia and Desdemona, and Cleopatra herself" (*SMS* 41). For Cyril, the sonnets do not add up to a self-referential lyric whole but are instead a means of deciphering the relationship between the dramatic works and the individual who inspired them by eliciting Shakespeare's erotic desires. The difference between Cyril's approach to the sonnets and that of other late Victorian critics can be seen most clearly in his interpretation of sonnet 20. Rather than presenting the poem as the figural key that will unlock the meaning of the entire sonnet cycle, Cyril finds the actual name of the boy-actor punningly encoded in the sonnet's seventh line: "A man in hew, all <u>Hews</u> in his controwling." He thus asserts that the last name of the boy-actor must be "Hughes," because "in the original edition of the Sonnets, '*Hews*' is printed with a capital letter and in italics, and in this, he claimed, showed clearly that a play on words was intended" (*SMS* 42). His emphasis on Shakespeare's wordplay calls attention to both the materiality of language and its ability to reference a reality that exists outside the poems themselves.

While he claimed to have discovered the name Willie Hughes from the language of the poems, Cyril's overall erotic and embodied reading of the sonnets stands as an aesthetic interpretation that is also, simultaneously, an act of self-interpretation. Erskine declares, "Cyril Graham's theory evolved . . . purely from the Sonnets themselves." It depended "for its acceptance not so much on demonstrable proof or formal evidence, but on a kind of spiritual and artistic sense, by which alone he claimed could the true meaning of the poems be discerned. . . . He went through all the Sonnets carefully, and showed, or fancied he showed, that, according to his new explanation of their meaning, things that had seemed obscure, or evil, or exaggerated, became clear and rational, of high artistic import" (*SMS* 41–42). Cyril insists that the "true meaning" hidden within the poems does not take the form of empirically verifiable "evidence" that can be objectively adjudicated as either true or false. Instead, it can be "discerned" only by those who, like Cyril, have developed an attunement to the feelings expressed by the poems, "a kind of spiritual or artistic sense." To someone who has cultivated his aesthetic discernment by engaging with the homoeroticism of the sonnets, what had seemed aesthetic imperfections coalesce into something "of high aesthetic import." Erskine's use of loaded terms such as "obscure," "evil," and "exaggerated" implies that the elements transformed into something "clear and rational" by Cyril's spiritual or artistic sense are precisely the homoerotic references that caused critics like Henry Hallam such regret.

Essentially, Cyril knows that the Willie Hughes theory is true because he believes himself to share the same homoerotic desires that Shakespeare possessed. The logic Cyril deploys in defense of his de-lyricizing interpretation of the sonnets attempts to save them from the bloodless hermeticism of the late Victorian critical consensus by returning them to the embodied reality of Shakespeare's erotic desire for Willie Hughes. We soon learn, however, that Cyril's homoerotic interpretation of the sonnets has become untenable even to himself. Yet the reason why he loses faith in his interpretation is not because empirical evidence has failed to establish the historical existence of Willie Hughes. (Though, of course, it has.) Nor does he lose faith because he ceases to believe in the theory per se. Instead, Cyril ceases to believe in his belief in the theory.[51] When he realizes that his interpretation of the sonnets cannot escape the logic of the performative lyric utterance that he has tried so ardently to reject, Cyril begins to feel a self-estrangement that is created in and through the very act of articulating his subjective aesthetic impressions.

Erskine inadvertently forces this realization upon Cyril when he maintains, "Before the theory could be placed before the whole world in a really perfected form, it was necessary to get some independent evidence about the existence of this young actor, Willie Hughes" (*SMS* 43). Cyril does not become upset because he is afraid that there will be no evidence supporting his interpretation. To the contrary, he becomes agitated because Erskine refuses to echo his own unquestioning belief in the theory. According to Erskine, Cyril became inordinately disturbed by the suggestion that they search for empirical evidence in support of the historical existence of Willie Hughes. Cyril "became a good deal annoyed" by what he called Erskine's "philistine tone of mind, and indeed was rather bitter on the subject" (*SMS* 43). Cyril turns angry at the mere suggestion that Erskine needs external, empirical evidence to believe in his interpretation. According to Erskine, "we discovered nothing, of course," in the way of historical evidence, "and each day the existence of Willie Hughes seemed to me to become more problematical" (*SMS* 43). Erskine's loss of faith puts the increasingly frantic and desperate Cyril "in a dreadful state," such that he "used to go over the whole question again and again, entreating me to believe" (*SMS* 43–44). Cyril's worry is not whether the Willie Hughes theory is objectively true but instead that Erskine's failure to believe in the theory will somehow undermine Cyril's own belief.

His disturbance stems from the fact that Erskine's encounter with his impressionistic and homoerotic interpretation of Shakespeare's sonnets does not compel the "kind of spiritual or aesthetic sense" that induces immediate assent, a phrase that recalls one of the foundational works of idealist aesthetics, Kant's *Critique of Judgment* (1790). Kant asserts that aesthetic judgments characteristically take the form of what he calls "subjective universals." This apparently oxymoronic term means that one's aesthetic impressions are, on the one hand, entirely subjective and incommunicable between subjects; that is, the actual experience of an object's beauty cannot be given to someone else in or through language. Yet because these aesthetic judgments are disinterested and do not depend on private conditions, one feels, on the other hand, that this impression ought to be shared by others. People articulate their aesthetic judgments as if they were inherent properties of the aesthetic object or logical necessities: one typically says, "this is beautiful," rather than, "I believe this to be beautiful." Kant asserts that, because this subjective universal is not founded on an objective principle of reason or logic, it stems from "a subjective principle, which determines only by feeling rather than concepts, though nonetheless with universal validity, what is liked or disliked."[52] This is the principle known as the sensus communis.

While, for Pater, this aesthetic quality can enable the intersubjective communication of queer experience, as I discuss in chapter 2, things do not go so smoothly in Wilde's novella. Erskine's disbelieving "philistine tone of mind" presents a profound challenge to Cyril's "spiritual or aesthetic sense." Rather than providing Cyril with the experience of self-extension that is usually provided by the sensus communis, Erskine's refusal to share in Cyril's subjective experience of the sonnets presents a challenge not only to the Willie Hughes theory but also to the integrity of Cyril's subjectivity itself. Because Cyril's aesthetic interpretation of the sonnets is tied to his homoerotic desires, Erskine's refusal of the interpretation appears to be a rejection of Cyril himself. Erskine, by foreclosing Cyril's erotically motivated experience of the sensus communis so emphatically, forces him into a profoundly unsettling sense of isolation and incompleteness that throws him against the limitations of his own existence.

In a last-ditch effort to convince him of the theory's truth, Cyril presents Erskine with the eponymous painting *Portrait of Mr. W.H.* as proof of the objective historical existence of Willie Hughes and his significance for Shakespeare's literary genius. As the reader already knows, however, the portrait is a forgery. Both Cyril's attempt to return Shakespeare's sonnets to the material reality of his erotic desire and his attempt to prove the objective historical reality of that desire founder upon the limitations of the self. Cyril's forged painting reveals the limitations of the subject's capacity either to express or efface the self through aesthetic interpretation and the consequent impossibility of escaping the autotelic logic of the lyric utterance. The self-reflexive nature of this forgery is literally figured on the canvas itself, when we realize that the portrait of Mr. W.H. is, in fact, a portrait of Mr. Cyril Graham. As Erskine describes him, Cyril shares many physical qualities with the young man represented in the portrait. He is "effeminate" and "somewhat languid in manner," "the most splendid creature I ever saw, and nothing could exceed the grace of his movements, the charm of his manner" (36). He was "always cast for the girls' parts," in the student productions of Shakespeare mounted by Cambridge's Amateur Dramatics Company, "and when *As You Like It* was produced he played Rosalind. You will laugh at me, but I assure you that Cyril Graham was the only perfect Rosalind I have ever seen" (*SMS* 37). Perhaps most tellingly, Erskine asserts, "The two things that really gave [Cyril] pleasure were poetry and acting" (*SMS* 36).

Cyril's forged painting catches him in the performative logic of the lyric. In his attempt to prove the historical existence of Willie Hughes, and thus to supplant all traces of his own merely subjective impressions of the sonnets with hard evidence, Cyril has actually created nothing but a "realization of his own personality." The portrait literalizes the fact that, in the search to find the real person that inspired Shakespeare's poems, he has found only himself, dressed up as another. As Erskine presciently suggests, the forgery is itself a type of performative, an act committed for Cyril's sake only. Cyril tells Erskine that he commissioned the painting "purely for your sake. You would not be convinced in any other way. It does not affect the truth of the theory." Erskine replies, "The truth of the theory! . . . The less we talk about that the better. You never even believed in it yourself. If you had, you would not have committed a forgery to prove it" (*SMS* 46). Erskine is even more correct than he realizes: if Cyril had any doubt as to the truth of the Willie Hughes theory, then a forgery he knew to be a forgery would do nothing to assuage that doubt. If the painting convinced Erskine to believe in Willie Hughes, Cyril would always know that Erskine's belief was elicited under false pretenses. Rather, the only truth confirmed by Erskine's belief would be that the Willie Hughes theory is an interpretation that can be believed by someone other than Cyril himself. Even if the historical existence of Willie Hughes could never be proven conclusively, Erskine's belief would at least confirm for Cyril that the theory, and the homoerotic desires it expresses, are objectively meaningful—that they have some sort of coherent existence outside of his own head and can perhaps be shared by others.

The inability to confirm a literary interpretation would hardly seem the stuff of compelling fiction, but "Mr. W.H." shows that the problem of intersubjective confirmation is more than just epistemological. In response to Erskine's accusation, Cyril shoots himself with a revolver "in order to show [Erskine] how firm and flawless his faith in the whole thing was" and "to offer his life as a sacrifice to the secret of the Sonnets" (*SMS* 46). Yet, as Erskine states, "a thing is not necessarily true because a man dies for it" (*SMS* 47). He implies that Cyril found it impossible to continue living in the face of the apparent failure of the Willie Hughes theory. It has betrayed him on three counts: not only has the theory resisted confirmation through recourse to empirical evidence and failed to establish that his homoerotic desires could be shared by anyone else, but, most devastatingly, it has entirely undermined Cyril's faith that he could ever find a coherent and meaningful sense of self or a community of like-minded individuals.

As Wilde's novella goes on to demonstrate, however, the profound sense of existential meaninglessness that drives Cyril to suicide is the result of a fundamental confusion regarding the relationship between language and self. Cyril interprets Erskine's failure to reciprocate his belief in the theory as evidence of his own damaged and isolated subjectivity, one that has been perverted by homoerotic desire. This is because he believes that his failure to communicate his subjectivity in and through language reflects his own in-adequacy, rather than being merely a property of language itself.[53] Wilde's narrator, however, comes to the opposite conclusion: he discovers that language's inability to articulate his homoerotic desires proves that selfhood may persists beyond language's ability to articulate it.

"A Tragic Form of Scepticism"

Much to Erskine's surprise and dismay, the story of Cyril's "sacrifice to the secret of the Sonnets," instantly convinces the narrator of the truth of the Willie Hughes theory. "It is the only perfect key to Shakespeare's Sonnets that has ever been made," the narrator asserts. "It is complete in every detail. I believe in Willie Hughes" (*SMS* 47). In the next three sections of the novella, the narrator develops an elaborate interpretation of the sonnets based on Willie Hughes that encompasses a wide-ranging discussion of intellectual and cultural history, including the Neoplatonic revival, the role of boy-actors on the Renaissance stage, the famous "Dark Lady" of the later sonnets, and even the origin of the "Romantic Movement of English Literature" (which the narrator, somewhat remarkably, also traces back to the influence of Willie Hughes) (69). The narrator's ecstatic embrace of the theory is, however, followed by an account of his traumatic loss of faith, one that mirrors Cyril's own. Yet, in contrast to Cyril, the narrator survives this loss because he realizes that language's failure to capture the immutable truth of his erotic subjectivity can actually be personally and intellectually enabling. The narrator realizes that he can craft a linguistic utterance that gestures to the presence of a subjectivity that exists beyond language's limitations.

In the narrator's initial enthusiasm for the Willie Hughes theory, it becomes clear that he believes it not only to be "the only perfect key" to Shakespeare's sonnets but also the only perfect key to reveal the truth of his own sexual subjectivity to himself. "How curiously it had all been revealed to me!" the narrator exclaims. "A book of Sonnets, published nearly three hundred years ago, written by a dead hand and in honour of a dead youth, had suddenly explained to me the whole story of my soul's romance" (*SMS* 93). The narrator believes that the sonnet cycle expresses the absolute truth of his innermost self and desires, his "soul's romance," in its entirety. He explains that, in rereading the sonnets from the vantage point of the Willie Hughes theory, "it seemed to me that I was deciphering the story of a life that had once been mine, unrolling the record of a romance that, without my knowing it, had coloured the very texture of my nature, had dyed it with strange and subtle dyes" (*SMS* 91). The narrator represents his acquisition of erotic self-knowledge as a strange literary metempsychosis. In an almost delusional act of identification, the narrator relates that his experience of reading the sonnets is akin to remembering having actually experienced every detail of the love affair between Shakespeare and Willie Hughes: "Yes, I had lived it all," the narrator maintains. "I had stood in the round theatre. . . . I saw *As You Like It*, and *Cymbeline*, and *Twelfth Night*, and in each play there was some one whose life was bound up into mine, who realized for me every dream, and gave shape to every fancy" (*SMS* 92). Through this dramatic over-identification with the content of the sonnets, the narrator undergoes the collapse between subject and object characteristic of the Hegelian lyric performance. Though the narrator believes himself to have gained perfect erotic self-knowledge through this collapse, it becomes apparent that he experiences a near-complete loss of self through the act of literary interpretation. By imagining that he inhabited the mind, body, and soul of Shakespeare, the narrator allows the story of the sonnets to stand in for "the whole story of [his] soul's romance."

Although he eventually realizes the vacuity of his identification with the sonnets through his attempts to reconvince Erskine of the truth of the theory, the narrator first writes a letter to Erskine offering a "passionate reiteration of the arguments and proofs that my study had suggested to me." After sending the letter, though, the narrator discovers that having put "all [his] enthusiasm" and "all [his] faith" into convincing Erskine, he is no longer convinced himself: "It seemed to me that I had given away my capacity for belief in the Willie Hughes theory of the Sonnets," the narrator states, "that something had gone out of me, as it were, and that I was perfectly indifferent to the whole subject" (*SMS* 94). Feeling that he has been somehow emptied out of his capacity for belief by writing the letter and thus putting his subjective experience into language, the narrator admits to himself:

> "I have been dreaming, and all my life for these two months have been unreal. There was no such person as Willie Hughes." Something like a faint cry of pain came to my lips as I began to realize how I had deceived myself, and I buried my face in my hands, struck with a sorrow greater than any I had felt since boyhood. After a few moments I rose, and going into the library took up the Sonnets, and began to read them. But it was all to no avail. They gave me back nothing of the feeling that I had brought to them; they revealed to me nothing of what I had found hidden in their lines. (*SMS* 95)

In referring to his belief in Willie Hughes as a type of "dreaming," the narrator recognizes that his experience of deep identification was merely a fantasy. He acknowledges that his belief that the sonnets revealed to him, in objective form, the true "story of his soul's romance" was merely an elaborate self-deception. The reciprocal relationship he believed existed between him and the sonnets now seems merely the projection of his own desires: he "brought" feeling to the sonnets, but in return they gave him "back nothing."

This realization presents a profound challenge to the narrator's sense of self, one that parallels the challenge to Cyril's self that occurred when Erskine refused to mirror his unquestioning belief in the theory. Instead of feeling the exhilarating sense of self-extension promised by the Kantian *sensus communis*, the narrator must confront the limits of his own subjectivity. The romance that seemed to "really" exist in the sonnets was merely the projection of his own homoerotic desires that he mistook for objective reality. The narrator's loss of belief in the theory is, like Cyril's, completely devastating on a personal level. He admits that his current indifference is "a bitter disappointment," and that his self-deception strikes him "with a sorrow greater than any I had felt since boyhood" (*SMS* 94, 95). He tells Erskine, "'I wish I could believe the Willie Hughes theory,' . . . I would give anything to be able to do so. But I can't. It is a sort of moonbeam theory, very lovely, very fascinating, but intangible. When one thinks that one has got hold of it, it escapes one" (*SMS* 97–98). The narrator speaks openly of the anguish that Cyril's suicide only implied. His loss of belief in the "moonbeam" theory, and the self-interrogation following hard upon it, fills him with deep "sorrow." This is the result of his loss of a sense of connection and identification with the sonnets' homoeroticism. Once the capacity for belief "escapes one," one is left gazing dejectedly into the shallowness of one's own reflection.

Unlike Cyril, however, the narrator survives this loss of faith by realizing the true nature of his despair. He expresses this hard-won wisdom in his surprisingly empathetic reaction to Erskine's fake suicide. Although Erskine insists in a letter to the narrator that he will kill himself "for Willie Hughes' sake, and for the sake of Cyril Graham, whom I drove to death by shallow scepticism and ignorant lack of faith," the narrator soon learns that Erskine did not actually commit suicide (*SMS* 98). Instead, he wrote the note aware of his imminent demise from tuberculosis. Erskine's attempt to convince the narrator by presenting his death as a suicide is, in a sense, a type of "forgery" paralleling the forged painting Cyril used to convince Erskine of the Willie

Hughes theory. The narrator is initially confused by Erskine's motives for lying about his death, but eventually concludes that

> he was simply actuated by a desire to reconvert me to Cyril Graham's theory,
> and he thought that if I could be made to believe that he too had given his life
> for it, I would be deceived by the pathetic fallacy of martyrdom. Poor Erskine!
> I had grown wiser since I had seen him. Martyrdom was to me merely a tragic
> form of scepticism, an attempt to realize by fire what one had failed to do by
> faith. No man dies for what he knows to be true. Men die for what they want
> to be true, for what some terror in their hearts tells them is not true. (*SMS* 100)

Just as Cyril's decision to commission a forged painting suggested that he was afraid of not actually believing in the Willie Hughes theory himself, so too does Erskine's forged suicide indicate his own "terror" of doubting his faith in the theory. The narrator realizes that Erskine believed, just as Cyril did, that "reconverting" someone was the only way of assuaging that doubt.

The narrator, however, instead of exhibiting the sense of betrayal Erskine felt toward Cyril, feels nothing but pity. In contrast to the "shallow scepticism" Erskine says he directed toward Cyril, the narrator believes that Erskine's fake martyrdom is the result of a "tragic scepticism." This skepticism is tragic rather than shallow, the narrator suggests, because it arises from a self-doubt that is entirely unnecessary and misguided. It is an attempt to bridge the wholly imaginary gap between what men "want to be true" and "what some terror in their heart tells them is not true." In other words, the "tragic scepticism" the narrator identifies in Erskine describes the anguish one feels when forced to confront the apparently insurmountable gulf between the subjective experience of what one wants to believe (in this case, his belief in and identification with Willie Hughes) and one's ability to confirm that belief through a self-originating act, such as the act of linguistic self-interpretation via literary criticism. The "terror" that Cyril and Erskine feel is rooted in a fatal misunderstanding: they destroy themselves (or, in what ultimately amounts to the same thing, claim to have destroyed themselves) because they believe that language is unable to articulate their faith in Willie Hughes. They interpret this linguistic failure as a sign that their subjectivities are irrevocably damaged and inadequate because of their perverse homoerotic desires—the same understanding of queerness promoted by their homophobic society.

Meanwhile, the narrator's ability to recognize this skepticism as tragic, and the pity he feels toward "the pathetic fallacy" of Erskine's false martyrdom, suggests that he has "grown wiser" through his encounter with the Willie Hughes theory.[54] Yet the narrator chooses to convey the implications of this wisdom not through the actual content of his utterances but through the specifically aesthetic qualities of his narrative voice. Wilde's version of erotic negativity differs markedly from Pater's, but they share an understanding that the aesthetic is the realm where one can expand the limits of dominant understandings of the subject. It is within the aesthetic that Wilde locates the perdurable aspect of the subject that Gilbert in "The Critic as Artist" suggests must exist outside of the performative act.

The specifically aesthetic quality of subjectivity becomes most apparent in the last line of the novella, when the narrator admits to the reader, "I think there is really a great deal to be said for the Willie Hughes theory of Shakespeare's Sonnets" (*SMS* 101). This statement expresses, in highly condensed form, the narrator's realization that a form of perdurable subjectivity transcends language's ability to express it. The line at first seems a puckish refusal of closure: the narrator wants neither to confirm nor deny the viability of the theory. More significantly, though, the phrasing of the statement carefully sidesteps issues of both grammatical and personal agency, partaking of the aesthetic's relative freedom from the preexisting, socially determined laws that govern conceptual thought and lyrical language's sidestepping of logical cause-and-effect relations. Though he initially prepares the reader for an unequivocal statement of his beliefs by beginning with the assertion "I think," a clever deployment of the infinitive form allows him to float the abstract possibility of the theory's truth without indicating anything about his personal commitments. Yet this evacuation of linguistic agency does not entail the complete erasure of the narrator's subjectivity. On the contrary, the wry detachment conveyed by the narrator's tone and style, its aesthetic qualities, convey something of his personality and outlook, even though we learn nothing explicit about the discursive content of his beliefs. Unlike Pater's late style, this literary voice manages to convey the presence of the self without saying anything specific about it. The narrator adroitly avoids the problem of self-reflexivity by allowing literary voice to stand in for the articulation of selfhood. The narrator uses the aesthetic techniques of style and tone to gesture toward the presence of a subjectivity that is necessarily condemned to articulate itself within a fundamentally inadequate language but cannot be either created or destroyed by that language.

"Mr. W.H." presents a version of performativity that adheres neither to the sentimental humanism of gay studies nor to the skeptical anti-humanism of queer theory. Wilde's performative theory of the lyric demonstrates the psychic dangers inherent in both emotional overinvestment in the literary object *and* the assumption that the subject's coherence is merely an illusion constructed by language. One could assert that the studied seriousness of these two interpretive frameworks must inevitably fail to do justice to the studied frivolity of Wildean style. Yet, in crafting a distinct literary voice that expresses the subject's boundaries but also gestures beyond them, Wilde shows us a form of homoerotic desire that creatively refuses entrapment within the inevitable limitations of language. There is really a great deal to be said about the desiring subject, Wilde suggests, once one realizes one cannot say everything.

CHAPTER FOUR

Vernon Lee and the Specter of Lesbian History

In *The Handling of Words* (1923), a study Vernon Lee (Violet Paget) wrote late in her life, the historian, aesthetic theorist, and fiction writer describes her understanding of the logic underlying literature's development over time. Artistic innovation comes only through refuting the previous generation's accomplishments. "There would be none of the topsy-turveying of all the old habits of seeing, feeling and saying," she says, "unless these innovators, romanticists or futurists of whatever epoch, had not been bored to death or impotently exasperated by doing what their elders had done, or trying to do it or being admonished to do it."[1] As her phrasing suggests, she does not rely on an Oedipal model of development, where a new generation rejects what came before it, only to install a new orthodoxy that, in turn, elicits renewed rebellion from the next generation. Instead, writers "topsy-turvey" what came before them, reshuffling old ideas into new entities through a process motivated by feelings of frustration with the past. When it comes to understanding how artists engage their predecessors, "so true is it that, as the Hegelians teach, nothing is closer akin to an assertion than its negation."[2]

For Lee, the relationship between literary generations is an extended labor of the negative, a process by which new writers assimilate and rework the ideas of older writers until they create productions that only seem new. She realizes that this logic applies as much to her as to anybody. "Among my own contemporaries, especially in the one I know best," she admits, "I can recognize long preliminary stages of being *not oneself*; of being; *being* not merely *trying* to be, an adulterated Ruskin, Pater, Michelet, Henry James." She presents her own artistic development as an arduous process of first emulating, then breaking down and rearranging, the ideas of influential mentors and peers until "a late, rather sudden, curdling and emergence of something one recognizes (even if there is no one else to recognize!) *as oneself*."[3]

Among the authors she names, there was none whose ideas she engaged more deeply, or eventually rejected more explicitly, than Pater's. Her admiration led them to become friends after meeting at Oxford in 1881, remaining in close contact until Pater's death in 1894. Lee's biographer Vineta Colby says that her third volume, *Euphorion: Being Studies of the Antique and Mediaeval in the Renaissance* (1884), which she dedicated to Pater, was the first work of art criticism in English to make full use of his Hegelian account of art-historical development in *The Renaissance*.[4] Yet his influence can be seen as early as 1881, in the collection *Belcaro: Being Essays on Sundry Aesthetical Questions*, Lee's initial foray into discussions of aestheticism and the philosophy of art. The impact of both Pater and Hegel is definitive in this collection, which, as Stefano Evangelista states, "revisits the history of aestheticism that had been written by her male predecessors" and follows "what could be called a Hegelian path, focusing on individual features and using them to draw general conclusions about Greek art and, perhaps more generally, on aesthetics."[5] Although Lee was up to speed on Hegel's philosophy early in her career, these encounters were always mediated and inflected by Pater's aestheticism, which she "repeatedly felt the need to come to terms with, to re-read, and to rewrite."[6]

Laurel Brake suggests that the intellectual and personal affinities between Lee and Pater stemmed from the mutual recognition that they were rebels against Victorian heteronormativity.[7] Although Lee never used the word "lesbian" to describe herself, living during a time when the sexual meaning of that term was only just beginning to gain cultural currency, many critics and biographers have characterized her as a proto-lesbian avant la lettre. Her erotically charged friendships with Annie Meyer, A. Mary F. Robinson, and Clementina (Kit) Anstruther-Thomson, as well as her cultivation of a deliberately androgynous physical appearance, suggest that Lee was as close to fulfilling the modern definition of lesbian identity as any late nineteenth-century woman could be.[8] Patricia Pulham notes that John Addington Symonds "in consultation with his friend, sexologist Havelock Ellis ... considered that [Lee] and Mary Robinson 'might serve as a possible case-history for the section on Lesbianism' in *Sexual Inversion* (1896)," the first English medical textbook on homosexuality.[9]

Lee's affinities with Pater's queer aesthetics led her to embrace erotic negativity in her earliest writings. In the essay "Mediaeval Love" from *Euphorion*, Lee asserts that "there is, in all our perceptions and desire of physical and moral beauty, an element of passion which is akin to love; and there is, in all love that is not mere lust, a perception of, a craving for, beauty, real or imaginary, which is identical with our merely aesthetic perceptions and cravings."[10] This description of intermingling artistic and sexual desires bears remarkable similarities to, and likely derives from, Pater's description of Winckelmann's erotically inspired critical insights in *The Renaissance*. Lee initially understood herself to be, like Wilde, a respondent to Pater's call for a new generation of queer aesthetes who would undermine the binary opposition between sexuality and aesthetics in modern Western culture in search of new kinds of artistic experience, forms of identity, and modes of social critique. This was true until 1895, when in the valedictory essay of her collection *Renaissance Fancies and Studies*, she explicitly repudiated Pater and the entire Aesthetic Movement. After this, she would devote herself to working with her partner, Anstruther-Thomson, to discover an empirical theory of aesthetics derived from studies of mental and physiological responses to art. This led her to develop the theory of empathy that has recently proven appealing to many literary critics eager to develop non-idealist theories of aesthetics.[11] Yet despite her seemingly emphatic rejection of aestheticism, Lee's retrospective comments in *The Handling of Words* make it clear that this was the culmination of a long process of reshuffling and reworking Pater's ideas to her own ends, rather than an absolute repudiation.

In this chapter, I argue that Lee's supernatural tales of the 1880s and 1890s are where her "topsy-turveying" of Pater took place most intensely. Unlike other chapters in this study, in which I discuss the deployment of Pater's homoerotic version of Hegelian negativity in the writings of queer aesthetes, I follow Vernon Lee's own lead by analyzing her early career as *itself* an extended labor of the negative upon Pater's writings. Rather than tracking negativity as a recurrent *topos* in her works, I use erotic negativity as an interpretive framework for understanding how she transformed the damaging lack of explicit lesbianism, unmediated by the male gaze, in Western art history into the occasion for developing a more inclusive version of queer history than Paterian aestheticism was able to offer.

In "Winckelmann," Pater describes the negative force of hidden homoerotic desire when it is suddenly revealed to the conscious mind, and retrospectively understood to be a socially mandated withholding of sexual self-knowledge rather than mere absence. Lee's ghost stories demonstrate that this version of erotic negativity also applies to the history of sexuality itself. In her stories, the lack of lesbians in history becomes, retrospectively, a meaningful and significant elision and the material for constructing a new historical sensibility grounded in supernatural experience. In her essay "Faustus and Helena: Notes on the Supernatural in Art" (1880), she describes the supernatural as "what is beyond and outside the limits of the possible, the rational, the explicable" in a post-Enlightenment modernity otherwise devoted to scientific empiricism and the discovery of the absolute limits of pure reason. For Lee, the supernatural was the realm most suited to reimagining autonomy as the ability to stretch supposedly fixed and unchanging, yet actually historically contingent, boundaries of the self and the world.[12] She distinguished between supernatural and aesthetic forms of autonomy, I argue, because she believed the former was better suited to capturing the experiences of queer women.[13] For her, the major difference between how queer men and women related to art was their differing relationships to the concept of history. Queer male aesthetes could presuppose the existence of definitive historical representations of their desires in art that lesbians could not—and to this day, still cannot—access. Lee's stories use supernaturalism to explore how histories of lesbian identity can be constructed by and for queer women out of artistic representations of female desire from the past that are, at best, ambiguous and equivocal.

Pater's theory of erotic negativity, as developed in the Winckelmann essay and elsewhere, was supported by research into the ancient world and many references to "Greek love" in canonical texts that, although they caused embarrassment to many Victorian classicists, were nevertheless well known and documented.[14] Throughout her career, Lee challenged such empirical historicism for its masculine bias. She first won fame for her book *Studies of the Eighteenth Century in Italy* (1880), which Christa Zorn notes pioneered a "blending of fact and fiction" that "was most creative and provocative in the area of history writing, a traditionally 'masculine' genre" that, as Hayden White has notably argued, became increasingly professionalized in the nineteenth century through the embrace of "empirical and inductivist" methods.[15]

If empirical historiographic practices worked against the aims of women writers, this was doubly true for queer women. Unambiguous historical depictions of lesbian desire in art have always been difficult to come by. Susan Lanser writes that "one of the most frustrating problems for lesbian historiography is the degree to which sapphic texts and their travels get covered up."[16] As recently as 2017, Clare Barlow writes in the introduction to the book accompanying Tate Britain's major exhibit *Queer British Art, 1861–1967*, that "we have been constantly frustrated by the comparative scarcity of material related to intersectional identities—queer people of color, genderqueer identities, even queer women artists."[17] The invisibility of lesbianism in art history persists even when the image seems to be hiding in plain sight. Christopher Reed writes that most "presentations of lesbianism" that existed in the visual arts and literature in the nineteenth century "were conceived as attention-getting strategies among men" to gain an avant-garde credibility.[18] Terry Castle has shown that throughout Western cultural history, genuinely women-centered artistic representations of lesbian desire have been "spectral." The "literary history of lesbianism," she writes, "is first of all a history of derealization."[19] For Castle, "The lesbian remains a kind of 'ghost effect' . . . elusive, vaporous, difficult to spot—even when she is there, in plain view, mortal and magnificent." Accordingly, no strictly empirical method can even definitively identify an image from the past as incontrovertibly lesbian. This ambiguity is the effect of pernicious, patriarchal assumptions about women's sexuality, or lack thereof.[20] For Castle, this means that the apparitional lesbian can be recuperated only when we direct our attention to artworks from the past that are haunted by ghostly, barely visible traces of desire between women.[21]

Although Martha Vicinus argues that Lee's supernatural tales represent a "displacing of powerful homoerotic feelings onto an imagined past," unambiguous representations of lesbians are difficult to find in her writings.[22] This can partially be attributed to the limits imposed by Victorian reticence toward explicit sexual representations. Yet I argue that Lee's reserve was meant to reflect the fact that obvious representations of lesbianism cannot easily be found in art history. Accordingly, the protagonists in her supernatural stories discern and affirm ghostly hints of their sexuality that lie dormant in art from the past. She uses this spectral historicism to determine how Victorian women who desired women could develop a sense of identity without having access to the same historical evidence of their sexuality that male aesthetes like Pater believed they possessed. This project would have had special urgency in the late nineteenth-century. Sharon Marcus has argued that these decades were a crucial turning point in the history of women's sexuality. For most of the nineteenth century, mainstream society did not perceive desire between women to be subversive or pathological. Instead, "same-sex bonds" were "acknowledged by the bourgeois public sphere. . . . Female marriage, gender mobility, and women's erotic fantasies about women were actually at the heart of normative institutions and discourses, even for those who made a religion of the family, marriage, and sexual difference."[23] Yet, starting around the 1880s, sexology's growing cultural influence meant that same-sex desire started to be treated as a threat to the social order.

A strategy queer Victorian men used to combat stigmatization was composing histories that presented male same-sex desire as a healthy and beneficent cultural force of long standing rather than evidence of degeneration into a more "primitive" stage of cultural development. These authors drew on the Hellenic ideal of intellectual and personal freedom promoted by Victorian liberalism, such as in Symonds's privately published yet widely circulated *A Problem in Greek Ethics* (1883) and *A Problem in Modern Ethics* (1891).[24] Yopie Prins asserts that the Michael Field poets attempted to do the same thing for queer women, "open[ing] Victorian Hellenism to the possibility of a lesbian reading that allows for the circulation of Greek eros among women as well as men." Much like Lee, they did so by "claim[ing] the masculine authority of classical scholarship" but "us[ing] it transgressively, for their own purposes."[25] Yet Prins maintains that the queer content of their lyrics would not have been legible to their contemporaries. Their reconstruction of lesbian history "requires the mediation of reading: it will be left to the reader of the future to decipher this sign."[26] Their homoerotic history can be recognized only retrospectively, after the emergence of a culturally recognized lesbian identity in the twentieth century.

Lee, by contrast, devised a queer historicism that would be legible in her own day and age, one capable of responding immediately to sexological stigmatization. The sense of lesbian selfhood arising from this history would not be compromised despite its claims on empirical truth being, at best, highly ambivalent. The purpose of Lee's spectral histories was not to create an unassailable record of desire between women but to elicit the subjective feeling of having a stable, autonomous identity that would allow lesbians to stand apart from and critique their culture's emergent phobic renderings of their desires. As Angela Leighton states, for Lee "the ghost offers itself for interpretation or evaluation" but "without necessarily commanding belief."[27] The central issue in Lee's ghost stories was the ability of lesbians to cultivate deliberately an attitude toward art from the past that would fulfill their need to, in Christopher Nealon's memorable phrase, "feel historical" without necessarily *being* so in the strictly verifiable sense promoted by empirical historiography.[28]

Lee seems to anticipate what Valerie Traub refers to as the "unhistoricism" of recent works in queer studies by scholars such as Carla Freccero, Jonathan Goldberg, and Madhavi Menon.[29] According to Traub, these studies display "an antipathy to empirical inquiry that . . . is posed as antithetical to acts of queering."[30] Lee's fiction appears very similar to the historical method Freccero defines as "queer spectrality," an attitude toward history that "reject[s] a notion of empirical history and allow[s] fantasy and ideology an acknowledged place in the production of 'phantasmic' historiography."[31] Unhistoricist queer investigations are united by critiques of the notion of linear "straight time," which they view as inherently teleological, posing the contingent historical trajectory leading to the construction of modern identity categories as inevitable and inexorable. The goal of unhistoricism is to queer linear histories of sexuality and, in the process, disturb and deconstruct notions of coherent sexual identity altogether. Yet, as Traub notes, although identity categories may be fictitious, they nevertheless do important cultural work, and "there remain ample reasons to practice a queer historicism dedicated to showing how categories, however mythic, phantasmic, and incoherent, came to be."[32] Lee's goal is to cultivate in queer women a disposition toward historical knowledge that elicits a sense of sexual identity yet at the same time avoids the pathologizing essentialism of Victorian sexological discourse. The nonempirical, highly subjective historiography of Lee's supernatural tales does not deconstruct sexual identities but instead seeks to rebuild them better and stronger.

In "Faustus and Helena," Lee describes two types of aesthetic experience, one that she associates with productions she refers to as "art" and another with productions she refers to as "supernatural." The supernatural is a premodern aesthetic experience that embraces a characteristically feminine formlessness and ambiguity, allowing one to feel a greater subjective connection to the past, even if that feeling is disconnected from the empirical facts of history. She puts her theory of the supernatural into practice in the first ghost story she wrote, "Oke of Okehurst; Or, The Phantom Lover" (1886), which tells the story of Alice Oke, a woman who becomes obsessed with an ancient painting of an ancestor who looks exactly like her and whose doomed love affair she may or may not believe herself to be reliving in the present. Despite her ostensible heterosexuality, Alice's situation mirrors the predicament of the late Victorian lesbian, whose sense of personal autonomy derives from a subjective sense of historicity that cannot be objectively confirmed through recourse to historical evidence. Yet by using her supernatural identification with the artwork to develop a sense of self that stands apart from limiting sexological definitions of identity offered by her patriarchal and heteronormative culture, Alice enacts Lee's vision of lesbian historical consciousness. Lee's "topsy-turveying" labor of the negative upon Pater's aestheticism culminates in "Prince Alberic and the Snake Lady" (1896), which was written a year after Lee's public farewell both to him and to the Aesthetic Movement. In this story, about a prince who falls in love with a Lamia figure appearing out of an ancient tapestry, Lee explicitly addresses the theory of erotic negativity associated with male aesthetes. She demonstrates that queer women's apparent disadvantage regarding the lack of definite historical representation is ultimately beneficial. It allows them to develop a more sophisticated understanding of queer historical representation than male aesthetes, one that openly acknowledges the fictive element within all histories of sexual identity—including, most provocatively, forms of nonnormative desire and identity that have yet even to be imagined—but does not allow that fact to compromise the sense of personal coherence and autonomy that results from such spectral, speculative histories.

Art, Ghosts, and Feminine Histories: "Faustus and Helena"

In "The Child in the Vatican," *Belcaro*'s leading essay, Lee recounts a visit to the Vatican's Belvedere Gallery, the place where, as Pater tells us, Winckelmann was first enchanted and aroused by the muscular statue of Apollo. Yet in a notable early departure from Paterian aestheticism, she does not endorse Winckelmann's art-historical practice. She describes the museum as "a dismal place of scientific ostentation, like all galleries; a place where art is arranged and ticketed and made dingy and lifeless even as are the plants in a botanic collection."[33] She says that those statues that "once stood, each in happy independence, against a screen of laurel or ilex branches" are now "poor stone captives, cloistered in monastic halls and cells, and arranged, like the skeletons of Capuchins, in endless rows of niche, shelf, and bracket."[34] For Evangelista, statements like this challenge the empiricist historicism of "the Vatican galleries, which had been, since Winckelmann, the theater for a culturally sanctioned type of lovemaking between the male critic and the male body as represented by ancient statues like the Apollo Belvedere."[35] Lee advocates for the replacement of an empirical art-historical method, exemplified by the rationalized space of the museum and its association with male homoeroticism, with a supernaturalism that, Evangelista states, "openly rejects the classifications and canonizations of art proposed by art historians and classicists such as Winckelmann" and instead relies on an intuitive and implicitly feminine "emotional understanding of antiquities" characteristic of Victorian women's writing on art.[36]

Lee "appeal[ed] to the growing authority of cosmopolitan female amateurism" in the writing of art history "to claim a place of her own . . . in the canon of aesthetic criticism best represented by Pater."[37] She wore this amateurism as a badge of honor, stating that her authority in aesthetic matters came from her intuitive grasp of the subject, rather than the formal training of her male peers.[38] In the introduction to *Belcaro*, she states that although she has "read a great many books about all the arts . . . from Plato to Lessing, from Reynolds to Taine, from Hegel to Ruskin," she has instead decided to turn solely to her own personal responses to "art itself, to statues and music and pictures and poetry, to [her] own thoughts and feelings" to write the essays in that collection.[39]

Lee deploys the logic of negativity to transform an otherwise embarrassing lack of training in art-historical methodology into an advantage, foregoing "science and precise knowledge" of the past in favor of "images of spectrality," such as her striking personification of the statues' happy independence in an imagined outdoor setting. Lee's writings "go altogether beyond the art object to what has been entirely lost" to the historical record, Evangelista states, providing access to aspects of history that have left no material trace but instead can be experienced only through the exercise of one's supernatural imagination.[40]

Her later writings on the supernatural develop the spectral historicism of "The Child in the Vatican," adapting it to the needs of the queer woman aesthete, who must develop a relationship to the lesbian past that cannot and does not rely on empirical methods. Her stories will be the feminine equivalent of the museum's cultural sanctioning of desire between men, exemplified by Winckelmann's homoerotic ecstasies in the Belvedere Gallery. In the preface to her short story collection *Hauntings* (1890), she dismisses the empirical investigations of the "Society for Psychical Research," a group of scholars who used scientific methods to examine the paranormal (40). She says her phantasms are instead like the ghost stories of her friend and literary rival Henry James: psychological rather than material in origin, "things of the imagination, born there, bred there, sprung from strange confused heaps, half-rubbish, half-treasure, which lie in our fancy" (39). Unlike James, however, Lee specifies that these "things of the imagination" do not arise spontaneously from subconscious desires. Instead, ghosts can be used intentionally, conjured to mediate between the contending impulses to identify with the premodern past while also acknowledging its inevitable and radical alterity from the present. This liminal state cannot be captured by scientific historiography. Lee instead states that "the Past, the more or less remote Past, of which the prose is clean obliterated by distance—that is the place to get our ghosts from. Indeed we live ourselves, we educated folk of modern times, on the borderland of the Past, in houses looking down on its troubadours' orchards and Greek folks' pillared courtyards; and a legion of ghosts, very vague and changeful, are perpetually to and fro, fetching and carrying for us between it and the Present" (39). Similar to Pater's description of survivals of pagan animism in Wordsworth's poetry, discussed in chapter 2, Lee's ghosts move between two incommensurate worldviews: disenchanted, post-Enlightenment modernity and the medieval and classical past when people believed unquestioningly in the reality of the supernatural. Lee does not believe we can ever truly bridge the gap between past and present in our imaginations. As she states in the introduction to *Euphorion*, we "must never hope to evoke any spectres which can talk with us and we with them."[41] Yet although she knows "it may be impossible to ever truly touch or know the past," as Kristin Mahoney notes, ghosts are an aesthetic expression of "the desire and attempt to do so."[42] Ghostly experiences fulfill our desire to feel as if we are gaining a true sense of the past, while also allowing us to maintain awareness that our reconstructions are, to a greater or lesser extent, fictional.

This is the disposition toward history that women, and lesbians especially, needed to cultivate to transform their lack of empirical history into an intellectual advantage over both queer male aesthetes and professional historians. In her literary-critical essay "Faustus and Helena," Lee provides the fullest account of her theory of ghostly supernaturalism begun in "The Child in the Vatican," explaining why it provides a superior understanding of the past compared to empiricist historicism. This is especially true, she implies, for women, whose subjective experiences have often not found their way into the historical record. Her supernatural tales build upon this theory to craft a supernatural historiography for lesbians, for whom this problem is exacerbated.

Lee's essay draws a sharp distinction between "artistic" and "supernatural" aesthetic experiences. Although she says they might "appear closely allied" because they are both "born of imagination," they actually belong to two different historical epochs (294). The difference lies in their respective handling of form: "The supernatural is necessarily essentially vague," she says, "and art is necessarily essentially distinct" (295). She associates the worship of definite aesthetic form with post-Enlightenment modernity's fetishizing of the boundaries created and enforced by the discourses of reason and empiricism, which prevent one from gaining a sense of what life was like in a premodern past that accepted the irrational as part of everyday life. The supernatural—and, especially, the spectral—is the only holdover from the premodern world that can elicit the feeling that one has momentarily escaped rationalized modernity and entered an enchanted vision of reality. There is an implicit gender dynamic to Lee's distinction. She portrays artistic formalism as a kind of masculine violence against premodern beliefs and associates the supernatural's ability to elicit a convincing facsimile of premodern enchantment through its ability to conjure the feminine sexual allure of Helen of Troy's ghost in the Faust legend.

Lee defines the supernatural as "the effect on the imagination of certain external impressions, it is those impressions brought to a focus, personified, but personified vaguely, in a fluctuating ever-changing manner; the personification being continually altered, reinforced, blurred out, enlarged, restricted by new series of impressions from without" (296). This description is inspired by Pater's aesthetic impressionism in *The Renaissance*, where he describes the "impressions, unstable, flickering, inconsistent, which burn and are extinguished with our consciousness of them."[43] The supernatural's characteristic lack of formal definition makes it the external equivalent of the mind's constantly flowing welter of impressions. These continuously morphing figures are, for Lee, "the real supernatural, born of the imagination and its surroundings, the vital, the fluctuating, the potent" (299). The vagueness of the supernatural is the source of its aesthetic power, as it achieves the illusion of liveliness and creative energy by appearing to objectively embody the mind's alert and attentive perceptual attunement to its environment.

Yet, according to Lee, over time what she calls "art" gradually overtook the supernatural as humanity's dominant technique for creating aesthetic representations of the world. It took "the vague, fluctuating impressions oscillating before the imagination like . . . the pattern of a shot silk, interwoven, unsteady, never completely united into one, never completely separated into several" and "rudely seized and disentangled" them, resulting in the "diminution—nay, destruction of their inherent power" (304). Her rhetoric implies that art's imperative to fix subjective impressions into definite objective forms is akin to an act of productive violence against the mind itself, a labor of the negative that results in the creation of artistic beauty:

As, in order to be moulded, the clay must be separated from the mound; as, in order to be carved, the wood must be cut off from the tree; as, in order to be re-shaped by art, the mass of atoms must be rudely severed; so also the mental elements of art, the mood, the fancy must be severed from the preceding and succeeding moods or fancies; artistic manipulation requires that its intellectual, like its tangible materials, cease to be vital, but the materials, mental or physical, are not only deprived of vitality and power of self-alteration; they are combined in given proportion, the action of the one on the other destroys in great part the special power of each. (304)

Beauty arises out of the process described by Hegelian negativity: the destruction of our subjective impressions of the world is the necessary prelude for the creation of art. Aesthetic productions come into being not, as one might suppose, through inspired acts of creativity but instead through an aggressive process of "diminution," "severing," deprivation, and restriction of the mind's impressions. Art rationalizes the supernatural by giving it "proportion" but also simultaneously "destroys" its lived vitality. Through the imposition of form, art murders to dissect the lived immediacy of the mind's subjective perception of the world, killing off the dynamic elements of those perceptions that cannot fit within its limits.

For Lee, beauty is produced by the violence of negation and serves as the artistic counterpart to Kant's enlightened philosophical project of defining the absolute limits of our mental and perceptual capacities. One of modernity's defining qualities is the brutal transformation of the supernatural into a perfected aesthetic form that disenchants the world. For the modern artist, "the gods, or the saints, which were cloudy and supernatural to the artist of immature art, are definite and artistic to the artist of mature art; he can think, imagine, feel only in a given manner; his religious conceptions have taken the shape of his artistic creations; art has destroyed the supernatural, and the artist has swallowed up the believer" (305).

Despite the apparent historical triumph of rationalized art, Lee asserts that there remains one "species of supernatural which still retains vitality" in the modern age: namely, "ghosts" (309). These are the "only modern equivalent" to "the gods of primitive religion": the same psychological structures that gave rise to primitive beliefs in the supernatural also elicit our modern experience of ghostliness. They are the product of the interaction between our minds and the external environment, "the damp, the darkness, the silence, the solitude," which gives rise to "a vague feeling we can scarcely describe, a something pleasing and terrible which invades our whole consciousness, and which, confusedly embodied, we half dread to see behind us, we know not in what shape, if we look round" (310). Ghostliness is the only experience still available to modern individuals that captures the vagueness and dynamic vitality of the premodern supernatural. For Lee, ghosts are what anthropologist Edward Burnett Tylor calls a "survival," as discussed in chapter 2, the holdover of a primitive, supernatural religious belief that persists in modern society. As in Pater's late writings, the "survival" for Lee is not simply cultural detritus from the past but a phenomenon that still holds aesthetic value for present-day viewers when it appears in artistic productions. Like Pater's aesthetic rendering of the survival, the irruption of premodern ghostliness in the present performs the labor of the negative on one's subjective experience of modern culture. It destroys faith in the historical triumph of secular rationality but also, dialectically, creates a new vantage point for understanding the contingency of modern intellectual structures.

The survival of ghostliness renders it not only a powerful agent for historical understanding, as Lee indicates in "The Child in the Vatican," but also brings to light the irretrievable losses entailed by the advent of Enlightened modes of thinking. Lee states that, although "we none of us believe in ghosts as logical possibilities, . . . we most of us conceive them as imaginative probabilities; we can still feel the ghostly, and thence it is that a ghost is the only thing which can in any respect replace for us the divinities of old, and enable us to understand, if only for a minute, the imaginative power which they possessed, and of which they were despoiled not only by logic, but by art" (309). When one feels as if he or she is in the presence of a ghost, one inhabits, if only for a moment, a premodern version of reality that allows us to comprehend, on an almost bodily level, the felt experience of past human existence. This insight is necessarily tempered, however, by our modern inability to "believe in ghosts as a logical possibility." The moment of historical sympathy carries with it a reminder of the pervasive and domineering force of reason. To feel oneself to be in the presence of a ghost is to be reminded of modernity's destruction of genuine supernatural belief. Spectral experience calls one's attention to the inescapable force of logic as a form of violence, a reminder of the vast realms of human experience destroyed by reason.

Lee's ghosts are closely akin to Jonathan Loesberg's description of the Kantian-Hegelian aesthetic as "structures meant to stand apart from reason and value" and thus available to critique a universalizing Enlightenment worldview while still enmeshed within its restrictive limits.[44] Lee shows the immense appeal of supernatural aesthetics in her account of how male intellectuals associated with the Enlightenment were unable to resist their desire to escape the rational and scientific modern worldview for the pleasures of the premodern supernatural. "It was from this sickness of the prosaic," she writes, "this turning away from logical certainty, that the men of the end of the eighteenth and the beginning of this century, the men who had finally destroyed belief in the religious supernatural, who were bringing light with new sciences of economy, philology, and history—Schiller, Goethe, Herder, Coleridge—left the lecture-room and the laboratory, and set gravely to work on ghostly tales and ballads" (312–13). These four men, in addition to their well-known literary pursuits, are also famous for their devotion to the Enlightenment notion of "universal history," the scientific and teleological understanding of human progress over time that eventually led to the development of Victorian scientific historiography, which would join "economy" and "philology" as one of the new social sciences promoting the nineteenth century's vision of the human as what Foucault calls an "empirico-transcendental doublet."[45] Despite their supposed dedication to empiricism and rationality, these men still desired the feeling of transcendence from "the sickness of the prosaic" they helped to create. Lee suggests there is an innate human desire to transcend the supposedly absolute limits of the natural and social worlds, what Pater calls "the incurable thirst for the sense of escape, which no actual form of life satisfies," but which finds its closest equivalent in artistic experience.[46] But while Pater believes art in general is the proper sphere for this testing of limits, Lee affirms that the ghostly supernatural is the only remaining venue where this can occur. For Lee, the supernatural embodies the quasi-conceptual quality of the Kantian-Hegelian aesthetic better than "art" itself does, insofar as it is freer from the rules governing rational thought.

Given her interest in the boundary-expanding capacities of the supernatural, it is no surprise she turned to the Faust legend for her examples of ghostly experience. Lee takes the title of her essay from an episode from the legend when Faust uses his pact with the devil to summon Helen of Troy's specter. She compares Goethe's modern rendering of this scene in *Faust* (1829) with Marlow's premodern version in *Doctor Faustus* (1592). Although she acknowledges Goethe's version is better written and more historically accurate than Marlow's, she says it is unsuccessful as an aesthetic experience. It is "laboured and abortive," a failed attempt to create what she calls "a conscious and artificial supernatural" within a modern, rationalist worldview (293, 314).

Although "born of deep appreciation of antiquity, the essentially modern, passionate, nostalgic craving for the past," it fails to resonate with audiences because the writer no longer genuinely believes in the supernatural, which makes his writing self-conscious and emotionally distant (315).

Marlow's premodern play is, by contrast, "unthinking and imperfect" in its representation of Helen and "forgets the scholarly interest in her" entirely (293, 316). Yet it successfully expresses "real passion for a real woman, a woman very different from the splendid semi-vivified statue of Goethe" (316). Marlow is better able to capture Faustus's powerful sexual attraction to Helen because he has no interest, or even concept, of the modern goal of historical verisimilitude and empirical accuracy. "His Helen was essentially modern" for Marlow's age, she says, because "he had probably no inkling that an antique Helen as distinguished from a modern could exist. In the paramour of Faustus he saw merely the most beautiful woman, some fair and wanton creature, dressed not in chaste and majestic antique drapery, but in fantastic garments of lawn," like the beautiful women of his own day (318). Because he lived in a world that had not yet developed the rationalism of Enlightenment universal history or Victorian scientific historiography, Marlow was better able to elicit the subjective feeling of having encountered the past, even if that experience had no grounding in historical "facts."

Implicit in Lee's comparison is that Goethe failed because he was devoted to historical empiricism, which meant he had no way of accessing female subjectivity because accounts of women's interior lives are nearly impossible to find in the historical record. Instead, he merely creates a "semi-vivified statue . . . with only the cold, bloodless, intellectual life which could be infused by enthusiastic studies of ancient literature and art, gleaming bright like marble" (316). Marlow, by contrast, was able to create a convincing version of femininity simply by looking to the women around him for models.

Yet Lee recognized that post-Enlightenment subjects, like her, live in a world where we notice such anachronisms and allow them to mar our aesthetic experiences. Although Lee says Marlow's play is also ultimately a failure, the problem lies not with him but with us. Because we, like Goethe, now "feel [the supernatural] as it can be felt only in days of disbelief," we are barred from the subjective, supernatural engagement with the past that was a vital part of premodern art (312). Though we can still access such an experience, she says, we cannot give it material expression without destroying its fundamental character. "We have all of us the charm wherewith to evoke for ourselves a real Helen," she says, "on condition that, unlike Faustus and unlike Goethe, we seek not to show her to others, and remain satisfied if the weird and glorious figure haunt only our own imagination" (319). Because the rationality and formal definiteness of "art" has now completely triumphed over the supernatural, we can only experience ghostliness as a lived experience, not through literary representation.

Lee did not follow her own advice, however, publishing her first ghost story six years later. Catherine Maxwell and Patricia Pulham suggest she changed her mind after realizing that supernatural effects can be achieve in fiction through "imaginative suggestion in the ephemeral and insubstantial form of memories, impressions, associations, relics, and fragments [that] trigger ghostly occurrences," rather than through attempts to present such experiences concretely (291). Yet this description of the representational techniques Lee developed does not account for the motivations that led her from writing primarily in the genres of history and aesthetic theory to supernatural tales. In her stories, ghostliness allows queer women to develop a new relationship to the past that allows them to feel historical by privileging subjective experience over rationalism and empiricism. She expresses this new historiography through the experience of Alice Oke, the main character of her first supernatural tale, "Oke of Okehurst."

Supernatural Historicism's Queer Subject: "Oke of Okehurst"

"Oke of Okehurst" begins with a dedication to Lee's friend, the Russian poet Count Peter Bourtourline, expressing misgivings about supernatural writing similar to those found in the conclusion of "Faustus and Helena": "To write is to exorcise, to dispel the charm," she says, and "printer's ink chases away the ghosts that may pleasantly haunt us, as efficaciously as gallons of holy water" (105). Her story is not really about ghosts, however. It is about what happens when a woman refuses to submit her subjective experiences to the scrutiny of men. Lee's story is narrated by an unnamed artist, who has been commissioned to paint a portrait of William Oke, an unremarkable country squire, and his beautiful wife, Alice. Upon arriving at Okehurst, the couple's Jacobean manor, the painter discovers Alice is a very different woman from what he expected. He says she is "exquisite and strange,—an exotic creature" who fascinates him, even as he finds it impossible to capture her image definitively on canvas (115). For the narrator, her charm comes from her obsession with her seventeenth-century ancestor, also named Alice Oke (the modern William and Alice being first cousins), whose portrait reveals her to be the exact double of the modern Alice. She is fascinated by the legend of her ancestor, who supposedly conspired with her husband, Nicholas Oke, to kill her lover, a cavalier poet named Christopher Lovelock. She strongly suggests to her husband and the artist, but never states unequivocally, that Lovelock's ghost is attempting to seduce her. Alice's obsession, which includes mimicking the appearance of both the historical Alice and, on one occasion, Lovelock, leads her to withdraw almost completely from the concerns of the modern world. Eventually, in a fit of jealous rage against Lovelock's ghost encouraged by Alice, William inadvertently kills her and then himself.

According to the narrator, Alice has "no interest in the present, but only an eccentric passion in the past" (122). Lee shows how Alice uses her relationship to history to maintain a sense of identity independent of the limiting definitions of femininity offered by her patriarchal, heteronormative culture, by developing the gendered dynamic between art and the supernatural established in "Faustus and Helena." Her sexualized relationship with a painting of a beautiful woman from the past who looks exactly like her mirrors the predicament of the late Victorian lesbian, who seeks historical aesthetic representations of women like her to gain a sense of autonomy from dominant pathologizing discourses but must also contend with the fact that identities that seem continuous over time are often equivocal and, perhaps, completely fictional. Alice exploits the supernatural's inherent ambiguity to sustain herself in a *Hamlet*-like situation, refusing to affirm if she does or does not genuinely believe herself to be the reincarnation of Alice Oke. Rather than indicating a split or divided subjectivity, however, this ambiguity allows her to sustain her autonomy through her subjective relationship to the past. Alice's experience of history is mediated through a supernatural work of art that does not rely on empirical evidence for the sense of truth it conveys. In this way, Lee models the relationship lesbians must develop toward history to gain a stable, but not essentialist, sense of self. Alice gains subjective coherence by maintaining resistance to both heteronormativity and the pathologizing discourse of sexology.

The modern Alice's all-consuming historical passion seems, in the first instance, a refuge from the interminable dullness of life with her husband. Despite his aristocratic lineage, William Oke is the very personification of modernity's "sickness of the prosaic." The narrator says he is "absolutely like a hundred other young men you can see any day in the Park, and absolutely uninteresting from the crown of his head to the tip of his boot" (107). He betrays the romantic associations of his ancient name, which can be traced "back to Norman, almost to Saxon times," through devotion to the rationalized and bureaucratized administration of the modern state: "The condition of his tenants and his political party—he was a regular Kentish Tory—lay heavy on his mind" (120). This leads him to spend "hours every day in his study, doing the work of a land agent and a political whip, reading piles of reports and newspapers and agricultural treatises," rather than paying attention to his wife (117). William Oke's conservatism, far from the heroic Toryism of the past embodied by Lovelock, stems from conformity to the social norms of his milieu and a pragmatic concern with the running of his estate, not romantic devotion to the grandeur of his family's lineage.

According to the narrator, Alice's turn to history stems from "a perverse desire to surprise and shock . . . her husband, and thus be revenged from the intense boredom which his want of appreciation inflicted upon her" (116). Her obsession with a work of art from the past is not just an expression of the "incurable thirst for the sense of escape" from one's own historical moment that Pater associated with aesthetic experience.[47] In contrast to Pater, Alice's embrace of supernatural historicism is a gendered strategy she uses to resist her husband's attempts to force her into a future-oriented, heteronormative paradigm. Although William has no interest in his family's past, he is terribly concerned about its prospects. When he tells the narrator, "I don't care for children one jackstraw, you know, myself; can't stand how anyone can, for my part," the narrator informs us that "if ever a man went out of his way to tell a lie, I said to myself, Mr. Oke of Okehurst was doing so at the present moment" (112). Later in the story, the squire tells of the "prophecy" uttered in the seventeenth century by Nicholas Oke on his deathbed: "When the head of his house and master of Okehurst should marry another Alice Oke, descended from himself and his wife, there should be an end of the Okes of Okehurst." He says that "it seems to be coming true. We have no children, and I don't suppose we shall ever have any. I, at least, have never wished for them" (134). Oke's obvious upset about his lack of progeny implies the real motivation underlying Alice's "perverse" desire to be "revenged" on her husband. She has used her preoccupation with the prophecy as an excuse not to have children after a miscarriage, thereby taking control of her sexuality and reproductive capacities. More than this, however, she ensures there will be no future for the Oke family by making sure Nicholas Oke's prophecy comes true.

Alice's rejection of motherhood marks her as "perverse" in more ways than one. By refusing to propagate another generation of worthless aristocrats, Alice also rejects what Lee Edelman calls the ideology of "reproductive futurity" propelling social reproduction. This concept, which is at the heart of the association between heterosexuality and the idea of sociality itself, demands that one delay the pursuit of desire in the present for the sake of the future, which is embodied in the figure of the Child.[48] Edelman notes that this ideology is authorized by certain assumptions about temporality: normative heterosexual reproduction becomes privileged because it appears in sync with an understanding of time as linear and sequential, which posits that the present's primary function is to prepare for the future. Consequently, other kinds of sexuality are portrayed as both temporally and socially "aberrant."[49] It is no coincidence that Alice rejects heterosexual futurity through a non-linear understanding of history. The "prophecy" authorizing her refusal to reproduce rests on an understanding of temporality where the present is beholden to the demands of the past rather than the claims of the future. Her obsession with history instead of maternity confounds William's desire to continue the family line and marks her as "perverse," turned the wrong way: away from her husband, away from children, and away from the future. This is the adjective the narrator most often uses to describe Alice, appearing eight times in the text.

Yet while Edelman, like other "unhistoricist" queer critics, believes coherent sexual identity categories are so closely tied to teleological understandings of history that to repudiate one is necessarily to repudiate the other, Alice's temporal perversity allows her to develop a coherent and independent sense of self through acts of resistance. She does so by drawing upon the supernatural's ability to elicit a sensually and emotionally engaging, subjective relationship to the past that defies the modern demand for objective, empirically accurate understandings of history. When the narrator casts doubt on the historical accuracy of Lovelock's legendary murder at the hands of Nicholas and Alice, the modern Alice responds by showing the painter what he initially believes will provide evidence of the manner of Lovelock's death, "a large bundle of papers, some printed and some manuscript, but all of them brown with age" (126). Yet he soon learns that these documents contain art rather than data. They are Lovelock's love poems, addressed to the historical Alice. The modern Alice responds to these documents in an intensely visceral, erotic manner. The narrator says she touched "the yellow papers with delicate and reverent fingers" before reading "some of them out loud in a slow, half-audible voice":

> She held the papers in one hand, and leaned the other, as if for support, on
> the inlaid cabinet by her side. Her voice, which was delicate, shadowy, like her

person, had a curious throbbing cadence, as if she were reading the words of a melody, and restraining herself with difficulty from singing it; and as she read, her long slender throat throbbed slightly, and a faint redness came into her thin face. She evidently knew the verses by heart, and her eyes were mostly fixed with that distant smile in them, with which harmonised a constant tremulous little smile in her lips. (126–27)

This "one hand" reading of Lovelock's poetry has obvious masturbatory overtones. The "throbbing cadence" of Alice's voice, which is manifested physically in the throbbing of her throat, the tense interplay between her self-restraint and eruption into song, the "faint redness" in her face and the "distant smile" in her eyes which culminates in a "tremulous little smile in her lips" suggest, none too subtly, that her rendition of these poems brings her to orgasm. The historical art object allows Alice to self-stimulate and access perhaps the most basic form of nonheterosexual, nonreproductive eroticism, a primordial expression of female sexual independence and autonomy.

She receives more than just sexual pleasure from Lovelock's poems. Alice believes her arousal proves the historical truth of the legend. "Can you doubt of the reality of Christopher Lovelock now?" she asks after recovering from her performance. The painter comments to the reader that "the question was an illogical one, for to doubt of the existence of Christopher Lovelock was one thing, and to doubt of the mode of his death was another" (127). The narrator is right to say that Alice's belief in the truth of all aspects of the Alice-Lovelock legend has no relationship to the poems' status as empirical evidence. For her, the fact that they elicit a powerful erotic response in her is enough to confirm their veracity. Elizabeth Freeman has termed this sexualized understanding of the relationship between past and present "erotohistoriography," a method of investigation that "uses the body as a tool to effect, figure, or perform [the] encounter with history" by admitting that "contact with historical materials can be precipitated by particular bodily responses . . . that are themselves a form of historical understanding. It sees the body as a method, and historical consciousness as something intimately involved with corporeal sensation."[50] Implicit in this method, especially as practiced by Alice, is that the relationship between the knowledge created by the erotic encounter with the object and the material facts of history is a matter of indifference to the erotohistoriographer. The standard against which this knowledge is to be judged is whether it creates a subjective sense of connection to the past, rather than empirically verifiable knowledge.

The narrator, however, is unable to distinguish between Alice's aims and culturally dominant understandings of historiography and thereby confuses her subjective belief with objective historical truth. He says he "somehow . . . did feel convinced" by her performance of the poems, despite admitting that this is an illogical conclusion if one is seeking for the literal truth of the legend (127). This leads him to make a specific and limited inference about Alice's sexual desires. Despite the obvious autoeroticism of the scene, he believes her erotic attachment to Lovelock's poetry necessarily indicates that she was somehow supernaturally inhabited by the spirit of the historical Alice: "What struck me on thinking over the scene," he comments, was "that this strange being read these verses as one might fancy a woman would read love-verses addressed to herself" (127). He believes that Alice's intense response indicates that she must have been inhabiting the subject position of the person to whom the poems are addressed—the Alice Oke of 1626—and is thus straightforwardly heterosexual.[51]

Yet Lee leaves the object of Alice's desires deliberately vague. As she states at the end of "Faustus and Helena," if we wish to "raise a real spectre of the antique . . . we seek not to show her to others, and remain satisfied if the weird and glorious figure haunt only our imagination." When we attempt to give definite expression to the supernatural in a modern world that has been overtaken by rationality and the definiteness of artistic form, we destroy the part of it that is vital and that gives us a subjective sense of historical connection. As a model for the lesbian historiographer, the modern Alice shows how one can maintain a subjectively meaningful historical identification with the past by refusing the imperative to give unambiguous expression of one's subjective, erotohistoriographic experience. In the poetry reading scene, it is far from certain whether Alice desires or desires to be the historical Alice. It is equally plausible or implausible to assume that the modern Alice desires Lovelock, that she desires the historical Alice, that she identifies with the historical Alice as the object of Lovelock's desire, that she identifies with Lovelock as the object of Alice's desire, that she is aroused by her voyeuristic glimpse into the erotic dynamics of the Alice-Lovelock affair, et cetera. The only definite object of Alice's desires in the poetry-reading scene is the art object itself—the "yellow papers" that she caresses "with delicate and reverent fingers." Alice gives neither the narrator nor the reader any explicit account of her experiences while undergoing these supernatural, erotic encounters with history.

The ambiguity of Alice's desire is only compounded by the events leading up to her death at the hands of William. In the story's final pages, Alice becomes the agent of her own demise by suggesting to her increasingly delusional husband that she is courting the ghost of the historical Alice's lover. "It was probably Lovelock" she says to William, when he thinks he sees a man looking through their window (146). After he starts becoming visibly distraught at the mere mention of "your eternal Lovelock," Alice goads him by saying, "If you saw any one with me, it must have been Lovelock, for there certainly was no one else" (147). Eventually, when William inadvertently kills Alice while attempting to shoot Lovelock's ghost, the painter offers readers one last image of the mistress of Okehurst, finally satisfied in death: "Her mouth was convulsed, as if in that automatic shriek, but her wide-open white eyes seemed to smile vaguely and distantly" (152). Alice's eerie smile can be interpreted many ways. She could be happily reunited in death with Lovelock, whose actual ghost causes her demise (unlikely, given Lee's opinion of "spurious ghosts"). Alternatively, she could be smiling in triumph, having tricked her humdrum husband into killing her in a fit of mad romantic passion, thereby fulfilling her desire to reunite with Lovelock and making him the unwitting agent of Nicholas Oke's prophecy. Or she could be satisfied because, by enabling the killing of Alice Oke, she has finally realized Lovelock's murderous desires. In driving her husband to kill her by convincing him of the existence of a ghost, Alice commits the act that, in a more traditional supernatural tale, would have been committed by Lovelock's ghost himself. While this is undoubtedly a Pyrrhic victory for Alice, she goes to her grave on her own terms and as the result of her own machinations. Her haunting, enigmatic smile figures a perdurable selfhood that persists even in death through its enigmatic resistance to categorization and interpretation, much like Pater's famous description of the mysteriously smirking Mona Lisa, "dead many times" but symbolizing "the fancy of a perpetual life" (*R* 99).[52]

Alice's supernaturally mediated historical identification allows her to maintain an autonomous sense of self that solidifies around her ability to resist co-optation by both the hetero-futurity of her husband and the artist-narrator's attempts to pathologize and essentialize her identity through psychological diagnosis. His obsession with categorizing Alice through recourse to new definitions of sexual pathology intertwines with his desire to assert his masculine authority over her supernatural ambiguity by capturing it within the limits of his portrait's aesthetic form. The narrator embodies the masculine violence inherent in art's relationship to the supernatural Lee describes in "Faustus and Helena," its association with the post-Enlightenment rationalist, scientific imperative to discover and enforce normative boundaries that the supernatural seeks to contest and expand. He delights in his imagined intellectual superiority to both Okes by ostentatiously displaying his knowledge of recent psychological theories, and he associates his acuteness as a diagnostician with his skills as a painter. He mentions how, although "it seemed so unfair that just [Oke] should be condemned to puzzle for ever over this enigma [of Alice's obsession], and wear out his soul trying to comprehend what now seemed so plain to me," he would nevertheless make "no attempt to explain psychological problems to him" (140). Later, when Oke begins to believe that he has seen Lovelock's ghost, the painter "pour[s] out volumes of psychological explanation" to relieve him of his supernatural delusions but to no avail (149). Despite Oke's obtuseness, the narrator reveals to the reader his scientific explanation of Alice's obsession: "I am tempted to think," he says, "that the psychological peculiarity of that woman might be summed up in an exorbitant and absorbing interest in herself—a Narcissus attitude—curiously complicated with a fantastic imagination, a sort of morbid day-dreaming, all turned inwards" (116).

Although the term "narcissism" would not appear in print until 1887, one year after the publication of "Oke of Okehurst," the painter's use of the phrase "Narcissus attitude" to describe Alice's "morbid day-dreaming, all turned inward" is not just a mythological reference. It anticipates the term's use in sexological studies of autoeroticism, indicating both his and Lee's familiarity with the cutting edge of research in scientific psychology. The term first appeared in an article by French psychologist Alfred Binet in the *Revue philosophique* that described cases of extreme sexual fetishism as displaced expressions of autoerotic desire, in a manner very similar to Alice's fetishistic, onanistic encounter with Lovelock's poems.[53] Later, the term was used for the first time in English in an 1898 article on autoeroticism in the *Alienist and Neurologist* by Lee's friend, the sexologist Havelock Ellis. He described "the Narcissus-like tendency sometimes found, more especially perhaps in women, for the sexual emotions to be absorbed, and often entirely lost, in self-admiration," much like Alice's erotic obsession with the mirror image of herself in the portrait of the historical Alice.[54] Given the close relationship between Lee and Ellis, it is quite possible that she learned of this psychological theory before it found its way into print and expressed her distaste for its misogynistic, pathologizing overtones by ascribing it to her vain and sexist narrator.

The painter believes that diagnosing Alice's psychosexual disorder will allow him to control her through psychological manipulation and make it easier to capture her "essence" in his portrait. Ironically, this quest becomes his own neurotic obsession. He says he "pursued her, her physical image, her psychological explanation, with a kind of passion which filled my days, and prevented my ever feeling dull" (116). He is able to endure the "monotonous life of solitude" at Okehurst only because he has "the interest of a strange psychological riddle to solve, and of a great portrait to paint" (116). The painter actively encourages Alice's "very harmless psychological mania" for the legend of Lovelock for "the sake of the portrait [he] had undertaken" (122). Immediately after Alice's orgasmic reading of Lovelock's poetry, the narrator exclaims to himself, "That is how I would wish to paint her!" (127). He "derives a morbid and exquisite pleasure" in drawing out her historical obsession because "it completed her personality so perfectly, and made it so much easier to conceive a way of painting her" (128–29). By encouraging her supernatural delusions, the painter attempts to make her "Narcissus attitude" more visible on the surface of her body, making her psychological condition more amenable to being captured and contained by the portrait's aesthetic form. The painter attempts to do for the sake of art what Foucault says the sexologists attempted to do for the sake of science, trying to show her pathology, like the homosexual's, "written immodestly in [her] face and body because it was a secret that already gave itself away."[55]

The painter is an aesthetic sexologist working in the medium of painting, motivated primarily by the will to know, and thus to discipline, Alice's sexuality. He says he must paint Alice "in the yellow room" where she read Lovelock's poetry and where the painting of the historical Alice is located: "Mr. Oke might resent it," he states. "Mrs. Oke even might resent it; they might refuse to take the picture, to pay for it, to allow me to exhibit; they might force me to run my umbrella through the picture. No matter. That picture should be painted, if merely for the sake of having painted it; for I felt it was the only thing I could do, and that it would be far away my best work" (129). This display of artistic mastery depends on his mastery of the mind and body of Alice Oke. He manipulates her erotically and psychologically to get the painting he wants, and he will continue to do so despite anyone's objections, including her own.

Yet, despite his protestations of intellectual superiority and artistic virtuosity, the painter finds it impossible to create an accurate representation of Alice's "essence," the core of her being. Her refusal to confess the nature of her subjective supernatural eroticism makes it impossible for him to capture her within the limits of artistic form. In the days before her murder, the narrator says that he has had Alice sit for 130 sittings because he "somehow could never get beyond preparatory sketches with her," and, of course, he never does (143). The narrator explains the hard-won wisdom he eventually gained through struggling and failing to paint Alice's portrait: "I don't believe, you know, that even the greatest painter can show what is the real beauty of a very beautiful woman in the ordinary sense," he says. "Something—and that the very essence—always escapes, perhaps because real beauty is as much a thing in time—a thing like music, a succession, a series—as in space" (115). Alice is a woman who defies "being fixed and defined by those around [her], even seeming to cross the boundaries of time and space," as Catherine Maxwell states.[56] The narrator's bizarre, tragic, and artistically futile encounter with Alice has taught him a truth about women more generally: that specifically feminine forms of "beauty," even of the "conventional" sort, obey an eccentric, boundary-defying temporal logic incompatible with the static form of his traditional portrait-painting techniques. The artist-narrator asserts that he has come to his realization because the encounter with Alice has forced him to reckon with a woman whose "very essence" indicates the existence of an autonomous core of selfhood yet confounds the formalist impulse of his rationalist, diagnostic approach to artistic representation.

Alice resists both painter and husband by refusing to articulate to them or, by extension, the reader the precise nature of her historical obsession with a painting. By doing so, she embodies the relationship late Victorian lesbians can develop to their own history. By turning to works of art to "feel historical," they must look beyond scientific and empiricist historiographies and instead accept that their subjective feeling of identification across time elicited by an aesthetic encounter is itself a sufficient basis for developing a stable sense of self, refusing to submit to empirical accounts of either history or identity. This is true even if there is no essential or provable connection between one's sexual identity in the present and someone else's in the past.

The efforts queer women must put into developing this relationship to history would seem to put them at a disadvantage compared to queer men, who had the privilege of knowing for certain that there were men in the past who desired other men. Yet, as Lee shows in her story "Prince Alberic and the Snake Lady," this was actually a disadvantage. Queer women are much better acquainted with the fact that knowledge of the past, and especially the history of sexuality, always contains elements of fictiveness and wish fulfillment. Lee's story expresses her realization that, because queer men like Pater did not have to confront this fact, their aesthetic impressionism rested on an untheorized historical positivism that militated against the goal of pushing back against the limits of received cultural knowledge. Lee returns to Pater's theory of erotic negativity to explore the damaging effects of this unacknowledged element in the historical consciousness of the queer male aesthete.

Gendering the Aesthetic *Bildung*:
"Prince Alberic and the Snake Lady"

"Prince Alberic" describes a young man brought into maturity through his relationship with a mythological Snake Lady who physically materialized out of a tapestry and whose legend specifies that her transformation into a half-snake, half-human hybrid can be reversed only by a lover's sexual devotion. This relationship offers a narrative of male psychological development that bears strong affinities to the erotic negativity that drives the queer aesthetic *Bildung* described in Pater's "Winckelmann." Yet while Pater believed his ideal aesthetic critic gained queer self-knowledge by encountering artistic representations of male homoerotic desire from the past, Lee's story places Prince Alberic's desire for a mythical, shape-shifting Lamia figure at the center of his personal trajectory. The Lamia is an ancient Greek myth of a beautiful Libyan queen who turns into a serpentlike demon. It received renewed attention in the nineteenth century because of the popularity of John Keats's poem "Lamia" (1820), as Diana Wallace, Ruth Robbins, and Martha Vicinus have remarked in their discussions of Lee's story, and Andrew Smith notes that "Prince Alberic" forms part of the Victorian tradition of associating the Lamia with the process of artistic representation.[57] Lee uses the Lamia to critique the masculinist bias of Pater's version of homoerotic negativity, which rests on the near-instantaneous historical identification between the male viewer's homosexuality and the content of the art object. This experience was, effectively, available only to queer men in the late nineteenth century.

Yet, in Lee's story, the Snake Lady comes from a mythical past that shares more similarities with the realm of supernatural aesthetics than with empirical history. Her constant transformations elicit an alternative version of erotic negativity for the prince that inheres not in his successful identification with her but instead in his *desire* for such an identification that she actively and continually resists. By embodying the supernatural's characteristic resistance to resolving into a definite form, the Snake Lady fuels his sexual desire and motivates his psychological growth, encouraging him to embrace what lies "outside the limits of the possible, the rational, the explicable" and to challenge the normalizing, boundary-enforcing imperatives of Kantian rationalist modernity. For Lee, the Snake Lady is a figure not just for lesbianism but for any form of desire that departs from cultural norms, including those forms of queerness that have yet even to be imagined. In this story, Lee's supernatural "topsy-turveying" labor of the negative upon Pater's aestheticism shows how any form of queerness can derive a sense of autonomy by turning toward the past and away from present-day social opprobrium, thereby grounding its sense of coherence in its ability to continually resist formalization into sexual essentialism or an impossible historical facticity.

Lee explicitly repudiated Pater's aestheticism in the valedictory essay of *Renaissance Fancies and Studies* in 1895, where she asserted, approvingly, that Pater "began as an aesthete, and ended as a moralist," using his supposed transformation to justify her newfound belief that aesthetic experience is ineffable and that the writing and reading of art criticism is merely a distraction from the direct experience of art itself.[58] I argue, however, that though this essay was her official public farewell to Paterian aestheticism, she had not yet completed her negation of his influence. This finally occurred in "Prince Alberic and the Snake Lady," which appeared the next year in the *Yellow Book*, the most famous periodical associated with fin-de-siècle aestheticism and decadence, and is the true culmination of the labor of the negative upon Pater that began with her implicit rejection of Winckelmann in "The Child in the Vatican."[59]

The first line of her story mocks the rhetoric of empiricist Victorian historiography: "In the year 1701, the Duchy of Luna became united to the Italian dominions of the Holy Roman Empire, in consequence of the extinction of its famous ducal house in the persons of Duke Balthasar of Maria and of his grandson Alberic, who should have been third of the name" (182). Despite her academic tone and seeming precision and specificity, complete with references to the "real" past of the Holy Roman Empire, Luna is an entirely fictional place. In this and the other "facts" she sprinkles throughout her story, Lee parodies historical writing's pretensions to objective truth, showing how the veneer of authority relies on the aesthetic effect created by a dull prose style. As she states in the next sentence, "Under this dry historical fact lies hidden the strange story of Prince Alberic and the Snake Lady" (183). She indicates that her tale narrates a history that takes place not in the materially verifiable past but rather "under" it, in a "strange" realm not governed by the rationalism and empiricism of official historiography—in other words, in the realm of the supernatural.[60]

The narrative proper begins when Duke Balthasar, a narcissistic and ty-rannical ruler, enters the rooms of his grandson, Prince Alberic, for the first time since his birth. Up to this point, Alberic has spent his entire life alone in his chambers and his garden, with almost no contact with the outside world. In a nod to Paterian accounts of aesthetic *Bildung*, the narrator tells the story of Alberic's psychological development through reference to his preoccupation with a beautiful tapestry hanging on his wall. In early childhood, Alberic spends his days gazing at the borders of the tapestry, "satisfied with seeing the plants and animals . . . and looking forward to seeing the real thing only when he should be grown up" (185). As he grows older, however, his attention gradually moves from the tapestry's periphery to its center, as he spends his days puzzling out the intricate geography of the rustic scene represented there.

Alberic reaches sexual maturity and self-awareness at the moment he can discern two faint figures woven into the center of the faded fabric. These figures "seemed like ghosts, sometimes emerging and then receding again into vagueness. Indeed, it was only as he grew bigger that Alberic began to see any figures at all; and then, for a long time he would lose sight of them. But little by little, when the light was strong, he could see them always" (186). Once he learns to accept the supernatural formlessness of the figures, rather than searching to discover their definite forms, he can finally recognize them as a knight and a lady. Although Alberic acknowledges that the knight and his horse are beautiful, he "got to love the lady most," even though the lower half of her body is covered by a crucifix set upon a chest of drawers, obscuring the skirt "he want[ed] so much to see" (*H* 187). One day, when Alberic's nurse rearranges the furniture in response to his growing maturity, so that "the child should cease to sleep in her room," it is revealed that the lady's lower half "ended off in a big snake's tail." The narrator tells us that Alberic "loved the beautiful lady with the thread of gold hair only the more because she ended off in the long twisting body of a snake. And that, no doubt, was why the knight was so very good to her" (*H* 187–88). Duke Balthasar's eventual removal of the tapestry occasions Alberic's first act of defiance against authority. He refuses food and begins to "pine away" because "the tapestry had been his whole world; and now it was gone he discovered he had no other" (*H* 188). The story maps Alberic's maturation from childish naïveté to sexual awakening and self-possession onto his growing ability to discern the forms at the center of the artwork. Once he learns that he can perceive the "ghostly figures" without having to resolve them into a definite form, the Snake Lady becomes the object of his erotic desire and provides the motivation for his first assertion of individuality in the form of adolescent rebellion.

Alberic's relationship to the tapestry bears many similarities to the narrative of aesthetic development offered in Pater's "Winckelmann." Pater asserts that Winckelmann's critical insight into the formal qualities of ancient Greek sculpture, much like Alberic's ability to recognize the figures represented in the tapestry, is associated with the initiation into sexual self-knowledge. In Winckelmann's case, however, it is crucial that the object mirrors his own desires back to him exactly. The fact that Winckelmann and the ancient Greek sculptors both are men and desire men creates a relationship of identification that spans the historical distance between them, which Pater calls Winckelmann's "reconciliation with the spirit of Greek sculpture" (*R* 152). This reliance on historical identification causes the aesthetic critic to operate within a closed circuit, where the ability to discern the formal qualities of art objects reflects the desires of the viewing subject.

In Lee's story, however, Prince Alberic does not gain erotic self-knowledge in tandem with the proper recognition of aesthetic form per se but with his acceptance that the desired historical object will never exactly match his expectations. Alberic embodies a radical sexual openness to the object that departs from both heteronormativity and the definitively male homoerotics of Pater's aestheticism. He loves the lady "only the more" and comes to realize the nature of erotic desire by speculating that "the knight was so good to her" specifically because she unexpectedly has the body of a snake. While the Snake Lady is, as her soubriquet would suggest, a woman, her serpentine body has traditionally signified an amorphous gender identity that confounds binary distinctions. While many readers have interpreted Prince Alberic's relationship with the Snake Lady to be a coded expression of lesbian desire, Zorn maintains that they share a "bond" that undermines the very concept of a gender binary.[61] "The relationship between the Snake Lady and the Prince does not produce a new dualism," she argues, because "without the boundaries of gender, norms like heterosexuality are undercut and direct us to other possible relationships."[62] This new vision of queer eroticism is open to, but not absolutely defined by, desire between women.

Alberic does not desire the Snake Lady simply because she takes on a serpentine form but because she refuses to settle into any definite form. She enables Alberic to embody a sexual subjectivity grounded in the ambiguity of a supernatural experience that accommodates many kinds of difference. As a supernatural artwork come to life, she actively resists becoming a fully knowable, or even partially comprehensible, object. Throughout the story, she appears in various guises: as a snake; as Alberic's godmother, who provides maternal protection and companionship; and as Lady Oriana, the beautiful woman who, according to family legend, fell in love with the prince's ancestor, also named Alberic, and who can be released from the curse of being a serpent only through the prince's sexual fidelity. The parallels between the myth of Prince Alberic and the Snake Lady and the myth of Alice and Lovelock in "Oke of Okehurst" indicate that Lee seeks to explore the relevance of the supernatural lesbian historiography developed in the earlier story for a wide range of queer sexualities.

Alberic's desire for the Snake Lady, like Alice Oke's desire for the historical Alice, is suggested but never definitively affirmed by the text: "Children sometimes conceive an inexplicable shyness, almost a dread," the narrator states, "of knowing more on some subject which is uppermost in their thoughts; and such had been the case of Duke Balthasar Maria's grandson" (201). Instead, it is merely suggested that his sexual attraction is sustained by his continually frustrated attempts to know more about the Snake Lady. The narrator informs us that, once Prince Alberic grows "into a full-grown and gallant-looking youth," he becomes increasingly obsessed by the story of Lady Oriana:

> He thought of it more than ever, and it began to haunt his dreams; only it was now a vaguely painful thought; and, while dreading still to know more, he began to experience a restless, miserable craving to know all. His curiosity was like a thorn in his flesh, working its way in and in; and it seemed something almost more than curiosity. And yet, he was still shy and frightened of the subject; nay, the greater his craving to know, the greater grew a strange certainty that the knowing would be accomplished by evil. (204)

The narrator's suggestive language in this passage, the "restless miserable craving," the "thorn" that slowly penetrates his "flesh," his ever-increasing "craving," suggests that Alberic struggles to separate his erotic from his epistemological desires. His growth into psychological and sexual maturity can be accomplished only through an encounter with unresolvable ambiguity, which manifests itself as Lady Oriana's resistance to taking a definite form that will unambiguously fulfill his desires.

Her shape-shiftings stop only when she is killed by Duke Balthasar's men while she is in the form of a snake and finally transforms into Lady Oriana for eternity. Much like Alice Oke, the Snake Lady embodies in her very being a supernatural aesthetic that resists sexual essentialism. Her story offers a vision of supernatural resistance to artistic form and empiricist historicism, and it offers a version of erotic negativity that elicits psychological and sexual development by embracing the unknowable without relying on the exclusionary, gendered assumption of sameness found in Paterian erotic negativity. Significantly, Lee mounts her critique of male aestheticism not by rejecting it wholesale but by reworking and adapting it through the "topsy-turveying" labor of the negative. Lee's story represents the culmination of the project begun in her supernatural writings of the 1880s. Through this "curdling and emergence" of her own philosophical account of aesthetics, Lee's supernatural writings perform the labor of the negative on Pater's homoerotic aestheticism to create an account of how art can enable the development of a range of coherent sexual identities that gain self-sufficiency through their ability to maintain resistance to heteronormative and essentializing discourses.

The vision of erotic negativity embodied in her supernatural writings strengthen its power as a theory of how queers of all kinds can transform their feelings of social alienation into a sense of autonomy from cultural norms. Recently, Traub has called for a new paradigm for queer historicism, one that deemphasizes the binary oppositions between theories of continuous versus discontinuous notions of sexual identity and instead focuses on what she calls "explanatory metalogics" that "might profitably be understood as *cycles of salience*—that is, as forms of intelligibility whose meanings recur, intermittently and with a difference, across time."[63] Lee presents her supernatural version of erotic negativity as just such an explanatory metalogic, one that shows how any form of sexual difference that might emerge and crystalize in the future can develop a salutary sense of historicity without having to affirm a transhistorical essentialism. In this, Lee's supernatural tales look not just back toward the lesbian past but also forward toward the queer future, providing a theory of historical consciousness for the heretofore unimagined versions of desire that will come to be.

CHAPTER FIVE

Queering Indifference in Michael Field's Ekphrastic Poetry

In the opening sentence of their preface to *Sight and Song* (1892), the two women who wrote under the pseudonym Michael Field state that "the aim" of this volume of poetry "is, as far as may be, to translate into verse what the lines and colours of certain chosen pictures sing in themselves; to express not so much what these pictures are to the poet, but rather what poetry they objectively incarnate."[1] This statement was radical. As I discuss in chapter 3, the post-Romantic nineteenth century's dominant expectation of lyric poetry was that it was the ultimate expression of individual subjectivity, the poet's speaking of himself to himself. But Katharine Bradley and Edith Cooper, the "Michael Field" poets, state that their translations of paintings into poems "demands patient, continuous sight as pure as the gazer can refine it of theory, fancies, or his mere subjective enjoyment."[2] They frame their version of ekphrasis, which James Heffernan defines as "the verbal representation of visual representation," as an experimental method for removing the temptation to introduce one's own personal feelings into the lyric.[3]

Julia F. Saville has argued that the poor reception that greeted *Sight and Song* can be attributed to this rejection of the emotionality expected of Victorian women poets.[4] William Butler Yeats's largely negative review condemned Bradley and Cooper for not staying within their own subject positions by "singing out of their own hearts and setting to music their own souls. They have poetic feeling and imagination in abundance, and yet they have preferred to write a guide-book to the picture galleries of Europe, instead of giving us a book full of the emotions and fancies which must be crowding in upon their minds perpetually" (*MF* 361). Their friend, the art critic Bernard Berenson, echoed this view in a letter to the poets, saying that they "ha[d] confused the material of poetry, which is <u>feeling</u> with colour & outline the material of painting" (*MF* 84).[5]

Fear of being limited to speaking only from a gendered subject position initially led Bradley and Cooper to write under a male pseudonym. "The report of lady-authorship will dwarf & enfeeble our work at every turn," they wrote to Robert Browning, an early supporter, after he revealed their identities in 1884. "We have many things to say the world will not tolerate from a woman's lips."[6] They were largely correct. Although their early blank-verse dramas, *Callirrhoe & Fair Rosamund* (1884) and the first volume of lyric poetry they published together, *Long Ago* (1889), were warmly received by critics and audiences, later volumes drew gradually less attention from the literary world. This compounded the alienation they already felt from late Victorian modernity and encouraged their retreat into a private world of art appreciation and historical research, culminating in conversion to an idiosyncratic form of Catholicism in 1907.

In April 1895, during Wilde's trials for "gross indecency," Cooper wrote in a letter to Bradley that she dreamed of a confrontation with a woman who had "heard things against [them]," culminating in Edith fearfully telling her aunt to remain calm and "remember the Oscar scandal."[7] Cooper's dream suggests that the distance they felt from mainstream society as women aspiring to speak beyond the confines of gender was exacerbated by their sexually unorthodox personal lives. In addition to being aunt and niece, Bradley and Cooper were also lovers. In *Works and Days*, the journal they kept jointly for most of their shared lives, they call themselves "closer married" than the iconic couple Robert and Elizabeth Barrett Browning and habitually refer to each other as "husband" and "wife."[8] Yet, in addition to this primary relationship, the two women also cultivated romantic feelings toward other men and women throughout their lives, such as Berenson and his wife Mary Costelloe, as well as their friends Charles Ricketts and Charles Shannon, who were themselves a gay couple. In a letter describing the wedding of sexologist Havelock Ellis, they explicitly reject monogamy, referring to the "modern sacrament of marriage" as "revolting. 'Free love, free field' is sacreder."[9]

I argue in this chapter that Bradley and Cooper's ekphrastic poems show how "disinterested" (or, alternatively, "indifferent") aesthetic judgments can elicit in readers a sense of gender and sexual fluidity that frees them from both the strictures of normative, queer-phobic Victorian morality and the limitations of nascent pathological categories of sexual identity, creating an experience similar to the erotic mutability they sought in their personal lives.

For Kant, the judgment we exercise in determining something to be beautiful is defined by the fact that the pleasure derived from the object is due solely to its beauty. If we value an object because it gives us pleasure in some other way, then this is not a truly *aesthetic* judgment, because the viewer is not indifferent to the other uses or purposes of the object in making her assessment. In traditional interpretations of Kant, aesthetic indifference means that the pleasure one derives from an artwork is divorced entirely from one's immediate needs and desires. Yet, in their poetry, Bradley and Cooper showed that disinterested judgment can result from an artistically mediated experience of erotic desires that are not actually one's own. In the process, they discovered the key to representing personal autonomy in an era when scientific advances made it increasingly difficult to distinguish between responses to physical appetites and genuine acts of free will: embrace bodily desire, rather than attempt to transcend it. Bradley and Cooper's account of aesthetic judgment sexualizes Amanda Anderson's insight that, in Victorian culture, the cultivation of "detachment" from merely personal interests that was the "aspiration" of the liberal subject was always dialectically bound to individual idiosyncrasies.[10] Their poems show how aesthetic disinterest, by enabling one to experience what it is like to possess sexual interests foreign to one's own appetites, allows one's consciousness to transcend the limits of the merely personal biological impulse, thereby enabling their readers to regain a sense of autonomous subjectivity.

The version of aesthetic disinterest developed in Bradley and Cooper's ekphrastic poetry would seem to anticipate, by nearly a decade, the notion of aesthetic "empathy" developed by Vernon Lee along with her partner, Kit Anstruther-Thomson, in the latter half of Lee's career. As I discussed briefly in the previous chapter, Lee publicly rejected Pater and aestheticism in 1895 in favor of developing an experimental science of embodied artistic perception. Marion Thain notes that "Bradley and Cooper may not have wanted to be associated" with Lee, calling her "an intellectual Vampire." Yet, despite this, "they knew her, and her work, very well."[11] Whitney Davis recounts that, for Lee, the observer of art "forges an eroticized connection with the possibility (perhaps even the proximity) of another body seen or remembered to be taking (its own) corporeal pleasure [in the artwork]." Yet "this erotic energy seems to be wholly absorbed *into* the work of art, to become its intrinsic objective motive."[12] Lee's notion of empathy is very much an "interested" theory of aesthetic response, arising from the viewer's desire for another viewer, mediated by the form of the artwork. In Bradley and Cooper's poems, however, it is aesthetic judgment's disinterestedness, its detachment from the immediate desires of one's own body, that frees us from being shackled to the limits of our own sexual appetites. This eroticized version of aesthetic disinterest was implicit in Walter Pater's belief that his literary style could convey the subjective feeling of queer erotic negativity to a non-queer audience, as I have discussed in chapter 2, but Bradley and Cooper's poetry presents it as a foundational principle of artistic experience tout court.

Their experiment in ekphrasis has important implications for the modern critical notion of "queering" the artwork as an emancipatory project. Much modern criticism implies it is the viewer's job to reject the notion of aesthetic disinterest by unearthing an erotically "interested" queerness within a work of art and thereby to expose its socially subversive intentions. Yet Bradley and Cooper's writings show that it is precisely the normativity of disinterested aesthetic judgement that allows the entrance into multiple erotic subject positions that marks the viewer's emancipated selfhood.

Their poetry expresses a formalist theory of aesthetic spectatorship inspired by Pater's Hegelian theory of painting in "The School of Giorgione" (1877), an essay that was deeply influential on Bradley and Cooper and one which notably departs from the subject-centered aesthetics that characterizes most of his writings.[13] Although they eventually lamented what they saw as Pater's apparent turn to a more traditional Victorian morality, they nevertheless followed his writings closely throughout his career, and, as Angela Leighton states, his aesthetic criticism was "the single most important influence on their writing."[14] This is nowhere more apparent than in *Sight and Song*, a copy of which they personally inscribed to him. His immense influence on the Fields was recognized as early as Richard le Gallienne's review of the collection in 1892.[15] Many of the artists who appear in this collection are also discussed in *The Renaissance*, and echoes of Pater's language can be found throughout the poems. This has led Thain and S. Brooke Cameron to read Bradley and Cooper's picture-poems as an extension of Pater's aesthetics, an experiment in using poetry's inherently diachronic language to capture the synchronic experience of looking at a painting.[16]

Yet I argue that these lyrics express a version of negativity that departs significantly from Pater's. As we have seen in chapter 1, Pater's erotic negativity is almost entirely an internal, subjective phenomenon. Though the homoerotic work of art serves as the external trigger to the process, the shattering and subsequent reconstruction of consciousness occurs entirely within the mind of the queer viewer. Bradley and Cooper, by contrast, are more interested in negativity as an objective quality embodied by the artwork itself. This, I maintain, is at the root of their desire to write poems based on paintings. Pater's formalist account of painting in "School of Giorgione" departs from the subjectivism that characterizes most of his work, relying instead on Hegel's definition of painting as the aesthetic practice par excellence for giving objective form to negativity through the quality he calls *Schein*, the ability to create a convincing representation of the real world on a two-dimensional canvas. *Schein* allows painting to render sensually humanity's capacity for freedom, serving as the objective, formal equivalent of the subjective act of disinterested aesthetic judgment. Similarly, when Bradley and Cooper translate painterly form into the language of poetry, they highlight how aesthetic disinterestedness can elicit an experience of erotic negativity. Their poems transform the alienation incumbent upon embracing sexual fluidity in a culture insisting on strict gender and sexual binaries in all aspects of life, including poetry, into a liberating sense of transcending the normative limits of identity.

Bradley and Cooper express their formalist version of autonomy in the lyrics "To Apollo—the Conqueror" (1878) and *Sight and Song*'s "L'Indifférent." These poems, which are inspired by Pater's Hegelian aesthetics and Johann Joachim Winckelmann's art-historical writings, anatomize the eroticism at the heart of experiences of formal beauty and prove that sexual desire is a vital element even of ostensibly disinterested aesthetic judgments. Their poems based on paintings of Saint Sebastian demonstrate the gender and sexual motility that becomes possible when erotic desire is mediated by the aesthetic, showing the poets imaginatively projecting themselves into a male homoerotic subject position. The process of aesthetic judgment enabling this mediation is represented in the poems based on paintings by Leonardo da Vinci. In these lyrics, Bradley and Cooper show that attentiveness to sexuality's role in artistic creation and reception is necessary for insight into an artwork's historical significance. In contrast to the abstract universality ascribed to aesthetic judgment by Kant and Hegel, the Leonardo poems show how assessments of canonical ideals of beauty contain traces of the erotic desires that originally inspired the work, traces that divert the desires of the viewer away from her own sexual appetites. These poems present a challenge to the notion that queering an artwork necessarily entails rejecting any normative ideal of beauty and highlight the queer potential inherent even in socially endorsed aesthetic judgments of canonical works of art. Although much modern criticism implies it is the critic's task to "queer" art objects by revealing their erotically interested subversiveness, Michael Field's ekphrastic poems show that it is precisely the normativity of disinterested aesthetic judgments that queers viewers and readers of art by detaching them from their limiting containment within a single gender and sexual identity. More than this, it shows how the aesthetic is the space best suited for queers to imagine how oppressive cultural norms might be radically reformed.

Pater, Hegel, *Schein*

Bradley and Cooper, like most late Victorian artists and intellectuals, inhabited a milieu where basic knowledge of Hegel's writings was expected. A somewhat condescending 1881 letter from John Addington Symonds included Hegel's *Aesthetics* as part of a recommended reading list, and Edith Cooper received a solid grounding in the German idealism dominating British academic philosophy in the late nineteenth century as a student of philosophy and classics at University College, Bristol.[17] Thain argues that their poetic career can be understood as "rooted within a quintessentially Victorian and, more precisely, Hegelian, process that draws meaning from recognising the self as founded upon contradiction."[18] Yet the most decisive influence on Bradley and Cooper's ekphrasis was not Hegel himself but Pater's Hegelian, formalist theory of painting. They reworked this into their own object-oriented version of erotic negativity, distinct from the subject-oriented version of negativity dominating Pater's own writings on queer sexuality.

Pater's "The School of Giorgione" was inserted into the third edition of *The Renaissance* in 1888, after appearing in the *Fortnightly Review* in 1877.[19] This perhaps accounts for Pater's departure in this essay from the subjective impressionism that characterizes the other pieces in that collection. In "The School of Giorgione," Pater famously states that "all art constantly aspires to the condition of music" (*R* 106). Although each genre of artistic production—architecture, sculpture, painting, poetry, and music—elicits a particular imaginative response from the observer that is unique to that genre, he also says that "each art may be observed to pass into the condition of some other art, by what German critics term an *Anders-Streben*—a partial alienation from its own limitations" (*R* 105). Musicality is the goal toward which all artistic productions strive because music comes closest to fulfilling art's ultimate purpose, which is to "obliterate" the distinction between form and content (*R* 106). Andrew Eastham argues that Pater's claim was inspired by "Hegel's system" of aesthetics, where "it is music that fulfils the Romantic spirit of subjective inwardness. . . . [I]t is the negative qualification of subjectivity which refuses sensuous embodiment."[20] Music, in other words, is the genre that comes closest to representing the subject's capacity for transcendent freedom. This freedom finds its only material equivalent in the medium of sound, which actively resists solidifying into a fixed and definite shape by existing only within duration, rather than space. Sound, like the autonomous subject, refuses to be captured once and for all within the limits of form.

Approximations of this phenomenon can be found in other art forms as well, as an aspect of their *Anders-Streben*. The quasi-musical element that can be found in painting is what Hegel refers to as *Schein*, which is translated as either "to shine" or "to appear" (R 106). Negation is at the heart of *Schein*. Benjamin Rutter explains, quoting the *Aesthetics*, that for Hegel "the fundamental character of painting" is that the soul "appea[rs] not so much as *free*, but *freed*, as having overcome natural particularity [and] pain."[21] To accomplish this, however, painting must first represent the limitations of the natural world, in order to demonstrate painting's ability to transcend them. Hegel asserts that it must "'negate the immediacy of feeling' . . . [f]or only in his 'involvement with concrete reality' does 'the free subjective individual . . . prove himself in his own eyes to be concrete and living.'"[22] The pleasure one derives from viewing a painting comes from the painting's ability to create a convincing representation of the world on a two-dimensional surface. This evidences the artist's ability to gain mastery over the painful and constricting limitations of the material world through her skill and creativity. In turn, the viewer's enjoyment comes from the recognition that she too, like the painter, possesses a spirit that is not limited by concrete reality but can transcend it. This is how painting can give sensual expression to humanity's capacity for subjective autonomy. The freedom embodied by a painting comes not from its ability to transcend the givens of the world entirely, in a utopian sense, but in the recognition that the apparent limits of the concrete world are not truly absolute but can be surmounted by the human spirit.

Schein is Hegel's word for this process of aesthetic negation, painting's superlative ability to create a virtual imitation of the material world by creating the illusion that a three-dimensional object is really present before us, despite our awareness that we are really looking at a flat, two-dimensional canvas. *Schein* is the illusion created by the painter through a combination of realistic depiction and trompe l'oeil. Painting negates the material world by depicting its limitations: if physical reality can be convincingly captured on a two-dimensional canvas, we must confront the fact that our world is finite and limited compared to the ineffable immensity of *Geist*, or "spirit." Dialectically, however, *Schein* transforms painting's negation of the world into an affirmation of human freedom. If the painter can create a convincing representation of the natural world, this shows that the spirit is not imprisoned by the givens of material reality. The ability to identify with the skills of the artist does not reside in the content of the painting but is instead communicated by its formal effects.

A key element of *Schein*'s negativity is the painter's use of visual elements on the canvas's surface to create a formal effect that mimics the formlessness of sound in music. Hegel calls this an "objective music, a peal in colour" that is the "subjective recreation of externality in the sensuous elements of colours and lighting." He explains that "just as in music the single note is nothing by itself but produces its effect only in its relation to another . . . so here it is just the same with colour. . . . The single colour as such does not have this gleam which it produces; it is the juxtaposition *alone* which makes this glistening and gleaming."[23] The artist's ability to create the illusion of actual physical presence that is *Schein* through this "musical" use of color and form is painting's formal equivalent to music's evocation of subjective inwardness, the *Anders-Streben* that allows painting to negate reality by reproducing it on the surface of the canvas and enabling the painter and, by extension, the viewer to experience the closest material equivalent to the ineffable freedom of the subject.

Jacques Rancière argues that Hegel's emphasis on the negativity of *Schein* was a response to changes in the nineteenth-century culture of art viewing. This culture was produced by the same Enlightenment political ideals expressed in Hegel's philosophy. Public art galleries owed their existence, according to Rancière, to the rise of democratic nationalism in Europe in the late eighteenth and early nineteenth centuries, when interest arose in making artworks available to the common people to develop a sense of communal identity. Yet the organizers of these museums had to contend with the fact that the content of these great works of art from the nation's history catered to the refined tastes and knowledge of the cosmopolitan aristocrats who patronized artists and collected their works. Consequently, Rancière argues that displaying these paintings in the radically different context of the public museum changed the very notion of what "Art" was and who it was for: "The idea of art as patrimony needed to impose itself: art as the property of the people, the expression of its forms of life, but also as a common property whose works belong to this common place now called Art, and that materialized itself in the museum."[24] Hegel recognized that changes in artistic display and the concept of art as the patrimony of the people required a new theorization of what constituted beauty in painting. In an age that celebrated universal human freedom, an art collection presented as belonging to a nation's history and embodying its cultural practices must be shown to represent the common people's desire and capacity for freedom, not the preferences and prejudices of its upper classes. Rancière thus claims that Hegel redefined beauty in painting not as the elite subject matter of its represented content but instead as the abstract forms that constituted its *Schein*, which would be visible to anyone who gazes upon it. "The freedom of the work signifies its indifference to its represented content," he writes:

> This freedom can thus appear purely negative: it relies only on the status of the
> works in museums where they are separated from their primary destination.
> Religious scenes or royal portraits, mythological compositions or domestic
> scenes, the paintings that yesterday were used to illustrate the truths of faith,
> to figure the grandeur of princes or to adorn aristocratic life, are offered in the
> same way to the gaze of anonymous visitors, ever less attentive to the meaning
> and the destination of paintings. This indifference could mean that, from now
> on, painting is a simple matter of shapes and light, lines and colours.[25]

As Hegel states in the *Aesthetics*, a painting's value lies not in its subject matter but entirely in its surface qualities, "the pure appearance which is wholly without the sort of interest which the subject has."[26]

Hegel's ideal of *Schein* takes Kant's notion of the disinterestedness of the viewer's aesthetic judgment and instead makes it a quality of the art object itself, showing it to be, in Rancière's words, "not only the subjective property of judgment, but also the very content of painting, and especially the content of painting as such."[27] More than any other art form, we look to paintings "for the pure 'disinterested' pleasure of enjoying the play of appearances. And it is this play of appearances that is the very realization of the freedom of mind."[28] As Hegel states in the *Aesthetics*, when it comes to art the viewer "leaves it free as an object to exist on its own account; he relates himself to it without desire, as to an object which is for the contemplative side of the spirit alone."[29] The viewer's ability to gain satisfaction by letting her gaze wander freely over a canvas's lines and colors, uninterested in any of the more practical or material desires the painting might embody, thus attests to the individual's capacity for freedom in the form of autonomous self-determination. This new concept of art also, in turn, transforms how one understands what the painting actually represents. *Schein*'s indifference to content is understood by Hegel to be "the realization of . . . an inner necessary freedom" that was *really* the true subject of the painting all along. As Rancière states, for Hegel "the play of appearances, light effects, and jauntiness of the canvas must not arrive on top of the painting independently of the subject. They must reveal its true subject. . . . [T]his indifferent treatment makes the non-vulgar, spiritual content of these subjects visible."[30] This is the essence of the Hegelian *Schein*, painting's ability to affirm the subject's transcendent freedom through aesthetic negation of the physical world.

Pater comes to a similar conclusion about painting in "The School of Giorgione." The aesthetic value of Giorgione's paintings derives from their ability to be appreciated even (perhaps especially) when they are detached from the original political and religious context in which they were produced. They are "easily movable pictures," he says, "which serve neither for uses of devotion, nor of allegorical or historic teaching" but instead are "typical of that aspiration of all the arts toward music . . . toward the perfect identification of form and matter" (*R* 110–11). Eastham here identifies Pater's turn away from Kant's abstract, viewer-centered version of disinterest that is similar to Hegel's redefinition of Kant. Pater historicizes "aesthetic modernity" to narrate how "the autonomous artistic media emerge from . . . social conditions. . . . [W]hat he describes is a fundamental change in the conditions of art, which becomes autonomous and private but also mobile and capable of global diffusion," insofar as their formal qualities produce a sense of subjective autonomy that in no way depends on the local conditions and historical context of the artwork's production.[31]

Bradley and Cooper's ekphrastic poetry seeks to win for modern poetry the same ability to represent freedom that Hegel and Pater ascribe to the paintings from the past hanging on the walls of the newly democratized museums they visited throughout Europe in the process of composing *Sight and Song*. As Yeats noted sardonically in his review, their collection does indeed form something of a guidebook to these new picture galleries. The poems draw from hundreds of pages of copious notes on paintings they saw in their travels, and the heading of each poem records the museum where they saw the picture. These included both the great public art collections founded in the nineteenth century, such as the National Gallery and the Louvre, as well as formerly private aristocratic collections that had been made available to the public, such as the Grand Duke's Palace at Weimar, the Ducal Palace at Venice, and Lord Dudley's Collection, among others (*MF* 83).

The possibility of capturing the *Schein* of painting within the "musical" language of poetry was inspired by their experience in these art museums and inflected by Paterian-Hegelian reflections on *Anders-Streben*. These issues are in the background of a conversation about ekphrastic language that occurred between Bradley and Oscar Wilde, which occurred while the Michael Fields were briefly back in England in the midst of their European tour. At a gathering at the London home of the American poet Charles Moulton, Bradley and Wilde discussed the relationship between color in painting and the musical qualities of poetic language. The fact that their conversation about the relationship between color and sound immediately turned into a discussion of a painting, rather than nature itself, suggests that Wilde and Bradley may have had Pater's historicist account of painterly formalism in mind. Bradley records in the *Works and Days* journal that, after she and Wilde both agreed that Pater was the "only [<one>] man in this century who can write prose," he brought up the fact that "French is wonderfully rich in colour words." Bradley writes that they both

> agreed English was poor in such—I instanced <u>bluish</u>-grey as a miserable effort, & he dwelt on the full pleasantness and charm of the French colour words ending in âtre bluâtre &c. But we should grapple with this colour difficulty. It should bear <u>faith</u> that everything in the world can be expressed in words. I spoke of <u>L'embarquement pour Cythère</u> [Antoine Watteau's painting, which would become the subject of the final poem in *Sight and Song*]—of the impossibility of expressing what was happening at that fairy-water. (*MF* 240)

The concerns expressed by Bradley and Wilde during this exchange are implicitly Hegelian and Paterian. "<u>Bluish</u>-grey" may be literally accurate as an analytical description of a color, but Bradley notes that the quotidian sound of the words is not in any way equivalent to the subjective experience of actually seeing the color, which is better conjured by the mellifluous sound of French "âtre" color words. Essentially, they agree it is difficult for the English language to recreate the *Schein* of painting because it lacks the "objective music" that could recreate in sound the illusion of reality so successfully captured by the color patterns on the surface of the canvas.

Concerns of the sort expressed in this conversation with Wilde inspired the task Bradley and Cooper set themselves in *Sight and Song,* where they "grapple with this colour difficulty" by transforming visual experience into the verbal music of poetry, recreating in language the act of looking at a painting. They seek to synthesize the free visual play of aesthetic perception with the descriptive powers of linguistic expression. Following the democratic impulse of *Schein*'s indifference to content, it is these formal elements, and not what they signify, that for Bradley and Cooper make the pictures "sing in themselves" and "objectively incarnate" poetry. One must eliminate from the gaze all "theories," "fancies," and "subjective enjoyment," divorcing one's experience of the artwork from any knowledge or desire that preexists the immediacy of the visual encounter. Ana Parejo Vadillo associates this quality of their poetry with John Ruskin's notion of "innocence of the eye," the idea that "to be able to see any art object, the gazer must be free of all historical and cultural constructions of the visual."[32] Consequently, their poems are not concerned with uncovering what might be understood as painting's represented content: the historical, mythological, allegorical, or political meanings signified by the image. One does not need any prior cultural knowledge to see the poetry embodied in a painting. Indeed, such knowledge interferes with the purity of the gazer's vision. The poetry to be found in a painting can be accessed by anyone with eyes to see it, because it inheres in the surface of the canvas itself, not the cultural knowledge she may bring to the encounter.

And, as Pater states in the closing paragraph of "Winckelmann," it is poetry, and not painting, that is the art form most suited to representing contemporary existence, because its complexities can find adequate expression only through the medium of language. It is the sole "form" that can "command that width, variety, delicacy of resources, which will enable it to deal with the conditions of modern life" (*R* 184). Although music is the form of art best suited to the representation of transcendent human freedom, painting is the genre that comes closest to giving it material and spatial form, insofar as visual delight in an object's surface signifies the individual's capacity to free herself from external constraints. Poetry, in turn, is the art of modernity par excellence, insofar as its unparalleled capacity for description is the only aesthetic form capable of representing the complexity of the mind's struggle against its own limitations. Under the influence of Pater's Hegelian account of painting, Bradley and Cooper determined that a picture-poem could synthesize these three aesthetic modes in a way that can give the modern individual an equivalent of the sense of freedom: hence their title *Sight and Song* to name a book of poetry. In a culture where philosophical and scientific writing on art increasingly emphasized how, as Benjamin Morgan states, "beauty dominates us and prevents us from experiencing the sort of freedom that Kant or Hegel describes" by appealing to our embodied sensorium, the Michael Fields used the resources of poetic language to show how physical, erotic impulses can actually free the subject from the limits of material determinations.[33] As I will show in the rest of this chapter, their ekphrastic poems accomplish this by transforming sexual desire, which in the late nineteenth century was taken to disprove the subjective self-determination of queer individuals, into a force that creates the intersubjective relationship between the freedom of the artist and the viewer produced by the formal effects of *Schein*.

The Erotics of Disinterest: Winckelmann and Watteau

As discussed in the introduction, scientists, physicians, and sexologists presented the possession of nonnormative sexual desires as evidence that their possessor was incapable of self-determination. Foucault famously argues in *The History of Sexuality*, volume 1, that Victorian scientific and medical authorities consolidated their power to define the subject by portraying sexual perverts as unwilling victims of their pathological biologies, locked in the bodily prison of their desires. To challenge this notion, Bradley and Cooper returned to the ideas of Winckelmann, one of queer aestheticism's key forerunners. Chapter 1 addressed how Pater's early writings were a call for queer aesthetes who would be modern-day Winckelmanns, finding their freedom from oppressive cultural norms through aesthetic experience. Bradley and Cooper, like Wilde and Lee, responded to this call. Winckelmann was one of Bradley and Cooper's major intellectual influences throughout their careers. Poems such as Edith Cooper's early composition "To Apollo—the Conqueror" and *Sight and Song*'s "L'Indifférent" explore the role eroticism plays in "disinterested" aesthetic judgments, which is one of the submerged themes of Winckelmann's *History of the Art of Antiquity* (1764). These poems show that sexual desire plays an important role in one's appreciation of aesthetic object but only if the desires one experiences are not actually one's own. It is only by abandoning preexisting impulses and allowing the art object to redirect libidinal energies into new and unexpected avenues that one can experience in poetry the feeling of subjective autonomy that is the effect of painterly *Schein*.

Edith Cooper's Winckelmann-inspired ode "To Apollo—the Conqueror," written early in her poetic career at the age of sixteen, shows how aesthetic judgment facilitates exchanges between sexual sensibilities. Although it did not find a place in *Sight and Song*, it is one of the earliest ekphrastic lyrics written by either of the Michael Field poets. It expresses the speaker's admiration of a statue of Apollo, which initiates her into heterosexual desire: "I watch thy sculptured form, while my heart guesses / The awful beauty of thy

Apollo Belvedere (marble statue), Roman copy of a Hellenistic bronze, original made ca. 350–325 by the Athenian sculptor Leochares. Cortile del Belvedere, Museo Pio Clementino, Vatican Museums. © Vanni Archive / Art Resource, NY.

aureate life," she begins.[34] Stefano Evangelista remarks that the speaker's description develops "an intertextual relationship with Winckelmann's canonical description of the [statue of] Apollo Belvedere, which surfaces in her description of the 'wave of scorn' on Apollo's lip, of his 'clear brow' which fuses beauty and pride, and of the impressive masculine hardness (the 'manhood's might') made soft by the curly hair."[35] The speaker goes on to describe herself as becoming feminized and sexualized through an imagined sexual encounter with Apollo, which makes her into "a mother to all beauteous things" through being "conquered, wedded" to the god. This leads Evangelista to assert that "Cooper's investment in the Apollo is, like Winckelmann's, erotic as well as aesthetic: she rereads Winckelmann's suffused male homoeroticism in a female heteroerotic key."[36]

It is not the male homoeroticism of Winckelmann's description per se that is of interest to the speaker, however. Instead, her ability to adapt his erotic language to her own female sexual experience depends on the description's cultural canonicity. When Cooper wrote her ode in the late nineteenth century, the passage on the Apollo Belvedere from the *History of the Art of Antiquity* she cites had become the normative account of sculptural beauty in Western culture, and her Winckelmann-infused vocabulary suggests her sexual impression of the statue has been primed by knowledge of its elite status. Although the speaker begins with a normative aesthetic judgment of the sculpture's "awful beauty," this judgment does not necessarily compel her to hew to the cultural status quo regarding sexuality. Her desire to be "conquered" by Apollo appears to enact stereotypical feminine submissiveness, but, as Evangelista notes, her plea to the god to "dower me with thine own lips" connects the poem's images of sexual union with the "transmission of the poetic tradition from antiquity to modernity in which the exchanged good is not, or rather not only, *eros* but language."[37] The speaker legitimizes the poetic representation of her sexual desire by placing it squarely within the otherwise male-dominated Western poetic tradition, calling upon Winckelmann's homoerotic appreciation of the Apollo Belvedere for its cultural authority and prestige but adapting it to her own feminine subject position. By transforming the erotic appreciation of the male body into an indicator of culturally approved artistic taste, the canonization of Winckelmann's aesthetic judgment makes it possible for a woman to figure her heterosexual libido as a source of poetic inspiration.

As I discuss in chapter 1, Pater makes clear that Winckelmann's understanding of ancient Greek sculpture derived not from his uninspiring childhood education in the classics but from the frisson of sexual desire inspired by their visual forms. But when Kant and Hegel drew upon Winckelmann's writings to articulate the concept of aesthetic disinterestedness they abandoned the erotic component of his thought. Pater, however, shows that, despite Winckelmann's influence on Kant and Hegel's theorizations of art's "purposiveness without purpose," his art-historical writings do not themselves display aesthetic disinterest, properly speaking. He shows that Winckelmann's sense of beauty was inspired by his erotic interest in men and that his insights into ancient Greek sculpture came about through his historical identification with the sculptors, because both they and he were men who desired other men.

Although, as Pater shows, subjective sexual interests condition aesthetic judgments, Whitney Davis argues that there is still something to be said for a version of aesthetic disinterestedness that embraces erotic desire. He suggests that Kantian-Hegelian disinterest can refer to what we experience when we view artworks that exhibit the features of "canonical beauty," that is, works that feature the formal qualities our culture has deemed to be beautiful but which do not answer to our own personal sexual appetites.[38] This was to be the fate of Winckelmann's aesthetics in Western culture. Although his sexual interest in men is what initially inspired his instinctual appreciation of ancient Greek sculpture, by the late nineteenth century such an appreciation had become simply an expression of the viewer's refined and educated tastes. For Davis, this means that culturally normative aesthetic judgments contain radical sexual potential: "disinterested judgments of ideal beauty," he asserts, can "effect a queering of personal interested judgments of taste."[39] In other words, when a man who personally desires women looks upon an ancient Greek sculpture of a male athlete and admires its beauty, his "disinterested" aesthetic judgment allows him to experience for a moment what it is like to be a man who desires men. This queerness inheres not in the erotic content of the artwork per se but in the artwork's ability to draw the viewer into another type of sexual subjectivity by means of its socially endorsed, canonical status.

Winckelmann's writing, and Cooper's adaptation of it, show that aesthetic normativity and sexual (hetero)normativity do not work in tandem but are often at odds with one another. In "To Apollo—the Conqueror," the canonicity of Winckelmann's description of Apollo's beauty makes it available to grant artistic authority and legitimacy to anyone who eroticizes the male body. Though the poem makes strategic use of the fact that it has lost its male homosexual particularity by becoming a culturally agreed upon signifier of refined sensibilities, the speaker *herself* never makes a truly disinterested assessment of the statue's beauty. In the first and last instance, the description of the statue is wedded to the speaker's personal romantic and erotic interest in the masculine body it represents, what she calls the "guesses" of her "heart." Consequently, the poem does not offer the same insights into the society and culture that produced the work that Winckelmann's art-historical

L'Indifférent, 1716 (oil on panel), Jean Antoine Watteau (1684–1721).
Louvre, Paris, France / Bridgeman Images.

writings offer. Any knowledge of the art object itself is made subordinate to
the legitimation of the speaker's poetic authority. Despite the poem's innovative re-gendering of lyric vocation, the speaker remains "wedded" to her own
sexual subjectivity and does not achieve the object-oriented purity of vision
for which Bradley and Cooper's later ekphrastic lyrics strive.

By contrast, *Sight and Song*'s opening poem presents a speaker whose sexual desire for a figure represented in a painting is frustrated by her inability
to transform the artwork into anything other than an object of disinterested
contemplation. The appropriately titled "L'Indifférent" illustrates the aesthetic principles of Bradley and Cooper's preface through negative example.

It describes Antoine Watteau's eighteenth-century painting of a young man absorbed in the act of dancing, indifferent to the gaze of both the audience presumably watching him from just outside the frame of the canvas and the audience looking upon his representation hanging in the Louvre. Nicholas Frankel argues that the inattentive dancer embodies just the sort of aesthetic autonomy vaunted by the preface, but the poem is structured around two direct addresses that attempt to interrupt the dancer's abstraction.[40] Julia Saville reads these as enacting "the viewer's wish to see in an image the confirmation of the fantasies it evokes beyond its own framing."[41] More specifically, though, the poem shows how these fantasies overwhelm the image itself when the viewer ceases to allow her gaze to play freely over the abstract forms that constitute the image's *Schein* in favor of her own "theories, fancies, [and] mere subjective enjoyment."

The poem's speaker allows her vision to be clouded by subjective interests lying beyond the purview of the painting, thus showing herself incapable of attaining the aesthetic disinterestedness represented by the image itself. The first stanza reads:

> He dances on a toe
>   As light as Mercury's:
> *Sweet herald, give thy message!* No,
> He dances on; the world is his,
> The sunshine and his wingy hat;
>   His eyes are round
>   Beneath the brim:
> To merely dance where he is found
>   Is fate to him
> And he was born for that. (*SS* 1)

The speaker gazes at Watteau's painting to uncover the "message" she presumes lies hidden in the image. Yet the simile that begins the poem indicates she has not purified her gaze of preexisting cultural knowledge. She conveys a sense of the visual lightness of the dancer's movement by comparing him to the god Mercury. Though the colon at the end of line 2 suggests she will begin expanding upon or clarifying the comparison, line 3 shifts to a direct command to the figure in the painting, one that is visually set off from the rest of the stanza by italics. The speaker asks the dancer, whom she now calls a *"Sweet herald,"* to *"give thy message!"*—a request immediately met with an abrupt "No." The speaker's search for the significance of the image causes her to lose focus on the actual visual details represented on the canvas: she no longer sees a dancer but the human embodiment of the messenger-god. These opening lines demonstrate the consequences of failing to purify one's vision before viewing a painting. The speaker's comparison of the dancer to Mercury is not merely an attempt to give a verbal equivalent to the visual lightness of the painted figure but a revelation of the speaker's desire to find discursive meaning, a "message," that lies behind the *Schein* created by the lines and colors of the painting's abstract form. The dancer's refusal to return the speaker's address both awakens her to renewed attentiveness to the visual details of the canvas and, as Vadillo notes, grants the object its own autonomous agency, the aesthetic "indifference" named in the poem's title.[42] The dancer "dances on; the world is his," and the ignored speaker has no recourse but to describe the image's exterior details. The stanza ends with the speaker's apparent acceptance of the indifference: "to merely dance where he is found" is the "fate" of both the dancer and the image that represents him; they signify nothing more, or less, than what their external visual appearance presents them to be.

It becomes clear in the second (and final) stanza, however, that although the speaker is ready to concede that the image has no message beyond its external form, she is not prepared to gaze upon it with aesthetic disinterest. Instead, she attempts to make the image personally significant by transforming it into the object of her sexual desire. Unlike the statue of Apollo in "To Apollo—The Conqueror," whose imagined erotic response legitimizes the poet, the dancing figure in the painting remains steadfast in resisting the speaker's attempt at seduction. The second stanza reads:

> He dances in a cloak
>> Of vermeil and of blue:
> *Gay youngster, underneath the oak,*
> *Come, laugh and love!* In vain we woo;
> He is a human butterfly;—
>> No soul, no kiss,
>> No glance nor joy!
> Though old enough for manhood's bliss,
>> He is a boy,
> Who dances and must die. (*SS* 1)

This direct address to the dancer rewrites the previous stanza's demand for discursive meaning. It is now an erotic invitation, an enticement to "*come, laugh and love.*" Much like the allusion to Mercury (as well as the references to Winckelmann in "To Apollo—the Conqueror"), the speaker's desires are motivated by information lying outside her immediate visual encounter with the artwork. Kit Andrews comments that "the French nineteenth-century Watteau reception, and its continuation by Pater [in his Watteau-inspired short story "A Prince of Court Painters"] considered the apparent indifference ascribed to both the painter and the figures that appeared on his canvases to be a ruse, an attempt to obscure the 'desire hidden beneath a pose of distant, refined uncaring.'"[43] Sexual desire comes to occupy the same structural position here as discursive meaning did in the previous stanza. In both instances, the speaker attempts to find hidden within the aesthetic object the subjective interests that reside within her own consciousness: a desire for personal significance bolstered by knowledge external to the visual encounter with the object.

Yet "in vain we woo," the speaker admits: she still perceives the dancer to be unresponsive. Just as he refused the fulfill the role of messenger-god projected upon him, so too does he reject the speaker's assumption of his sexual repression, which is derived from her familiarity of the literature surrounding Watteau rather than from her immediate visual encounter with the artwork. He remains a cipher when it comes to anything other than his objective visual appearance, his *Schein*, which is the only aspect of his being that it is within the painting's remit to capture. Rather than shifting her attention back to the work's objective appearance, however, the dancer's sexual rejection causes her to give up altogether the attempt to describe visual form within language. Her focus instead becomes entirely negative, as she imagines the dancer to be withholding his erotic attentions: "No soul, no kiss / No glance nor joy." Like a spurned lover, she resentfully imagines the dancer's unresponsiveness to her advances as signifying an impotent lack of interest in "manhood's bliss" altogether. This, in turn, is understood to indicate the lack of vitality of the artwork itself. Instead of the eternal life in art promised at the end of the first stanza, the speaker now concludes that although he "dances," he "must die": the speaker ascribes to the painting a morbidity that is unattached to any concrete visual detail of the painting but present only to her own imagination, as the subjective fantasy the image refuses to confirm.

The speaker of "L'Indifférent" fails to capture the "poetry" of the original painting because she cannot derive pleasure merely from its lines and colors alone. She is, in other words, unable to experience *Schein*'s negation of the world, which would have been the guarantee of the viewer/speaker's subjective autonomy. Despite the speaker's efforts, the poem ultimately expresses an inwardly subject-oriented, rather than object-oriented, gaze. Because the viewer/speaker cannot separate her vision of the painting from preexisting discursive and sexual paradigms, she sees it as nothing more than a dead thing. The poem demonstrates why an ekphrastic lyric composed without aesthetic disinterest fails: it prevents the gazer from transcending her own limitations and understanding the art object on its own terms. Yet, as Bradley and Cooper's poems on paintings of Saint Sebastian make clear, attaining a disinterested aesthetic judgment of an artwork does not mean foregoing sexual desire altogether. These lyrics show them exercising their subjective autonomy by imagining themselves into and embracing a male homoerotic subject position—a perspective that was definitionally and, for that reason, attractively foreign to their own personal desires as women.

Free Love, Free Field: The Saint Sebastian Poems

Despite Bradley and Cooper's cultivation of what Thain calls a "deliberately amorphous sexual identity" through the many hetero- and homoerotic attachments they cultivated throughout their lives, as well as the wrinkle of their incestuous romance, *Sight and Song* continues to be read almost exclusively in a lesbian context.[44] Beginning with Chris White's influential essay "'Poets and Lovers Evermore': Interpreting Female Love in the Poetry and Journal of Michael Field" and continuing in important studies by Ana Vadillo, Krista Lysack, Jill Ehnenn, and Hilary Fraser, critics have interpreted Bradley and Cooper's ekphrastic lyrics to be part of a lesbian-feminist literary project set on rejecting what Vadillo calls the "phallocentric" celebration of self found in the writings of Pater.[45]

Yet, in their poems based on paintings of Saint Sebastian, Bradley and Cooper liberate themselves from being fixed into a single gendered subject positions by strategically embracing a male persona. This development was occurring at the same time in their personal lives. By the time they started composing the lyrics that would become *Sight and Song*, Bradley and Cooper had developed a set of male nicknames for each other: "Boy, Henry, Hennery, Henny, and Henney-Boy," for Cooper, and "Michael, Mick, and Sim" for Bradley.[46] Their embrace of masculinity both in their private writing and in their poetry was, I maintain, an affirmation of their freedom from a literary culture that attempted to shackle their poetic voices to a monolithic feminine subject position and punished them when they resisted. The Saint Sebastian poems build upon this gender and erotic flexibility. When Bradley and Cooper wrote these poems in the early 1890s, the figure of Saint Sebastian, a Roman martyr, was freighted with male homosexual meaning. Italian Renaissance paintings commonly portrayed him as a lithe young man tied to a tree or post and shot through with arrows. In late Victorian Britain, the suggestiveness of this pose made images of the saint iconic for male homoerotic desire.[47] This cultural context informs Bradley and Cooper's poems, which express the masculine, sadomasochistic qualities of Sebastian's spiritual suffering.

In "Saint Sebastian, Antonello Da Messina," it is not Sebastian's bondage itself that causes him to feel unfree but his mistaken self-understanding as being locked in pitched battle against the divine. This overinvestment in the self prevents him from transcending his physical captivity. Ehnenn argues that Bradley and Cooper imbue the saint's "suffering and isolation" with a "defiant tone" by presenting his pain as a heroic protest against a religion that condemns sexual, and especially homosexual, pleasure.[48] The poem makes clear, however, that Sebastian derives sexual pleasure from being denied his liberty, even if he does not recognize it as such. It certainly makes him self-aware of his own virility and the erotic appeal of his body:

> Sound in muscle is the boy,
> Whom his manhood fills
> With an acrid joy,
> Whom its violent pressure thrills. (*SS* 73)

Although Sebastian's "manhood" causes him "joy," it is nevertheless also "acrid," angry and embittered, because it is on the brink of being lost. The speaker's paradoxical phrasing reflects the contradiction at the heart of his predicament: God has seemingly confounded the purpose of his life by granting him superlative male strength and libido, only to take those powers away before they come to fruition. As the subsequent stanza asserts, "this force implanted in him must be lost / And its natural validity be crossed / By a chill, disabling fate" (*SS* 73). This seems evidence of, at best, cosmic indifference and, at worst, sheer spitefulness on the part of the divine.

Yet the speaker indicates that Sebastian finds masochistic pleasure in his struggle. Ruth Vanita remarks that Michael Field "uses phallic language to stress the nature of the deprivation Sebastian feels, which is explicitly described as consisting not in death but in the denial of pleasure."[49] It is the "violent pressure" of bondage that makes him "thrill": his struggle against the divine arouses his engorged virility like nothing else. Sebastian's enjoyment of his masculine powers is raised to a fever pitch by the very imminence

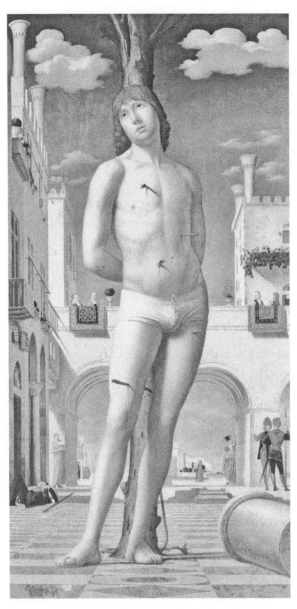

St Sebastian, 1475–76 (oil on canvas laid on board),
Antonello da Messina (1430–79). Gemaeldegalerie Alte
Meister, Dresden, Germany. © Staatliche Kunstsamm-
lungen Dresden / Bridgeman Images.

of their destruction. Rather than being confounded, his masculinity finds its fullest realization in the struggle against the fate decreed by God. The poem presents sexual pleasure as recompense for the loss of self-determination. The struggle against his restriction is precisely what elicits an internal sense of sexual freedom, which no external force can ever destroy. Yet, rather than giving himself over to the masochistic pleasures of his struggle, Sebastian remains committed to a restrictive notion of heroic masculinity that believes anything other than complete triumph over one's opponent to be failure. When one's adversary is God, this will inevitably be a losing proposition. This is how "the virtue of his sex is shattered, cursed" (*SS* 73). Sebastian's suffering lies not in the destruction of his body, "not / In the arrows' sting," but instead in his misperception that the triumph of God is emasculating (*SS* 74).

In the poem "Saint Sebastian, Correggio," however, Sebastian wins spiritual freedom by embracing a vision of himself as an object of male homoerotic desire. The martyr is only one of nine figures portrayed on the canvas—indeed, art historians often refer to the painting as *Madonna and Child with Saints Sebastian, Geminian and Roche*—but Bradley and Cooper's title reinforces the poem's emphasis on the homoerotic gaze shared between the saint and the Christ Child. The first stanza reads:

> Bound by thy hands, but with respect unto thine eyes how free—
> Fixed on Madonna, seeing all that they were born to see!
> > The Child thine upward face hath sighted,
> > > Still and delighted,
> Oh, bliss when with mute rites two souls are plighted! (*SS* 32)

In contrast to the gaze of Da Messina's Sebastian, whose eyes are locked in fervent dispute with God, this Sebastian's eyes are "free," despite being constrained in their movement. Sebastian's gaze is "fixed on Madonna," and just as tightly "bound" as are his "hands." Rather than perceiving his life's purpose to have been confounded by the divine, this version of Sebastian realizes his eyes are "seeing all that they were born to see" when they meet Christ's gaze, despite his physical immobility. The poem's first line appears to set up a contrast between Sebastian's bodily captivity and his liberty of visual observation, but the second line makes clear that his sight will provide not freedom *from* servitude but freedom *within* servitude.

The visual liberty Sebastian experiences is obviously not physical in any sense, and neither does it depend on a sense of masculine self-assertion conveyed by the da Messina poem. He can transcend the imminence of his own

Madonna of Saint Sebastian, ca. 1524 (oil on poplar), Antonio Allegri da
Correggio (1489–1534). Inventar-Nr.: Gal. Nr. 151. Photo: Hans-Peter
Klut. Gemaeldegalerie Alte Meister / Art Resource, NY.

demise by inhabiting Christ's desiring gaze as it looks upon his own restrained body: "While cherubs straggle on the clouds of luminous, curled fire, / The Babe looks through them, far below, on thee with soft desire" (33). The poem's intimate, second-person address allows the speaker to blur the boundary separating the gazes of the saint and the Christ Child. In the line "The Child thine upward face hath sighted," whether Sebastian first catches Christ's eye or vice versa is ambiguous. The speaker presents this intermingling of gazes in specifically conjugal terms, a same-sex marriage where "two souls are plighted," another form of relation where, ideally, bodily restrictions lead to a higher spiritual freedom through the merging of two separate selves into one.

This manifests through the saint's experience of divine love, which the poem portrays as his ability to view himself erotically, just as Christ sees him. The speaker says that although "thou hast the peril of a captive's chances / Thy spirit dances, / Caught in the play of heaven's divine advances" (*SS* 32). Sebastian's "spirit dances" because he is no longer invested in the fate of his bound body, with its "captive's chances." This freedom of visual experience, routed through Christ's sexualized vision, liberates Sebastian from his physical suffering: "Though arrows rain on breast and throat they have no power to hurt, / While thy tenacious face they fail an instant to avert" (*SS* 33). Physical pain cannot "avert" Sebastian's fixed gazing upon Christ's gaze upon him, because he finds in that vision the spiritual freedom that renders him impervious to the body's demands.

Bradley and Cooper indicate that this is the proper route to autonomy for the modern subject: not through masculine self-assertion per se but through the ability to use self-reflection to alter one's perception of the world by seeing it through the eyes of another, an action made possible through eroticized aesthetic judgment. This mirrors the experience Bradley and Cooper would have undergone to compose these Saint Sebastian poems. By viewing the paintings of Sebastian and allowing their disinterested aesthetic judgment of the visual forms on the canvas to direct their libidinal energies into the saint's masculine erotic subject position, they demonstrated their ability to transcend the limited version of feminine subjectivity that their culture foisted upon them as women poets. More than this, such judgments prove that one's consciousness can exist apart from merely personal physical appetites and hence can act in a truly free manner. As they demonstrate in their poems based on paintings by Leonardo da Vinci, this can happen when one disengages oneself from one's own desires to allow oneself to enter into the erotic world built by the artwork itself. This ability properly belongs only to universal, disinterested judgments of beauty.

Universal Desires: The Leonardo Poems

In contrast to "To Apollo—the Conqueror" and "L'Indifférent," Bradley and Cooper's two poems based on works by da Vinci, "Drawing of Roses and Violets" and "La Gioconda," have speakers who rely on their immediate visual impressions to guide their historical understanding of the artwork. In the process, they redefine what Kant and Hegel refer to as the "universality," or normativity, of aesthetic judgment. This is one of the defining qualities of our individual experience of beauty in art. One *feels* as if beauty is a quality belonging to the beautiful object itself, rather than to one's own subjective experience of it. For this reason, one feels that everyone ought to share in that judgment and derive the same kind of pleasure from the artwork. Beauty, in other words, is a subjective experience that feels like an objective truth.

By juxtaposing one of Leonardo's little-discussed minor works to a canonical expression of feminine beauty, Bradley and Cooper highlight the idiosyncratic personal motivations embedded within universal aesthetic judgments. Looking at the two poems together reveals how normative judgments of beauty, rather than being abstracted from subjective interests, rely on the traces of sexual desires that can be found in works of art to create a sense of objectivity. Awareness of these remnants of eroticism, which is elicited by Bradley and Cooper's poems themselves, allows viewers to understand that universal aesthetic judgments can enable them to enter into different kinds of sexual subjectivity.

Critics have not put "Drawing of Roses and Violets" and "La Gioconda" in dialogue, even though poem pairings were, at Thain notes, "an important structuring feature" of their poetry collections throughout their career, a technique they borrowed from their mentor Robert Browning.[50] The poems' appearance together represents only one of two instances among the collection's thirty-one lyrics when paintings by the same artist appear sequentially. *La Gioconda*, more popularly known as the *Mona Lisa*, is one of the world's most recognizable images, and its notoriety was already established by the time Bradley and Cooper wrote their poem in 1892. Its hyper-canonical status can largely be traced (in the English-speaking world, at least) to Pater's well-known description of it in his essay on Leonardo from *The Renaissance*. Because of this fame, Bradley and Cooper's "La Gioconda" is one of their most frequently anthologized and discussed lyrics. It must be understood, however, as putting into practice the historical theory of viewing first outlined in "Drawing of Roses and Violets," which places the notion of libidinal sympathy at the center of its vision of aesthetic judgment and art-historical practice.

"Drawing of Roses and Violets" is, in many ways, an odd fit for *Sight and Song*. It is the only poem in the collection not based on a painting of human or humanlike figures. This makes the image markedly more difficult to translate into verse through personification. It is also of limited art-historical importance. Leonardo's drawing makes only a brief appearance in Pater's Leonardo essay, when he refers to "a stray leaf from [Leonardo's] portfolio dotted all over with studies of violets and the wild rose," as proof of his "fondness for particular flowers" (*R* 87). The drawing is a piece of ephemera, a formal study that served as practice for Leonardo's more finished, refined works. The poem itself acknowledges as much when the speaker associates his drawing of "the rose's amorous, open coil" to the "women's placid temples" in his later works, and his drawing of the violet to "the precious smile that weaves / Sweetness round Madonna's mouth" in his paintings of the Virgin Mary (*SS* 6–7). I maintain that Bradley and Cooper wrote a poem about this image, despite the formal challenges it presents to their practice of ekphrasis, because it is key to understanding the vision of eroticized aesthetic indifference that underlies their poetic project in *Sight and Song*.

Over the course of forty-four lines, the poem moves temporally from the historical moment of Leonardo's initial perception of the flowers to, finally, the moment in the present day when the speaker gazes upon Leonardo's drawing on the wall of Venice's Accademia museum. There, as the poem's final stanza states, the flowers will "not die / Like everything / Of ruin's blight / And April's flight" (*SS* 7). Bradley and Cooper dramatize the speaker's thoughts as she undergoes the process of forming a disinterested aesthetic judgment of the work. We observe her mind in motion as she attempts to divine the historical and aesthetic significance of the drawing. The poem presents aesthetic judgment as an iterative process where the mind continually doubles back to reassess its understanding of the artwork, a redoubling expressed by the opening line of every stanza, each of which repeats a subject-verb-object structure beginning with the word "Leonardo": "Leonardo saw the spring," "Leonardo drew the blooms," "Leonardo loved the still / Violet," and "Leonardo drew in spring" (*SS* 5–7).

In the first stanza, the speaker treats the drawing not as a work of art at all, but as a piece of historical evidence. "Leonardo saw the Spring / Centuries

Study of flowers, pen drawing on yellowish paper, with signs of silver point preparation, Leonardo da Vinci (1452–1519). Preserved in the Gallery of the Academy, Venice (Gallerie dell'Accademia), Venice, Italy. Alinari Archives, Florence / Bridgeman Images.

ago," she begins, asserting a basic, objectively true historical statement about the drawing: its mere existence testifies that Leonardo had firsthand visual knowledge of these flowers when they were in bloom (*SS* 5). Based on this empirical truth, the speaker ventures a conjecture regarding the artist's emotional attitude: he "saw the spring / And loved it in its flowers" (*SS* 5). The fact that he drew these highly detailed studies would strongly indicate his personal appreciation of the roses and violets and, by extension, the season when they were in bloom. These lines are a poetic restatement of Pater's assertion that the drawing evidences Leonardo's fondness for specific kinds of flowers. As in "L'Indifférent," the speaker's reliance on information from outside her immediate perception of the painting prevents her from making a

disinterested aesthetic judgment. Specifically, her belief that the drawing provides unmediated access to Leonardo's subjective disposition short-circuits
her attempt to understand precisely *why* he loved the flowers. In this first
attempt at analysis, the painting's status as evidence for Leonardo's partiality
for flowers causes the speaker to view the drawing forensically rather than
aesthetically.

The inadequacy of this initial perspective is made apparent by the second
stanza, which makes a second interpretive pass over the drawing, now purified of external historical commentary and following more closely the di-
rectives laid out in Bradley and Cooper's preface. The speaker begins not by
describing the content of the drawing but by imaginatively reconstructing
the moment of its creation: "Leonardo drew the blooms / On an April day"
(*SS* 6). The shift in perspective to the creative act allows the speaker to craft
a more sophisticated description of the work than the one in the first stanza,
which comprehends it as a series of representational choices made by the
artist. Instead of believing that she has unmediated access to Leonardo's
"love," this stanza indicates that his feelings can be divined only by the care
with which he drew them, what the speaker refers to as the "toil" of his
"subtle pencil" (*SS* 6). When the speaker begins to understand the drawing
as the result of artistic labor, she is allowed a moment of historical insight
into Leonardo's aesthetic judgment, what he found beautiful and why. He
lavished attention on floral studies, she realizes, not only because he loved
the flowers in themselves, but also because "he saw / In the rose's amorous,
open coil / Women's placid temples" (*SS* 6). Leonardo felt compelled to draw
the rose, the speaker suggests, because he recognized that its alluring shape
could be adapted into visually compelling representations of women. Rather
than coming to the painting armed with historical and critical knowledge,
the speaker comes to her own art-historical insight by proceeding from her
immediate visual perception of the painting's *Schein*. Unlike the speaker of
"L'Indifférent," this impression allows her to recognize that the form of Leonardo's drawing is indifferent to its represented content. It is not the flowers
themselves that make the drawing significant but the reappearance of the
work's floral forms in Leonardo's later canvases.

Significantly, this insight into Leonardo's aesthetic judgment in the past
depends upon the speaker's own critical, art-historical insight in the present—
specifically, her realization that the form of the rose reappears in his later
paintings of women. It is as if the speaker's imaginative recreation of his artistic "toil" in the past has allowed her to transcend the historical distance

that lies between her and Leonardo and to enter his consciousness, such that the speaker's present-day insight into Leonardo's artistic representation of flowers mirrors his own insights into the flowers themselves on that "April day" long ago. It is also undeniable that the moment of transhistorical identification carries strongly erotic overtones. The speaker implies Leonardo loved roses because he was attracted to the feminine sexuality suggested by their form, and the sensual language the speaker uses to describe the "amorous, open coil" of the rose and the "limpid curve" of "women's placid temple" suggests that the speaker, too, shares this desire for women. Her insights in this stanza could, perhaps, be inspired by the fact that both she and Leonardo desire women.

Some critics have interpreted this poem as just such an expression of lesbian desire. White discusses Bradley and Cooper's floral imagery as participating in a tradition of literary representations of desire between women, and Ehnenn has characterized the poem as part of *Sight and Song*'s overall strategy of eliciting a lesbian gaze through "sensual description gesturing toward hidden, secret pleasures" that "challenge patriarchal, heteronormative modes of seeing, perceiving, and signifying."[51] Although Ehnenn's overall argument that *Sight and Song* participates in the "long tradition of homoerotically inclined women using flowers to code female sexuality" is convincing, I maintain that Bradley and Cooper are doing something different in this particular poem: they eroticize the femininity of the flowers by inhabiting Leonardo's masculine subject position.[52] In contrast to Pater's description of Winkelmann's identification with the sculptor of the Apollo Belvedere, the connection between the speaker and Leonardo does not rely on a shared homoerotic disposition that preexisted his engagement with the artwork but instead on the speaker's ability to enter the creator's erotic subject position. This is facilitated by the aesthetic encounter itself. The image of Leonardo's "subtle pencil" toiling over "the rose's open, amorous coil" associates his artistic labors with specifically masculine, phallic desires. The speaker's description of Leonardo's women foiling "hearts in the luring way / That checks and dooms / Men" only reinforces this impression, by partaking of the femme fatale imagery typically associated with male heterosexuality (*SS* 6).

If the speaker's historical insights stemmed from a desire for women preexisting the poetic text, this would put her in the same position as the speaker of "L'Indifférent," unable to engage with the picture on its own terms because of a preoccupation with her own subjective interests. Instead, the speaker of "Drawing of Roses and Violets" gains insight into the artwork because her indifferent aesthetic judgment, elicited by the *Schein* of the drawing's formal elements, has allowed her to enter Leonardo's subject position. This is most apparent in the poem's third stanza, which uses intensely physical and sexually suggestive metaphors to associate Leonardo's drawing of violets with his objectification of the female body. This makes "Drawing of Roses and Violets" significantly different from the collection's more obviously lesbian poems, which Lysack says represent "female desire outside of the economy of a male gaze" through "the discursive formation of shared pleasure rather than possession."[53] By contrast, in this stanza Leonardo's drawing transforms the "violet" from a living entity that "blows" into an object of aesthetic consumption that is "still" (*SS* 6). By committing a representation of the violet to paper, Leonardo violently removes it from the natural environment that nurtures it, figuratively "pluck[ing] it from the darkness of its leaves / Where it shoots / From wet roots" (*SS* 6). This highly sexualized, metaphorical deflowering of the violet allows Leonardo to come into possession of its aesthetic form, such that he can later deploy it in "the precious smile" of the Madonna in subsequent works.

   Though these lines could be understood to expose the violence inherent in men's artistic objectification of femininity, the sensuality of the speaker's description of Leonardo's Madonna resists such a reading. The speaker describes

> the precious smile that weaves
> Sweetness round Madonna's mouth and heaves
>   Her secret lips, then goes
>   At its fine will,
>   About her face
>   He loved to trace. (*SS* 6)

This richly detailed language creates an odd moment of ekphrasis-within-ekphrasis. Since the speaker presumably gazes upon "Drawing of Roses and Violets" at this moment, the description must be based upon the speaker's imaginative conjuration of one of Leonardo's Madonna paintings as it appears in her memory. This moment of art-historical insight is thus also a moment of sexual fantasy as the speaker follows in her mind Leonardo's hand as it "traces" a path "at its fine will" around her mouth, lips, and face. The desire exhibited in this stanza is not specifically lesbian but evidences the merging of the speaker's and Leonardo's subject positions. The disinterestedness of the speaker's gaze has enabled her to experience what it is like to desire as someone else.

In "La Gioconda," Bradley and Cooper put into practice the eroticized art-historical method outlined in "Drawing of Roses and Violets" to demonstrate that the normativity of indifferent aesthetic judgments is not necessarily a *normalizing* procedure when it comes to sexuality. Critics have emphasized the transgressive quality of Bradley and Cooper's ekphrastic poems, arguing that they challenge the objectifying and possessive "male gaze" famously described by Laura Mulvey by presenting a queer vision of the art object.[54] Ehnenn, for instance, asserts "that their rendition of La Gioconda denounces the Othering effect of the male art critic's gaze," while Lysack argues that the poetic representation of the painting "refus[es] to reflect a male gaze."[55] Similarly, Fraser remarks that such a gaze is "subverted" by Bradley and Cooper's lesbian perspective on the artwork, what she calls a "gaze of gays."[56] These accounts assume that Bradley and Cooper challenge the presumed universality of the male gaze by introducing their own subjective, sexualized, and nonnormative vision of the art object, thereby exposing how ostensibly "indifferent" judgments of beauty actually reflect the desires of the heterosexual men who dominate cultural production and consumption. Such interpretations imply that normative aesthetic judgments are synonymous with the normalization of the viewing subject: that is, an aesthetically disinterested gaze causes one to accept patriarchal standards of feminine beauty as universally valid. Such a perspective can be undermined only through potent reminders that judgments of beauty are, contra Kant, not universal, but always and inevitably individual and interested.

"La Gioconda" shows, however, that aesthetic normativity does not necessarily reinforce the cultural status quo. While "Drawing of Roses and Violets" dramatizes how disinterested judgments can initiate one into a masculine and heterosexual subject position, "La Gioconda" shows that aesthetic normativity is politically and culturally neutral, as well as an unavoidable quality of a viewer's experience of art. Davis explains that "queering a norm cannot bring a culture back to nonnormativized or prenormativized conditions. It can only recalibrate it by queering it to a newly emergent norm."[57] The goal of the poem is not to subvert the male gaze but instead to harness the painting's cultural force as a universal embodiment of dangerous and seductive feminine beauty. The poem then works dialectically to decouple the painting's eroticism from the specifically female body represented on the canvas.

It reconfigures the viewer's experience of the artwork by recasting its beauty as a property of its abstract visual form, its *Schein*, rather than of its content. By reverse engineering the process by which normative aesthetic ideals come into being, this poem shows how the subjective experience of an artwork's universal beauty can allow one to experience a free-floating sexual desire detached from any specifically gendered object. In full, the poem reads:

Historic, side-long, implicating eyes;
A smile of velvet's lustre on the cheek;
Calm lips the smile leads upward; hand that lies
Glowing and soft, the patience in its rest
Of cruelty that waits and doth not seek
For prey; a dusky forehead and a breast
Where twilight touches ripeness amorously:
Behind her, crystal rocks, a sea and skies
Of evanescent blue on cloud and creek;
Landscape that shines suppressive of its zest
For those vicissitudes by which men die. (*SS* 8)

The first and most important word of this highly condensed lyric, "historic," announces the speaker's interest in the work's cultural significance, in addition to her immediate visual impressions. Although this may appear to be a violation of Bradley and Cooper's injunction that art be viewed without any preconceived theories or fancies, the reference to Mona Lisa's famously ironical, "side-long" expression suggests that the image displays awareness of its own referentiality and is thus self-aware of its own historicity. The painting's historical resonance is not projected onto the painting externally, as in "L'Indifférent," but is instead a response to a demand internal to the picture itself. In the late nineteenth century, critical consensus was that the *Mona Lisa*'s importance derived from its embodiment of certain universal ideals of feminine beauty in art. Ehnenn finds evidence of such veneration in W. Stillman's 1891 article on Leonardo in the *Century*, where he quotes from Vasari's *Lives of the Artists* (1550) that Mona Lisa's smile was so "charming that it was a thing more divine than human to see, and it was held so wonderful a thing that the living person could not be beyond it."[58] She also references the assertion made by Symonds, Bradley and Cooper's friend and erstwhile mentor, that the smile "was to Lionardo a symbol of the secret of the world, an image of the universal mystery."[59]

However, neither Stillman nor Symonds characterizes the image's universality as erotic in nature. Their ideal is more akin to the spirituality of a Madonna rather than a femme fatale. Yet Bradley and Cooper suffuse the poem with a dark sexuality, such as the Mona Lisa's "breast / Where twilight touches ripeness amorously." Their understanding of the relationship between the painting's historicity and its eroticism appears most clearly in the diary entry Cooper wrote after seeing it in the Louvre in 1890. She enumerates the painting's various visual details, its "Sea, Rocks, Atmosphere" in addition to what she is already referring to as "sidelong, historic, implicating eyes," and remarks that these qualities "all are infamously, perfectly treacherous to the point of infatuation—& ~~with~~ to the ~~extent~~ [<] measure [>] of universality. It is no portrait, it is a dream of power and occult influence" (*MF* 238–39). Like Stillman and Symonds, she recognizes that the image's historical importance derives from its "universality" as the embodiment of an idealized, canonical aesthetic norm. Unlike them, however, her definition of universality includes the painting's ability to inspire sexual "infatuation" with its abstract visual forms alone, despite its being "no portrait" of an individual. For Ehnenn, this evidences Bradley and Cooper's recognition that their culture saw Mona Lisa "not as a real woman, but as a series of male fantasies," but nothing in Cooper's tone in the diary entry indicates she finds this blameworthy.[60] Instead, for Cooper the image is remarkable precisely because its ability to inspire desire does not depend on its represented content. *La Gioconda* clearly expresses eroticism even though no one who views the painting sees her as a real woman but instead only as a "dream of power and occult influence."

This is how, as Kathy Alexis Psomiades states, the poem presents "the femme fatale without the femme," a woman who "does not exist except as a constellation of formal devices."[61] I maintain, however, that "La Gioconda" celebrates, rather than critiques, this formalism. Bradley and Cooper's inspiration for doing so came from the most famous English-language account of the painting: again, Pater's description in "Leonardo," which readers have long recognized as the most obvious influence on their poem. Pater also offers an eroticized rendering of the painting's "historic" embodiment of a universal ideal of beauty, describing *La Gioconda* as "expressive of what in the ways of a thousand years men had come to desire" (*R* 98). The image's potency derives from the fact that its abstract form is composed of the many different forms of erotic desire that have existed throughout human history. In his words, "all the thoughts and experience of the world have etched and moulded there, in that which they have of power to refine and make expressive the outward form" (*R* 98). Pater's description offers a historicist account of how individual sexual interests transform, over time, into a seemingly disinterested and abstract aesthetic norm. This comes across most clearly in the final sentences of his description, where he states, "The fancy of a perpetual life, sweeping together ten thousand experiences, is an old one; and modern philosophy has conceived the idea of humanity as wrought upon by, and summing up in itself, all modes of thought and life. Certainly Lady Lisa might stand as the embodiment of the old fancy, the symbol of the modern idea" (R 99). Myriad experiences of desire enter the realm of the aesthetic by being abstracted from their individual embodiment and molded into an abstract visual form that effectively summarizes them. When this occurs, the image becomes a "symbol" for a universal ideal of desire because of the many traces of different types of embodied erotic desire layered within it.

The painting is what the poem calls "historic" in two senses: first, it is itself a type of historical record, the visual condensation of the various ways male sexual desire has manifested throughout history; second, it has become art-historically important as the utmost embodiment of a normative ideal of feminine beauty. It is in this context that one must understand the description of the eyes as "implicating," in addition to "historic" and "side-long." Lysack and Fraser argue that the term reveals the poem's subversive intentions by figuring Mona Lisa's look as a rebuke to the viewer, Bradley and Cooper's attempt to imbue the figure on the canvas with the illusion of autonomous agency to challenge the objectifying, possessive male gaze. The painting and the poem both make clear, however, that the "side-long" glance is not directly confrontational. Rather than glaring directly out at the audience, the eyes are turned slightly inward and away. The effect is, Bradley and Cooper suggest, more conspiratorial than adversarial: the viewer is implicated along *with* rather than *against* the painting. *La Gioconda* invites the viewer to uncover the sexual meanings latent within its depiction of universal, canonical feminine beauty.

The poem makes clear, however, that although the picture's aesthetic normativity derives from its summing up of the history of human eroticism, one should not look for the traces of individual sexual desires to be somehow hidden within its visual form. The speaker of "La Gioconda" resists approaching the painting as if it held a message secreted under its surface and avoids making the same mistake the speaker of "L'Indifférent" made. Instead, sexual meanings become visible in the poetic process of anatomizing the painting, as the speaker breaks the image down into its various formal components. Cameron notes that the preponderance of verbal phrases in the poem eliminates all temporality and narrative action. It also forecloses any possibility of ascribing subjectivity to the woman represented on the canvas, insisting on the image's radical superficiality. She possesses "calm lips the smile leads upward," as if the smile were an outside force acting upon the lips as passive objects, rather than the external signifier of an internal emotional state. While the speaker aims to convey the work's expressive qualities, she also makes certain that these cannot be taken as visible expressions of Mona Lisa's personal feelings. It is not she who possesses "patience" but her "hand," and the most potent descriptive phrase in the entire poem, the "cruelty that waits and doth not seek / For prey" is a negation of action that grammatically belongs to the abstract concept of rest. The poem rigorously maintains a distinction between form and content to militate against the illusion that the painting conveys anything of Mona Lisa's subjectivity.

The speaker emphasizes her awareness that the affective qualities of the painting do not emanate from a mysterious hidden force, and that the image is neither a symbol nor a secret, as Symonds or Pater might suggest. Instead, the poem insists that the painting is but a collection of aesthetic forms intentionally combined to elicit a response from the viewer. This becomes most apparent in the poem's second half, where the speaker's attentions shift toward the natural objects in the picture's background and at the same time become more insistently sexual. In her diary entry, Cooper remarks that "rocks & Seas in nature are the ~~powers~~ types of the inconstant & perilous— they are the chosen background with Da Vinci" (*MF* 239). By deliberately replacing the word "powers" with "types," Cooper expresses that external forms in nature do not serve as organic symbols for internal psychological states. The relationship is instead conventional and allegorical, and those forms were deliberately "chosen" by Leonardo to create a particular artistic effect. This is the Hegelian *Schein* that negates the physical world through the masterful aesthetic representation of it, thereby affirming the artist's and, by extension, humanity's freedom from the givens of material reality. Paradoxically, as the poem becomes more focused on inanimate forms, it also becomes more obviously erotic in its presentation of those objects. It is "twilight" that "touches ripeness amorously," as if the painting's abstract chiaroscuro quality possessed its own sexual agency. The masochistic "cruelty" that seemed only faintly related to the painting's human figure belongs most forcefully to the natural forms surrounding her, the "landscape that shines suppressive of its zest / For those vicissitudes by which men die." By the end of the poem, it becomes apparent that the traces of sexual desire sedimented within the image's normative beauty can be seen only if one focuses insistently on the painting's surface, maintaining awareness of the image as a collection of conventionally meaningful aesthetic forms, rather than succumbing to the illusion of psychological interiority that can attach to artistic representations of human figures.

"La Gioconda" thus detaches the subject's sexual desire from the gendered object. For a work of art like the *La Gioconda* to embody a universal ideal of feminine beauty where "all the thoughts and experience of the world have etched and moulded there," its form must contain within it traces of all the different forms human sexual desire can take, hetero- and homosexual, male-directed, female-directed, and otherwise. The poem demonstrates this by showing that any aesthetic form, not just Mona Lisa herself as a specifically feminine object of desire, has the potential to elicit an erotic response from the viewer: not just her eyes, hands, and breast but the abstracted "types" of rocks, seas, and the quality of light that surround her. The poem deploys an eroticized version of aesthetic universality to insist on form's indifference to content in painting, as well as to map onto that distinction sexuality's indifference to gender.

The representation of aesthetic judgment in *Sight and Song* not only revises traditional notions of subjective autonomy for Victorian modernity but also forces one to rethink the repudiation of that concept within contemporary queer studies. The queering of a work of art often involves an explicit or implicit rejection of the concept of aesthetic disinterest. In such readings, the normativity of aesthetic judgment is taken to be an impulse to "straighten" a work of art by making it conform to a culture's normative ideal of beauty and thus to the culture's definitions of normativity more generally, including heterosexual desire. It is thus the queer critic's job to reveal the erotically subversive interests that are actually expressed by the work. *Sight and Song* shows, however, that many erotic subject positions are always potentially available in a work of art, and that it is precisely the *normativity* of aesthetic judgments that allows the viewer to enter any number of these positions. Bradley and Cooper's poems not only queer aesthetics but also deconstruct the very opposition between normative and queer aesthetics, showing that it is only by inhabiting the sexual otherness inherent in canonical beauty that one can find evidence of one's capacity for subjective autonomy.

The queer potential within normative aesthetic judgments reinvigorates the sense of autonomy of those whose personal desires are otherwise culturally normative. It also renders the aesthetic a space where those who possess queer desires can discover a coherent sense of identity in a social world that actively prevents them from attaining self-knowledge. As I have discussed earlier in this chapter, aesthetic normativity and sexual normativity do not work in tandem but are often at odds with one another. Davis explains that engagement with culturally endorsed works of art has historically allowed queer viewers to "retrace the teleology of queer beauty, presented officially or canonically as an aesthetic or cultural norm, back to its echo and origins or its content and conditions in homosexual judgments of taste. Indeed, they could (re)discover their *participation* in the dynamic constitution of ideals of beauty in their culture."[62]

One may think of, for example, the pleasure experienced by a student who picks up a copy of *The Picture of Dorian Gray* at his local library, expecting an expression of the universal literary theme of "the double," yet instead finds his desires echoed in the beautifully rendered, all-but-explicit gay love triangle described in the novel's opening chapters. Such a reader might find a renewed sense of strength, solidarity, and coherence through his connection with Wilde and imagine a society where people like him are not just tolerated but celebrated. This is not simply because he shares a sexual orientation with a celebrated writer from the past. It is because he recognizes that, even within the limits of an otherwise phobic culture, art is a place where one can experience sexual difference not as a threat to the self but the source of a sense of self-determination gained through determined resistance to cultural norms and a commitment to social change. As a realm located within normative social life yet not strictly governed by socially predetermined concepts and forms of thought, the aesthetic is the venue most suited for queers to generate new concepts and reimagine how their culture might be radically reformed along practically realizable, nonutopian lines. Queer aesthetic experiences could be the source of an imaginative liberty and creativity that everyone in the world would desire for themselves, if only they could learn how to see it.

Coda

Unlike Dorian Gray, who immediately recognizes the nature of the "fresh influences at work on himself" when confronted by Lord Henry's dazzling language, I did not realize I was gay in an instant.[1] Though I have felt vaguely different from most other people for as long as I can remember, I initially struggled to reconcile my subjective sense of who I was with the images of queer people circulating in culture. Coming of age in the 1990s, most of the depictions I encountered were clichéd and one-dimensional: noble and tragic AIDS patients, sexless best friends, victims of hate crimes, protagonists of maudlin "coming out" stories, bogies of the religious right, targets of crude locker-room humor—in all cases, definitive outsiders to the fabric of social life. The thought that I might count myself among that abject and disparaged group did more than fill me with fear. I could not conceive how my internal perception of myself as a complex human being was in any way related to these radically diminished figures. *How could* I *be* that?

Being a bookish, academically inclined adolescent, my first impulse was to do research. Reading about being gay seemed much less threatening than talking about it. Over many months spent hidden in a corner of the local library, afraid to check out any books for fear of the looks I might receive at the counter, I read the writings of any queer author I could find: Oscar Wilde, Radclyffe Hall, James Baldwin, Rita Mae Brown, Armistead Maupin. Through these readings, I gradually came to see myself differently. A growing apprehension that I was, indeed, very much like the characters in these books contended with an appreciation of the beauty with which these authors portrayed queer lives. Out of this tension there arose a tentative, yet meaningful and empowering, sense of self that stood apart from negative cultural messages. Although I was aware that I was part of a homophobic society that placed practical limitations on what I could do and who I could be, I also realized for the first time that not following the narratives of development society presents as natural and inevitable was both possible and, potentially, wonderful. Through these artworks I discovered that I could, within limits, define for myself what my life would be. I consider this not only the moment when I finally accepted my sexuality but the birth of my critical consciousness. If what the dominant culture presented as the truth of queer identity had almost no relationship to my own newly developed sense of self, then what other supposed truths needed to be questioned?

Although many years have passed since first reading Wilde's novel, I consider my encounter with the exchange between Lord Henry and Dorian Gray to be the origin of this book, my contribution to urgent debates in the humanities about the purpose and value of the aesthetic. This discussion has a special but, I believe, insufficiently acknowledged significance for queers who first came to know themselves through immersion in the arts. In a recent issue of the *ASAP/Journal* special issue "Queer Form," Kadji Amin, Amber Jamilia Musser, and Roy Pérez assert that queer theorists must acknowledge that "aesthetic form is crucial" to "artists concerned with the structural conditions of social violences."[2] One of the purposes of this book has been to establish that this insight has a long lineage that reaches at least as far back as the creation of modern notions of sexual identity in the late nineteenth century. Queer aesthetes subtly but forcefully encouraged resistance to homophobia by turning to advantage the "obstacle" of their desires through the contemplation of erotic beauty in art. Through the process of Hegelian *Negativität*, this prompted the emancipation of a reconfigured, self-directed subjectivity.

Cultivating a conceptual vocabulary for queer aesthetic experience is still vital for understanding the unique contribution art makes to the development of oppositional social identities. Without one, it is difficult to articulate precisely why queer art from the past remains relevant for a modern audience. This was a central concern at the Tate Britain's 2017 exhibit on *Queer British Art, 1861–1967*, which commemorated the fiftieth anniversary of the UK's partial decriminalization of male homosexuality. One might assume that the exhibit would explore the joys and sorrows of queer lives lived during a difficult period of transition: after the death penalty for sodomy was abolished with the Offenses against the Person Act in 1861 but before the relative freedom allowed by the passage of the Sexual Offenses Act of 1967. This was an era when same-sex-loving people were allowed to exist but were burdened with official condemnation and harsh legal punishment. Yet Clare Barlow, the Tate's assistant curator of British art 1730–1830, writes in the book accompanying *Queer British Art* that the exhibit has the broader goal of "presenting a number of objects that have been considered to hold queer meaning in a range of different ways by certain people at certain times."[3] Rather than focusing on art explicitly by or about queer people, the curators instead relied on an "inclusive imprecision" that encompassed artists from the past who were definitively queer, those who were questionably queer, and those who were not queer at all but who created images with nonnormative erotic resonances to either historical or modern-day viewers.[4] Placing this curatorial philosophy in the context of "queer studies" writings by Judith Butler, Eve Kosofsky Sedgwick, and Michel Foucault, Barlow states that the exhibit aims to acknowledge "the radical shifts in the ways gender and sexuality were understood" rather than "to reassure ourselves that there were people like us in the past." Instead of encouraging historical identification between viewer and artist, Barlow (citing Laura Doan) claims that we might instead learn "to appreciate approaches to gender and sexuality that are radically different to our own."[5]

This aim is, perhaps, not so very different from that of Bradley and Cooper in *Sight and Song*. Yet one might wonder about the exact nature of the "appreciation" the exhibit seeks to encourage. Is it aesthetic, moral, ethical, historical, or philosophical? What precisely is to be gained from it? Is queer historical identification a more complex and difficult process than Barlow suggests in her dismissive comments? For queer Victorian aesthetes, the ability to bring one's desires into some vital relationship with erotic art from the past is more complex and consequential than the mere wish for the "reassurance" of sameness or an "appreciation" of difference. As I hope to have shown, aesthetes understood that encounters with art from the past entailed a difficult interplay of identification and abjection, sympathy and resistance, a Hegelian "tarrying with the negative" that, as Andrew Cole states, "requires the positing in advance of a truly unthinkable or inconceivable content—a content that is at the outer limits of thought and being."[6] Yet, when Barlow attempts to capture something of what she calls a "queer aesthetic" that is not reducible to "social or biographical contexts," she can only turn to the "camp aesthetic" famously described by Susan Sontag, which mediates queer social abjection by privileging style over content and celebrating grandiose yet failed artistic ambitions.[7] When she tries to describe what is particularly queer about works of art that do not partake of this camp aesthetic, she can only assert that "these images are open to queer interpretations that depend as much on sensibility as on subject manner."[8]

Victorian aestheticism helps us think about the language and the concepts necessary to describe this sensibility. The issue is not that Barlow's otherwise excellent and theoretically savvy introduction is uninterested in what is specifically *aesthetic* about queer art. It is that our present-day vocabulary for describing the role art can play in the creation of self-possessed queer identities is impoverished by queer theory's hesitance to engage with the history and theory of aesthetics and the possibility of autonomous subjectivity. In recent debates about the purpose of Victorian studies and its role in contemporary society, one of the liveliest conversations has been about the practice of "strategic presentism," a willingness to think dialectically about the relationship between past and present, rather than emphasizing the historical alterity between ourselves and the Victorians. David Sweeney Coombs and Danielle Coriale state that strategic presentism entails "think[ing] critically about the past in the present in order to change the present."[9] I have attempted to reconstruct queer Victorian aesthetes' theories of sexual subjectivity using their own nineteenth-century philosophical concepts. Yet my ultimate goal has been to demonstrate how a full appreciation of the Aesthetic Movement forces us to push against the intellectual limits of our present moment, to find new modes of thinking and ways of speaking about art and desire that will allow us to glimpse the otherwise inconceivable queers of the future.

Introduction

1. Wilde, *The Picture of Dorian Gray*, 19.

2. Wilde, *The Picture of Dorian Gray*, 22; Pater, *The Renaissance*. Subsequent references to this edition will appear in parentheses after the abbreviation *R*.

3. My use of "queer" and "homophobic" to refer to pre-twentieth-century sexual cultures is, of course, anachronistic. I embrace such terms strategically, as the best vocabulary at hand to name these writers' awareness of their same-sex attractions and their recognition that such desires were anathematized by their society. As Eve Kosofsky Sedgwick asserts in her influential definition of the term, while "queer" can signify many different practices of sexual and gender dissidence, "given the historical and contemporary force of the prohibitions against *every* same-sex sexual expression, for anyone to disavow those meanings, or to displace them from the term's definitional center, would be to dematerialize any possibility of queerness itself" ("Queer and Now," 8).

4. Glavey, *The Wallflower Avant-Garde*, 8.

5. For a discussion of Victorian art critic John Addington Symonds's idiosyncratic use of Hegel's historicism for queer purposes in his *Renaissance in Italy* (1875–77), see Davis, *Queer Beauty*, 99–134; on Edward Carpenter's queer critique of aestheticism from an anti-capitalist perspective, see Livesey, "Morris, Carpenter, Wilde, and the Political Aesthetics of Labor."

6. Ruti, *The Ethics of Opting Out*, 2.

7. Coole, *Negativity and Politics*, 43. In critical theory, the most influential poststructuralist rereading of Hegelian negativity is Žižek, *Tarrying with the Negative*. For poststructuralist negativity in literary studies, see Kurrik, *Literature and Negation*; and Budick and Iser (eds.), *Languages of the Unsayable*.

8. Hegel, *Hegel's Preface to the "Phenomenology of Spirit,"* 128–29.

9. Wilde, *The Soul of Man under Socialism*, 304.

10. Bersani, "Is the Rectum a Grave?," 218.

11. Yannis, "The Aesthete as Scientist."

12. Kant, *Kant: Political Writings*, 54.

13. Dowling, *Hellenism and Homosexuality in Victorian Oxford*, 60.

14. Pater, "Coleridge," 49.

15. Sedgwick, "How to Bring Your Kids Up Gay," 18–27.

16. Sedgwick, *Epistemology of the Closet*, 42.

17. Muñoz, *Cruising Utopia*, 12–13. Muñoz's version of negativity draws on Virno, *Multitude*; and Felman, *The Scandal of the Speaking Body*.

18. Hegel, *Hegel's Preface to the "Phenomenology of Spirit,"* 128.

19. Hegel, *Hegel's Preface to the "Phenomenology of Spirit,"* 128.

20. Cole, *The Birth of Theory*, 15.

21. Jacques Rancière has recently claimed that artistic experience creates a "distribution of the sensible" establishing new forms of perception that "change the cartography of the perceptible, the thinkable, and the feasible" within the dominant social and political order, with the aim of giving voice to the alienated and marginalized. I claim that aestheticism relies on Hegelian negativity to describe the changes that must occur within viewing, speaking, and thinking subjects for them to inaugurate this process of distribution (*The Emancipated Spectator*, 72–73).

22. On the difficulties of defining aestheticism, see Peckham, *The Triumph of Romanticism*, 218; Temple, "Truth in Labeling," 201–22; and Shrimpton, "The Old Aestheticism and the New."

23. The phrase "art for art's sake" is an Anglicization of *l'art pour l'art*, a slogan typically associated with the Théophile Gautier's preface to his novel *Mademoiselle de Maupin* (1835).

24. See Dellamora, *Masculine Desire*; Dowling, "Ruskin's Pied Beauty and the Constitution of a 'Homosexual' Code," and *Hellenism and Homosexuality in Victorian Oxford*; Morgan, "Reimagining Masculinity in Victorian Criticism"; Adams, *Dandies and Desert Saints*, 183–228; Evangelista, *British Aestheticism and Ancient Greece*, 23–54.

25. Reed, *Art and Homosexuality*, 76.

26. Reed, *Art and Homosexuality*, 77–78.

27. See Gagnier, *Idylls of the Marketplace*; Freedman, *Professions of Taste*; Psomiades, *Body's Beauty*; Schaffer, *The Forgotten Female Aesthetes*; and Psomiades and Schaffer (eds.), *Women and British Aestheticism*.

28. See Dowling, *The Vulgarization of Art*; Maltz, *British Aestheticism and the Urban Working Classes*.

29. Jonathan Loesberg notes that the notion that aesthetic philosophy was mere ideology "almost became the common belief of all literary theories of note at one point" (*A Return to Aesthetics*, 1). Characteristic statements of this position can be found in Bourdieu, *Distinction*; de Man, *Aesthetic Ideology*; Eagleton, *The Ideology of the Aesthetic*; and Levine (ed.), *Aesthetics and Ideology*. For readings of aestheticism as ideology, see Adorno, *Aesthetic Theory*, 225–61, and Bürger, *Theory of the Avant-Garde*, 47–49. Benjamin Morgan counters Adorno and Bürger by offering a materialist account of Paterian aestheticism; see "Aesthetic Freedom."

30. Accounts of Friedrich Schiller's influence on the aesthetes can be found in Hext, "The Limitations of Schilleresque Self-Culture in Pater's Individualist Aesthetics"; Brown, *Cosmopolitan Criticism*, 1–22; and Leighton, *On Form*, 113.

31. Kant, *Critique of Judgment*, 44.

32. Kaufman, "Red Kant," 711.

33. Bauer, *English Literary Sexology*, 3.

34. Mill, *On Liberty and Other Writings*, 60.

35. Ward, "Psychological Principles," 466; Montgomery, "The Unity of the Organic Individual," 318; both quoted in Cohn, "'One Single Ivory Cell,'" 189.

36. For an overview of scholarship on the relationship between British aestheticism and evolutionary thought, see Wilhelm, "Evolutionary Science and Aestheticism."

37. Pater, "Coleridge," 49.

38. Morgan, *The Outward Mind*, 22.

39. Foucault, *The Order of Things*, 347.

40. Pater, "Coleridge," 49.

41. Merquior, *Foucault*, 53.

42. Foucault, *The Order of Things*, 347.

43. Loesberg, *A Return to Aesthetics*, 3.

44. Foucault, *The History of Sexuality*, 43.

45. Ruehl, "Inverts and Experts," 167.

46. Foucault, *The History of Sexuality*, 101; Dellamora, *Masculine Desire*, 2–3.

47. This study joins Dider Eribon's *Insult and the Making of the Gay Self* in arguing for the importance of literary and philosophical works that existed apart from the "reverse discourse" for the history of queer world making.

48. Dellamora, *Masculine Desire*, 3.

49. Oscar Wilde, "To Leonard Smithers," 11 December 1897; quoted in Bristow, "'A Complex, Multiform Creature'—Wilde's Sexual Identities," 199.

50. Love, *Feeling Backward*, 53–71; Foucault, *The History of Sexuality*, 101.

51. See White, "'Poets and Lovers Evermore'"; Thain, *"Michael Field,"* 42–51; and Newman, "The Archival Traces of Desire."

52. Morgan, *The Outward Mind*, 9.

53. For a detailed account of German culture's introduction to early nineteenth-century Britain, see Ashton, *The German Idea*.

54. Willis, "The Introduction and Critical Reception of Hegelian Thought in Britain," 91.

55. Willis, "The Introduction and Critical Reception of Hegelian Thought in Britain," 97–98.

56. See Den Otter, *British Idealism and Social Explanation*, 10–51.

57. Stirling, *Jerrold, Tennyson, and Macaulay*, 98–99.

58. Andrews, "Walter Pater as Oxford Hegelian," 437; Wright, *Life of Walter Pater*, 2:211.

59. Smith and Helfand, *Oscar Wilde's Oxford Notebooks*, 17–34.

60. Glavey, *The Wallflower Avant-Garde*, 8.

61. An exception is Davis, "Walter Pater's 'Latent Intelligence.'"

62. Dowling, *Hellenism and Homosexuality in Victorian Oxford*, 98. Also see Davis, *Queer Beauty*, 23–50.

63. Kaye, "Gay Studies / Queer Theory and Oscar Wilde," 202; Bauer, *English Literary Sexology*, 4.

64. See Jameson, "Postmodernism and Consumer Society." Poststructuralism's anti-humanist strain can largely be traced back to the critiques of Hegel in the lectures of Jean Hyppolite and Alexandre Kojève, who counted among their students Jacques Derrida, Michel Foucault, Gilles Deleuze, and Jacques Lacan. See Lawlor, preface to *Logic and Existence*, by Hyppolite; and Muldoon, "Foucault's Forgotten Hegelianism."

I thank Christopher Vitale for calling my attention to the Hyppolite connection. This genealogy has led Rita Felski to argue that "literary studies has been shaped by a strong strand of anti-Hegelianism in twentieth-century French thought" (*Uses of Literature*, 30).

65. See, for example, Bersani, *Homos*; Edelman, *No Future*; and Love, *Feeling Backward*. See also the forum commentary by Caserio, Edelman, Halberstam, Muñoz, and Dean published as "The Antisocial Thesis in Queer Theory."

66. See Snediker, *Queer Optimism*; Muñoz, *Cruising Utopia*; and Glavey, *The Wallflower Avant-Garde*.

67. Ruti, *The Ethics of Opting Out*, 5.

68. Ruti, *The Ethics of Opting Out*, 58. On the submerged Hegelian provenance of Butler's theory of queer performativity, especially as it was expressed in her first book, *Subjects of Desire*, see Robbins, "'I Couldn't Possibly Love Such a Person.'"

69. Snediker, *Queer Optimism*, 25–26.

70. See Allan, "The Anti-subjective Hypothesis"; Anita Seppä, "Foucault, Enlightenment, and the Aesthetics of the Self"; and Norris, "'What Is Enlightenment?'"

71. Foucault, *The Foucault Reader*, 43.

72. Foucault, *The Foucault Reader*, 47.

73. Foucault, *The Foucault Reader*, 42.

74. Muldoon, "Foucault's Forgotten Hegelianism," 103.

75. Pater, "Poems by William Morris," 300.

76. Foucault, *The Foucault Reader*, 41.

77. Seppä, "Foucault, Enlightenment, and the Aesthetics of the Self."

Chapter 1 • *Homoerotic Subjectivity in Walter Pater's Early Essays*

1. W. E. Watson, "'Life of Bishop John Wordsworth'" (1915), quoted in Seiler, *Walter Pater*, 62.

2. Monsman, "Old Mortality at Oxford."

3. Inman, "Estrangement and Connection." Shuter has questioned Inman's conclusions, as well the critical impulse to "out" Pater's sexuality in "The 'Outing' of Walter Pater."

4. Dellamora, *Masculine Desire*, 1, 58–68; Brake, *Print in Transition*, 213–24.

5. Although, as Gowan Dawson argues, irreligiousness and sexual impropriety were readily associated in the Victorian imagination generally, studies of Pater have tended to focus on the circumstances specific to the homosocial/homophobic milieu of Victorian Oxford (*Darwin, Literature and Victorian Respectability*, 82–115).

6. Love, *Feeling Backward*, 71.

7. Halberstam, *The Queer Art of Failure*, 88.

8. The most extensive reading of Pater within the context of Oxford Idealism is Ward, *Walter Pater*; this line of inquiry has been continued in Shuter, "History as Palingenesis in Pater and Hegel"; McGrath, *The Sensible Spirit*; Morgan, "Aesthetic Freedom"; Whiteley, *Aestheticism and the Philosophy of Death*; Eastham, *Aesthetic Afterlives*, 16–35; and Andrews, "Walter Pater as Oxford Hegelian."

9. Andrews, "Walter Pater as Oxford Hegelian," 440.

10. Shuter, *Rereading Walter Pater*, 63.

11. Ward, *Life of Walter Pater*, 2: 211.

12. Willis, "The Introduction and Critical Reception of Hegelian Thought in Britain," 101.

13. Hegel, *Hegel's Preface to the "Phenomenology of Spirit,"* 6.

14. Den Otter, *British Idealism and Social Explanation,* 29–30.

15. Hegel, *Hegel's Preface to the "Phenomenology of Spirit,"* 128.

16. Hegel, *Hegel's Preface to the "Phenomenology of Spirit,"* 128–29.

17. Hegel, *Hegel's Preface to the "Phenomenology of Spirit,"* 129.

18. Kaufman, "Red Kant," 711.

19. Pater, *The Renaissance,* xxi. Subsequent references to this edition will appear in parentheses after the abbreviation *R.* Parkes, *A Sense of Shock,* 53.

20. Pater, "Coleridge," 383.

21. Hegel, *Hegel's Preface to the "Phenomenology of Spirit,"* 20.

22. Kaufman, "Red Kant," 682.

23. Davis, *Queer Beauty,* 3.

24. Stefano Evangelista identifies two major strands in the Victorian phobic response to Pater: one that criticizes his theory of passive aesthetic reception as "effeminate," and another that focuses on the specifically homoerotic element sin his writing. Mallock's novel forms part of the latter ("Walter Pater").

25. Mallock, *The New Republic.* The novel originally appeared as a series of sketches in the periodical *Belgravia* from June to December 1876.

26. The homoerotic overtones of Mallock's description of Pater are discussed in Denisoff, *Aestheticism and Sexual Parody,* 30–55.

27. Higgins, "No Time for Pater," 38. On the early twentieth-century gay reception of Pater, see Hassall, *Rupert Brooke,* 43; and Martin, "The Paterian Mode in Forster's Fiction." Philip Carey's decision to save Pater from the proposed "bonfire" of "the Great Victorians" in Somerset Maugham's *Of Human Bondage* is also characteristic (187–88).

28. Wellek, *A History of Modern Criticism,* 381.

29. Knoepflmacher, *Religious Humanism and the Victorian Novel,* 149–223; DeLaura, *Hebrew and Hellene in Victorian England*; and Monsman, *Walter Pater.*

30. Monsman, *Walter Pater,* 47.

31. Inman, *Walter Pater's Reading,* and *Walter Pater and His Reading*; Williams, *Transfigured World*; and Shuter, *Rereading Walter Pater.*

32. Love, "Exemplary Ambivalence," 25.

33. Evangelista, *British Aestheticism and Ancient Greece,* 34; and Davis, "Walter Pater's 'Latent Intelligence,'" 262.

34. Dellamora, *Masculine Desire*; Linda Dowling, *Hellenism and Homosexuality in Victorian Oxford,* and "Ruskin's Pied Beauty and the Constitution of a 'Homosexual' Code"; Morgan, "Reimagining Masculinity in Victorian Criticism"; Adams, *Dandies and Desert Saints,* 183–228; Evangelista, *British Aestheticism and Ancient Greece,* 23–54.

35. Lyons, *Algernon Swinburne and Walter Pater,* 31.

36. Harris, "Arnold, Pater, Wilde, and the Object as in Themselves They See It"; Hext, *Walter Pater,* 86; and Wallen, "Reflection and Self-Reflection."

37. Morgan, "Aesthetic Freedom," 733; and Hext, *Walter Pater,* 118.

38. Matz, *Literary Impressionism and Modernist Aesthetics,* 54–55.

39. Bersani, *The Culture of Redemption*; for a reading of Bersani's refusal of

redemption as itself a form of redemption, see Kurnick, "Embarrassment and the Forms of Redemption."

40. Love, *Feeling Backward*, 30; Halberstam, *The Queer Art of Failure*, 89.

41. This line of critique originated with the "Left" or "Young Hegelians" in the years immediately following Hegel's death. See Toews, "Transformations of Hegelianism."

42. Inman, "'Sebastian von Storck,'" 460.

43. Shuter, *Rereading Walter Pater*, 61–77; Hext, *Walter Pater*, 11.

44. Wolfgang Iser has identified Pater's understanding of the aesthetic as a space "in-between," where "reconciliation was not a dialectic movement toward synthesis; it was, rather, an interaction of opposites, a telescoping of incompatibles" (*Walter Pater*, 39); Winfried Fluck describes this in-between state as an "application of the idea of negation, one that also embraces negation itself" ("The Search for Distance," 181).

45. Pater, "The History of Philosophy," 6.

46. Whiteley claims that Pater's skepticism toward the Absolute in the "History of Philosophy" manuscript indicates the appropriateness of "the French post-structuralist tradition" as the "'toolkit' for discussing the complexities of Pater's response to Hegel" (*Aestheticism and the Philosophy of Death*, 6). Yet Pater's against-the-grain reading more closely anticipates the insights of modern Hegel scholars who have argued that the description of movement toward the Absolute is not as programmatic as its reputation would suggest. See Jameson, *The Hegel Variations*, and *Valences of the Dialectic*; Pippin, *Hegel on Self-Consciousness*; and Badiou, *The Rational Kernel of the Hegelian Dialectic*.

47. Muldoon, "Foucault's Forgotten Hegelianism," 110.

48. Hegel, *Hegel's Preface to the "Phenomenology of Spirit*," 20.

49. Varty, "The Crystal Man," 205.

50. Monsman, *Walter Pater*, 26.

51. Pater, *Miscellaneous Studies*, v. Subsequent references to this edition will appear in parentheses after the abbreviation *MS*. For an account of the implicitly homoerotic character of the Old Mortality, see Dowling, *Hellenism and Homosexuality in Victorian Oxford*, 81–85.

52. Monsman, "Pater's Aesthetic Hero"; and Carlyle, *On Heroes, Hero-Worship and the Heroic in History*, 218.

53. Mill, *On Liberty and Other Writings*, 67, 65.

54. Dowling, *Hellenism and Homosexuality in Victorian Oxford*, 85; Dellamora, *Masculine Desire*, 58–68; Morgan, "Aesthetic Freedom," 736; Hext, *Walter Pater*, 171.

55. Khalip, "Pater's Sadness"; Love, *Feeling Backward*, 59–63.

56. Hegel, *Science of Logic*, 439.

57. Hegel, *Phenomenology of Mind*, 112.

58. Williams, *Transfigured World*, 176.

59. Coole, *Negativity and Politics*, 51.

60. Dellamora, *Masculine Desire*, 64–65.

61. Engelstein, "The Allure of Wholeness," 754–55.

62. Potts, *Flesh and the Ideal*, 240.

63. Evangelista, *British Aestheticism and Ancient Greece*, 23–24.

64. The most extensive reading of Pater's criticism as autobiography is Levey, *The Case of Walter Pater*.

65. For discussions of Pater's identification with Winckelmann, see Dellamora, "The Androgynous Body in Pater's 'Winckelmann,'" 51; Clark, introduction to *The Renaissance*, 13; Hill, in Pater, *Renaissance*, 412; and Evangelista, *British Aestheticism and Ancient Greece*, 23.

66. Francis Roellinger argues that Pater had Winckelmann in mind when writing "Diaphaneitè" ("Intimations of Winckelmann in Pater's 'Diaphaneitè'").

67. Jonathan Loesberg argues that Pater departs from Hegel in this essay through a series of calculated revisions that "replaced Hegel's philosophical concept with an extra-philosophical, aesthetic concept," an impulse that led to Pater's repression of the more philosophical moments in the essay in subsequent revisions. I argue, however, that the extra-philosophical concept Loesberg identifies is precisely the labor of the negative that lies at the heart of the dialectic (*Aestheticism and Deconstruction*, 67).

68. Potts, *Flesh and the Ideal*, 240; Evangelista, *British Aestheticism and Ancient Greece*, 25.

69. Pater, "Winckelmann," 80. Subsequent references will appear in parentheses after the abbreviation "W".

70. For a detailed account of Kant's "straightening" of Winckelmann, see Davis, *Queer Beauty*, 23–50.

71. Richard St. John Tyrwhitt's infamously homophobic 1877 review of John Addington Symonds's *Studies of the Greek Poets* states that "Greek love and nature and beauty went frequently against nature" and makes reference to Symonds's embarrassing displays of "phallic ecstasy and palpitations at male beauty" (Tyrwhitt, "The Greek Spirit in Modern Literature," quoted in Dellamora, *Masculine Desire*, 87). Frank M. Turner points out that Victorian interpreters of Plato "were frequently perplexed by the morally troubling passages" of the dialogues, including Jowett's long and tortured account of Platonic homoeroticism in his *Dialogues of Plato* (1875) (Turner, *The Greek Heritage in Victorian Britain*, 424, 426).

72. Potts, *Flesh and the Ideal*, 252–53. Khalip similarly finds in Pater's writings a character "whose first act of descent is a death, a self depleted by the simultaneous disappearance of the fields of sociality which are available for its self-realization" ("Pater's Sadness," 141).

73. Dellamora, *Masculine Desire*, 115.

74. The key study of Pater's readings in the physical sciences and their influence on the "Conclusion" is Inman, "The Intellectual Context of Pater's 'Conclusion.'"

75. Hegel, *Hegel's Preface to the "Phenomenology of Spirit*," 20.

76. Taussig, *Defacement*, 135.

77. Adams, *Dandies and Desert Saints*, 160.

78. Pater, "Coleridge," 49.

79. Halberstam, *The Queer Art of Failure*, 3.

Chapter 2 • *Styles of Survival in Pater's Later Writings*

1. Field, *Works and Days*, 119.

2. The critical debate over the extent to which Pater's revises or repents the radical ideas presented in *The Renaissance* after the controversy has been discussed thoroughly in Williams, "On Pater's Late Style."

3. Kant, *Critique of Judgment*, 87.

4. Pater, *Appreciations*, 10.

5. Pater, *The Renaissance*, 110. Subsequent references to this edition will appear in parentheses after the abbreviation *R*.

6. Love, *Feeling Backward*, 58–59. The essay Love refers to is Sedgwick, "Shame, Theatricality, and Queer Performativity."

7. Barthes, *Writing Degree Zero*, 10.

8. Miller, "*Foutre! Bougre! Ecriture!*," 503.

9. Ohi, *Henry James and the Queerness of Style*, 1.

10. Maltz, *British Aestheticism and the Urban Working Classes*, 8.

11. Sedgwick, "Queer and Now," 9.

12. Williams, "On Pater's Late Style," 144.

13. Adorno, *Beethoven*, 123; Williams, "On Pater's Late Style," 157.

14. Goldstone, *Modernist Fictions of Autonomy*, 68, 69.

15. Stocking, *After Tylor*, 10. Although Robert Crawford believes Pater never read Tylor's work, instead borrowing the terms from the writings of mythographer Andrew Lang, Inman insists that internal evidence from Pater's writings indicates that he must have had firsthand knowledge of Tylor's theories ("Pater's Renaissance, Andrew Lang, and Anthropological Romanticism," 873); also see Inman, *Walter Pater's Reading*, ix–x. Additional support for Inman's assertion can be found in Shuter, *Rereading Walter Pater*, 100.

16. According to Stocking, Tylor's sociocultural evolutionism was not influenced by Charles Darwin or Herbert Spencer, but developed in parallel with them under the influence of eighteenth-century evolutionary theorists (*Victorian Anthropology*, 178). Similary, Sebastian Lecourt asserts that Tylor's teleological evolutionism has very little to do with Darwin and is essentially a reworked version of eighteenth century stadial history (*Cultivating Belief*, 62).

17. Evangelista, *British Aestheticism and Ancient Greece*, 41. Also see Whiteley, *Aestheticism and the Philosophy of Death*, 3.

18. Hegel, *Hegel's Preface to the "Phenomenology of Spirit*," 129.

19. In contrast to many of his contemporaries (including Tylor himself), Pater did not hesitate to apply the insights of anthropology to the classical origins of Western culture, thereby studiously avoiding the racist implications of Victorian accounts of primitivism. In a reference to the anthropological concept of "animism," Pater asserts, "the condition 'survives' . . . in the negro who thinks the discharging gun a living creature" but also "in the culture of Wordsworth and Shelley, . . . Goethe, . . . and in Schelling" (Pater, *Plato and Platonism*, 151).

20. Lecourt, *Cultivating Belief*, 130–62.

21. Hegel, *The Encyclopaedia Logic*, 203.

22. Lecourt, *Cultivating Belief*, 60.

23. Lecourt, *Cultivating Belief*, 60.

24. Tylor, *Primitive Culture*, 1.

25. Tylor, *Primitive Culture*, 15.

26. Shuter, "History as Palingenesis in Pater and Hegel"; Crawford, "Pater's Renaissance, Andrew Lang, and Anthropological Romanticism," 870; Connor, "Myth as Multiplicity in Pater's *Greek Studies* and 'Denys L'Auxerrois,'"32.

27. DeLaura, *Hebrew and Hellene in Victorian England*, 245.

28. Pater, "On Wordsworth," 458.

29. Crawford, "Pater's Renaissance, Andrew Lang, and Anthropological Romanticism," 878.

30. Tylor, *Primitive Culture*, 22–23.

31. Tylor, *Primitive Culture*, 428–29.

32. Tylor, "The Religion of Savages," 82–83.

33. Pater, "On Wordsworth," 458.

34. The image is from Wordsworth's poem "I Wandered Lonely as a Cloud" (1807).

35. Pater, "On Wordsworth," 458. The quote is from Shelley's "Peter Bell the Third" (1819).

36. Evangelista, *British Aestheticism and Ancient Greece*, 42.

37. Williams, *Transfigured World*, 240.

38. Alternatively, John Coates argues that Pater critiques the limitations of Tylor's anthropology in "Dionysus," especially his characterization of "primitive" people as childlike ("Pater and the Myth of Dionysus").

39. DeLaura, *Hebrew and Hellene in Victorian England*, 249.

40. Arnold, *Culture and Anarchy and Other Writings*, 128.

41. Arnold, *Culture and Anarchy and Other Writings*, 58–80.

42. Evangelista, *British Aestheticism and Ancient Greece*, 38.

43. Dowling, *Hellenism and Homosexuality in Victorian Oxford*, xiii, xv.

44. Evangelista, *British Aestheticism and Ancient Greece*, 38.

45. Lecourt, *Cultivating Belief*, 62.

46. Pater, *Greek Studies*, 18.

47. Iser, *Walter Pater*, 115.

48. Evangelista, *British Aestheticism and Ancient Greece*, 40.

49. Pater, *Greek Studies*, 43.

50. Pater, *Greek Studies*, 37.

51. Dellamora, *Masculine Desire*, 91; Dellamora cites Johnson, *Living in Sin*, 167.

52. Pater, *Greek Studies*, 37.

53. Dellamora, *Masculine Desire*, 176–80; Inman, "Estrangement and Connection"; and Hext, *Walter Pater*, 100–101.

54. Arnold, *Culture and Anarchy and Other Writings*, 128.

55. Denisoff, "The Dissipating Nature of Decadent Paganism from Pater to Yeats," 439. Although they wrote at the same time and both focused on the opposition between Apollo and Dionysus, there is no evidence that Pater ever read Nietzsche or vice versa.

56. For discussions of Pater's attempts to reconcile Apollonian and Dionysian modes of being in his fiction, see Monsman, *Pater's Portraits*; and Connor, "Myth as Multiplicity in Pater's *Greek Studies* and 'Denys L'Auxerrois.' "

57. Pater, *Greek Studies*, 37.

58. Pater, *Greek Studies*, 38.

59. Pater, *Greek Studies*, 39.

60. Pater, *Greek Studies*, 42.

61. Connor, "Myth and Meta-myth in Max Müller and Walter Pater."

62. On Pater's anachronism in *Marius* as an expression of the tension between his

belief in both historical continuity and historical difference, see Williams, *Transfigured World*, 169–234.

63. Pater, *Marius the Epicurean*, 110. Subsequent references will appear in parentheses in the main text with the abbreviation *ME*.

64. Logan, "On Culture."

65. Walkowitz, *Cosmopolitan Style*, 3.

66. Walkowitz, *Cosmopolitan Style*, 7.

67. Walkowitz, *Cosmopolitan Style*, 11.

68. Walkowitz, *Cosmopolitan Style*, 10.

69. Walkowitz, *Cosmopolitan Style*, 11–12.

70. Østermark-Johansen, "The Death of Euphues," 4.

71. Østermark-Johansen, "The Death of Euphues," 4. She cites from Morley, "Euphuism," 383.

72. Symonds, *Shakespeare's Predecessors in the English Drama*, 71. Cited in Østermark-Johansen, "The Death of Euphues," 8.

73. The *Oxford English Dictionary* defines Alexandrianism as a literary style that is, like Euphuism, "derivative, imitative, artificial, [and] addicted to recondite learning," associated with the literature produced in Alexandria under the Ptolmies.

74. Anonymous, "An Alexandrian Age," 31. See also De Quincey, "Style," 4.

75. Adams, *Dandies and Desert Saints*, 149–82.

76. Anonymous, "An Alexandrian Age," 31.

77. The late Victorian preoccupation with the intertwined degeneration of masculinity and the nation has been analyzed in Arata, *Fictions of Loss in the Victorian Fin de Siècle*, 79–104.

78. Tylor, *Primitive Culture*, 16.

79. Arnold, *Culture and Anarchy and Other Writings*, 35.

80. Wordsworth, "Preface to *Lyrical Ballads*," in *Prose Works*, 138–39.

81. Dowling, *Language and Decadence in the Victorian Fin de Siècle*, 104–74.

82. According to the *Oxford English Dictionary*, when the word "proletariat" entered the English language in 1847 it already carried its proto-Marxist meaning, referring to wage earners who have no capital and who depend for subsistence on their daily labor, i.e., the working classes.

83. Camlot, "The Victorian Critic as Naturalizing Agent," 490.

84. Price, "A Genealogy of Queer Detachment," 655.

85. Dellamora, "Critical Impressionism as Anti-phallogocentric Strategy," 133.

86. For more on the novel's challenge to the philosophy of Marcus Aurelius, see Behlman, "Burning, Burial, and the Critique of Stoicism in Pater's *Marius the Epicurean*," and Bassett, "'Golden Mediocrity.'"

87. McLynn, *Marcus Aurelius*, 511; and Turner, *Contesting Cultural Authority*, 319.

88. Arnold, *Essays in Criticism*, 285.

89. Arnold, *Essays in Criticism*, 279–80.

90. Turner, "Why the Greeks and Not the Romans in Victorian Britain?," 79.

91. Arnold, *Essays in Criticism*, 287.

92. Iser, *Walter Pater*, 142–43.

93. Wilde, *De Profundis*, 71.

94. Arata, "The Impersonal Intimacy of *Marius the Epicurean*," 131, 133.

Chapter 3 • *Oscar Wilde's Lyric Performativity*

1. Smith and Helfand, *Oscar Wilde's Oxford Notebooks*, 141.

2. Linda Dowling, introduction to Wilde, *The Soul of Man under Socialism*, xi–xii. Hereafter cited parenthetically by page number after the abbreviation *SMS*.

3. Ellman, *Oscar Wilde*, 47–52.

4. Ellman, *Oscar Wilde*, 47; Wilde, *De Profundis*, 64.

5. Danson, *Wilde's Intentions*, 13–14.

6. For more on these disagreements, see Donoghue, *Walter Pater*, 65–97.

7. Sinfield, *The Wilde Century*, 103.

8. Sedgwick, *Epistemology of the Closet*, 131–81; Arata, *Fictions of Loss in the Victorian Fin de Siècle*, 61.

9. Pease, "Aestheticism and Aesthetic Theory," 108.

10. Bashford, *Oscar Wilde*, 14.

11. Butler, *Precarious Life*, 27. Wilde's most explicit expression of his belief in the superiority of the individual over the social can be found in the essay "The Soul of Man under Socialism."

12. Kaye, "Gay Studies / Queer Theory and Oscar Wilde," 192.

13. Gee, "Gay Activism"; Ellmann, *Oscar Wilde*; Fone, *A Road to Stonewall*; Sedgwick, *Epistemology of the Closet*; Ed Cohen, *Talk on the Wilde Side*; Sinfield, *The Wilde Century*; and Schmidgall, *The Stranger Wilde*.

14. Kaye, "Gay Studies / Queer Theory and Oscar Wilde," 202.

15. Foucault, *The Foucault Reader*, 44.

16. Shakespeare, *The Riverside Shakespeare*, 1839.

17. Hallam, *Introduction to the Literature of Europe in the Fifteenth, Sixteenth, and Seventeenth Centuries*, 504. See de Grazia, "The Scandal of Shakespeare's Sonnets." For a provocative alternate account of homoerotic readings of the sonnets, see Matz, "The Scandals of Shakespeare's Sonnets."

18. Dowling, "Imposture and Absence in Oscar Wilde's 'Portrait of Mr. W.H.' "; Smith and Helfand, *Oscar Wilde's Oxford Notebooks*, 87–95; Saint-Amour, *The Copywrights*, 106–11; and Thomas, *Cultivating Victorians*, 160–65.

19. Gagnier, *Idylls of the Marketplace*, 17–48; Chedgzoy, *Shakespeare's Queer Children*, 142; and Danson, *Wilde's Intentions*, 106.

20. Bristow, " 'A Complex, Multiform Creature,' " 198–89.

21. According to William A. Cohen's deconstructive reading, the discovery of the name Willie Hughes encoded within the language of the sonnets is a figure for "the basic contradiction of language, the impossible striving after a univocal correspondence between signifier and signified. As the exemplary case of language's indexical capacity, the name can thus be understood as a false work that tells the truth about the falseness—that is, the arbitrary, unmotivated character—of language in general" (*Sex Scandal*, 198). Richard Halpern elaborates upon Cohen's account of the move from image to text by mapping it onto the conjunction between the discourses of sodomy and sublimity. Halpern argues that the Willie Hughes theory "circulates in, and is structured by, the [psychoanalytic] field of the transference," whereby "belief is always staged for, and in behalf of, a nonbelieving Other" (*Shakespeare's Perfume*, 46).

22. Lacan, *On Feminine Sexuality*, 48. Both W. Cohen's and Halpern's readings build

on Joel Fineman's deployment of deconstructive theory and Lacanian psychoanalysis in his account of Wilde's story as the telos of the quixotic literary project begun by Shakespeare's sonnets themselves. Fineman defines this project as "the literary problematic that derives from the effort to imagine a visible language, a language in which there would be no difference between the *imago* of presentation (the 'Portrait') and the *sign* of representation ('W.H.')," written in service of the impossible ideal of a self that is simultaneously both represented within and created by language (*Shakespeare's Perjured Eye*, 28).

23. Smith, "Philosophical Approaches to Interpretation of Oscar Wilde," 443–44.

24. Smith and Helfand, *Oscar Wilde's Oxford Notebooks*, 53; Shewan, *Oscar Wilde*, 63.

25. Smith and Helfand, *Oscar Wilde's Oxford Notebooks*, esp. 17–34.

26. Wilde makes a very similar claim in his 1886 essay on Thomas Chatterton, which he delivered at Birkbeck College in London. See Wilde, "Essay on Chatterton." For a reading of the Chatterton essay and "Mr. W.H." in the context of literary forgery and copyright law, see Saint-Amour, *The Copywrights*, 90–120.

27. Austin, *How to Do Things with Words*; Felman, *The Scandal of the Speaking Body*; Derrida, *Limited Inc.*; Butler, *Gender Trouble*, *Bodies that Matter*, and *Undoing Gender*; and Sedgwick, "Around the Performative."

28. Hegel writes: "Den Geist mit mallen seinen Konzeptionen der Phantasie und Kunst . . . für den Geist ausspricht" (*Vorlesungen über die Ästhetik*, 225). Quoted in Mieszkowski, "Derrida, Hegel, and the Language of Finitude," 27.

29. Mieszkowski, "Derrida, Hegel, and the Language of Finitude," 9.

30. Pater, *The Renaissance*, 110.

31. Hegel, *Hegel's Aesthetics*, 2:967.

32. Hegel, *Hegel's Aesthetics*, 2:968.

33. Mieszkowski, "Derrida, Hegel, and the Language of Finitude," 10.

34. Hegel, *Hegel's Aesthetics*, 2:1112.

35. Mieszkowski, "Derrida, Hegel, and the Language of Finitude," 10.

36. Mieszkowski, "Derrida, Hegel, and the Language of Finitude," 22.

37. Hegel, *Hegel's Aesthetics*, 2:1035.

38. Hegel, *Hegel's Aesthetics*, 2:1128.

39. Mieszkowski, "Derrida, Hegel, and the Language of Finitude," 11.

40. Kant, *Critique of the Power of Judgment*, 103.

41. Heraud, "A New View of Shakespeare's Sonnets: An Inductive Critique"; Anonymous, "New Views of Shakespeare's Sonnets: The 'Other Poet' Identified," and "New Views of Shakespeare's Sonnets: The 'Other Poet" Identified. II.-Resemblances."

42. Heraud, "A New View of Shakespeare's Sonnets: An Inductive Critique," 53; Schroeder, "*The Portrait of Mr. W.H*", 55.

43. Shakespeare, *The Riverside Shakespeare*, 1997.

44. Heraud, "A New View of Shakespeare's Sonnets: An Inductive Critique," 57.

45. Heraud, "A New View of Shakespeare's Sonnets: An Inductive Critique," 60.

46. Anonymous, "New Views of Shakespeare's Sonnets: The 'Other Poet' Identified," 751.

47. Anonymous, "New Views of Shakespeare's Sonnets: The 'Other Poet' Identified," 749.

48. Anonymous, "New Views of Shakespeare's Sonnets: The 'Other Poet' Identified," 753.

49. Anonymous, "New Views of Shakespeare's Sonnets: The 'Other Poet' Identified," 754.

50. Smith and Helfand, *Oscar Wilde's Oxford Notebooks*, 119. Wilde's reference is to Percy Bysshe Shelley's "To a Skylark."

51. Rachel Ablow argues that Wilde's portrayal of ambiguous belief in "Mr. W.H." indicates his engagement with the writings of Cardinal John Henry Newman, especially *An Essay in Aid of a Grammar of Assent* (1870). She maintains that Wilde's story "suggests that the beliefs we adopt in reading fiction represent only an extreme version of the beliefs we ordinarily regard as our own," and that the value of fiction is thus in its ability to allow us "to imagine who we are not." In making her case, however, Ablow brackets off the issue of homoerotic desire, which seems to me to be the central issue at stake in Cyril's crisis of belief ("Reading and Re-reading," 157–58, 172).

52. Kant, *Critique of Judgment*, 123.

53. Cyril's misguided belief that the failure of language indicates the "failure" of sexual subjectivity is also central to the negative turn in queer theory. See, for example, Edelman's discussion of the "sinthomosexual" in *No Future*, 33–66.

54. This term is, of course, borrowed from John Ruskin, whose writings were deeply influential for most mid- and late Victorian art critics, including Wilde. See "Of Pathetic Fallacy," in *Works*.

Chapter 4 • *Vernon Lee and the Specter of Lesbian History*

1. Lee, *The Handling of Words*, 295.

2. Lee, *The Handling of Words*, 295.

3. Lee, *The Handling of Words*, 295.

4. Colby, *Vernon Lee*, 67.

5. Evangelista, *British Aestheticism and Ancient Greece*, 58.

6. Evangelista, *British Aestheticism and Ancient Greece*, 56.

7. Brake, "Vernon Lee and the Pater Circle," 44.

8. Notable critical discussions of Lee's sexuality include Gardner, *The Lesbian Imagination*; Kathy Alexis Psomiades, "'Still Burning from This Strangling Embrace'"; Vicinus, *Intimate Friends*"; and Newman, "The Archival Traces of Desire." Colby insists that Lee's relationship with Mary Robinson was an essentially chaste "Boston Marriage" (*Vernon Lee*, 58).

9. Pulham, *Art and the Transitional Object in Vernon Lee's Supernatural Tales*, xiii.

10. Lee, *Euphorion*, 183–84.

11. Lee's work on a material and scientific account of aesthetic experience, especially her development of the concept of empathy, has received a great deal of attention in recent criticism. See Maltz, "Engaging 'Delicate Brains'"; Bristow, "Vernon Lee's Art of Feeling"; Fluhr, "Empathy and Identity in Vernon Lee's *Hauntings*"; Lanzoni, "Practicing Psychology in the Art Gallery"; Burdett, "'The Subjective Inside Us Can Turn into the Objective Outside'"; Morgan, *The Outward Mind*, 219–54.

12. Lee, *Hauntings and Other Fantastic Tales*, 296. In this chapter, subsequent references to this edition will appear in parentheses.

13. On the gender politics of Vernon Lee's interventions into male aestheticism, see

Maxwell and Pulham, introduction" to *Vernon Lee*; and Evangelista, "Vernon Lee and the Gender of Aestheticism."

14. See Dowling, *Hellenism and Homosexuality in Victorian Oxford.*

15. Zorn, *Vernon Lee*, xxix; White, *Metahistory*, 136.

16. Lanser, *The Sexuality of History*, 17.

17. Clare Barlow, introduction to *Queer British Art,* 17.

18. Reed, *Art and Homosexuality*, 79.

19. Castle, *The Apparitional Lesbian*, 34.

20. Castle, *The Apparitional Lesbian*, 2.

21. Castle, *The Apparitional Lesbian*, 3.

22. Vicinus, " 'A Legion of Ghosts,' " 599.

23. Marcus, *Between Women*, 13.

24. The first unabridged critical editions of these two works can be found in Brady, *John Addington Symonds and Homosexuality*. On the use of Symonds's work on ancient Greek homosexuality to challenge degeneration theory, see Chauncey, "From Sexual Inversion to Homosexuality," 134.

25. Prins, *Victorian Sappho*, 78.

26. Prins, *Victorian Sappho*, 79.

27. Leighton, *On Form*, 102–3.

28. Nealon, *Foundlings*, 8.

29. The works Traub refers to are Freccero, *Queer/Early/Modern*; Goldberg, *Sodometries*; and Menon, *Unhistorical Shakespeare.*

30. Traub, "The New Unhistoricism in Queer Studies," 34.

31. Freccero, "Queer Times," 488.

32. Traub, "The New Unhistoricism in Queer Studies," 35.

33. Lee, *Belcaro*, 18.

34. Lee, *Belcaro*, 18. For a broad discussion of Victorian representations of museums as sepulchers for art, see Siegel, *Desire and Excess*, 3–15.

35. Evangelista, "Vernon Lee in the Vatican," 38.

36. Evangelista, "Vernon Lee in the Vatican," 37.

37. Evangelista, "Vernon Lee in the Vatican," 38.

38. For a discussion of Lee's participation in an influential public culture of amateur women art historians who wrote for a popular audience, see Fraser, *Women Writing Art History*, 15–39.

39. Lee, *Belcaro*, 6. As Hilary Fraser has argued, this method especially appealed to Victorian women writers on art, who were routinely denied access to formal training in the methods of scientific historiography. See *Women Writing Art History*, 15–39.

40. Evangelista, "Vernon Lee in the Vatican," 38. For a reading of Lee's essay emphasizing Lee's transformation of her predecessors' historical materialist approach to art into a thoroughgoing idealism, see Siegel, "The Material of Form," 189–201.

41. Lee, *Euphorion*, 22.

42. Mahoney, "Haunted Collections," 61.

43. Pater, *The Renaissance*, 187. Subsequent references to this edition will appear in parentheses after the abbreviation *R*.

44. Loesberg, *A Return to Aesthetics*, 3.

45. See Parker, *The English Idea of History from Coleridge to Collingwood.*

46. Pater, "Poems by William Morris," 300.

47. Pater, "Poems by William Morris," 300.

48. Edelman, *No Future*, 1–33.

49. Edelman, *Homographesis*, 183.

50. Freeman, *Time Binds*, 95–96.

51. Other readers have disagreed with the painter's interpretation of this scene. Dennis Denisoff argues for an explicitly lesbian reading where the modern Alice's supposed supernatural inhabitation by the historical Alice expresses "the force of the same-sex bond" that "arises from the heroine's devotion to her namesake surpassing not only the portraitist's interest in the living Alice, but also the dead Alice's dubious attachment to a lover who may have never existed." For him, the painter's inadequate assessment of Alice's experience follows from the inherent bias toward masculine heterosexuality, expressed by his assumption that only a man can sexually arouse a woman (*Sexual Visuality from Literature to Film*, 104–5). Alternatively, Patricia Pulham offers a psychoanalytic reading that suggests Alice's desire for the historical Alice is overdetermined: the Alice Oke of 1626 is "the phallic mother," "the apparitional lesbian," and "the beautiful boy" who has "a particular role to play in the expression on homo-sexuality," a figure she eventually projects onto Lovelock (*Art and the Transitional Object in Vernon Lee's Supernatural Tales*, 130–31). For an account of this scene that in relation to discussions of "ancestral memory" in Victorian psychology, see Vrettos, "'In the Clothes of Dead People.'"

52. Denisoff, by contrast, argues that Alice is killed because her same-sex desires pose a threat to late-Victorian patriarchal society, a truth that the narrator obfuscates by portraying her as an active conspirer in her own murder (*Sexual Visuality from Literature to Film*, 104–6). For a reading of smiles as poetic figures for the persistence of queer subjectivity in the face of trauma, see Snediker, *Queer Optimism*, 43–78.

53. Shorter, *A Historical Dictionary of Psychiatry*, 184.

54. Ellis, "Autoeroticism," 280.

55. Foucault, *The History of Sexuality*, 43.

56. Maxwell, *Second Sight*, 142.

57. See Wallace, *Female Gothic Histories*, 109–15; Robbins, "Vernon Lee"; Vicinus, "The Adolescent Boy"; and A. Smith, *The Victorian Ghost Story*, 83.

58. Lee, *Renaissance Fancies and Studies*, 255. Colby notes that Lee embeds two alternative *Bildung* narratives in her eulogy: the first tells the story of what she believes to be Pater's spiritual maturation from aesthetic critic to spiritual counselor, and the second expresses Lee's own farewell to her career as a cultural historian and aesthetic critic (*Vernon Lee*, 76).

59. Christenson has analyzed the story's deep intertextual relationships with the periodical's other aestheticist writings. See "Cultural Decline and Alienation in Vernon Lee's 'Prince Alberic and the Snake Lady.'"

60. Stetz argues that Lee's facetious gesture toward historical empiricism was meant to signal the unspeakable history the tale really represents in displaced, allegori-cal terms: the trials and imprisonment of Oscar Wilde. See "The Snake Lady and the Bruised Bodley Head."

61. Zorn, *Vernon Lee*, 153. Jane Hotchkiss, Mary Patricia Kane, and Vineta Colby make much of the Snake Lady's place within a literary lineage of "phallic women," who

have been traditionally associated with nonnormative sexuality. See Hotchkiss, "(P)revising Freud"; Kane, "The Uncanny Mother in Vernon Lee's 'Prince Alberic and the Snake Lady' "; Colby, *Vernon Lee*, 230.

62. Zorn, *Vernon Lee*, 156.

63. Traub, *Thinking Sex with the Early Moderns*, 84–85.

Chapter 5 • Queering Indifference in Michael Field's Ekphrastic Poetry

1. Field, *Michael Field, the Poet*, 85. References to this text are hereafter cited in the main text by the abbreviation *MF*.

2. Field, *Sight and Song*, v. References to this text are hereafter cited in the main text by the abbreviation *SS*.

3. Heffernan, *Museum of Words*, 3. Marion Thain mentions that although Bradley and Cooper did not use the word to describe their poems about paintings, "the idea of ekphrasis . . . was important to cultural developments in the fin de siècle, even if the term had yet to gain prominence" (*Michael Field*, 68).

4. Saville, "The Poetic Imaging of Michael Field."

5. For a longer discussion of Berenson's dismissive attitudes towards women who wrote about art, see Fraser, *Women Writing Art History*, 1–2.

6. Field, *Works and Days*, 193.

7. Field, Journals, British Library, Add. Mss. 46783, 57V–58R; quoted in Evangelista, *British Aestheticism and Ancient Greece*, 158.

8. Field, *Works and Days*, 16.

9. Field, *Works and Days*, 193.

10. Anderson, *The Powers of Distance*, 5–7.

11. Thain, *Michael Field*, 77; Field, Journals, British Library, Add. Mss. 46783, 46V–47V, quoted in Thain, *Michael Field*, 47.

12. Davis, *Queer Beauty*, 182.

13. On the influence of this essay on Bradley and Cooper, see Thain, *Michael Field*, 70–72.

14. Leighton, *Victorian Women Poets*, 215. For detailed accounts of the relationship between Pater and the Michael Fields, see Saville, "The Poetic Imaging of Michael Field"; Vadillo, *Women Poets and Urban Aestheticism*, 187–95; Vanita, *Sappho and the Virgin Mary*, 182; and Evangelista, *British Aestheticism and Ancient Greece*, 111–13.

15. Le Gallienne, "Pictures Done into Verse."

16. Thain, *Michael Field*, 66–89; and Cameron, "The Pleasures of Looking and the Feminine Gaze in *Sight and Song*."

17. Schuller and Peters (ed.), *The Letters of John Addington Symonds*, 683–84.

18. Thain, *Michael Field*, 17.

19. Pater, *The Renaissance*, 384. Subsequent references to this edition will appear in parentheses after the abbreviation *R*.

20. Eastham, "Walter Pater's Acoustic Space," 200.

21. Rutter, *Hegel on the Modern Arts*, 77.

22. Rutter, *Hegel on the Modern Arts*, 77.

23. Hegel, *Hegel's Aesthetics*, 600.

24. Rancière, *Aisthesis*, 23.

25. Rancière, *Aisthesis*, 30–31.

26. Hegel, *Hegel's Aesthetics*, 162.

27. Rancière, *Aisthesis*, 31.

28. Rancière, *Aisthesis*, 32.

29. Hegel, *Hegel's Aesthetics*, 36–37.

30. Rancière, *Aisthesis*, 32.

31. Eastham, "Walter Pater's Acoustic Space," 200–201.

32. Vadillo, *Women Poets and Urban Aestheticism*, 21.

33. Morgan, "Aesthetic Freedom," 733.

34. Michael Field, *Uncertain Rain*, 58.

35. Evangelista, *British Aestheticism and Ancient Greece*, 94.

36. Field, *Uncertain Rain*, 59; Evangelista, *British Aestheticism and Ancient Greece*, 94.

37. Evangelista, *British Aestheticism and Ancient Greece*, 95.

38. Davis, *Queer Beauty*, 44.

39. Davis, *Queer Beauty*, 38.

40. Frankel, "The Concrete Poetics of Michael Field's *Sight and Song*."

41. Saville, "The Poetic Imaging of Michael Field," 186.

42. Vadillo, *Women Poets and Urban Aestheticism*, 26.

43. Andrews, "The Figure of Watteau in Walter Pater's 'Prince of Court Painters' and Michael Field's *Sight and Song*," 467.

44. Thain, *Michael Field*, 45. For a reading of Bradley and Cooper's poetry and life that focuses on the relationship between queerness, incest, and bourgeois class norms, see Tate, "Lesbian Incest as Queer Kinship."

45. Vadillo, "Sight and Song," 15–34; Fraser, "A Visual Field"; Lysack, *Come Buy, Come Buy*, 109–35; and Ehnenn, *Women's Literary Collaboration, Queerness, and Late-Victorian Culture*, 59–96. Saville also reads *Sight and Song*'s objectivity in gendered terms, but argues Bradley and Cooper placing themselves within a definitively male tradition of aesthetic objectivity. See "The Poetic Imaging of Michael Field."

46. Ehnenn, "'Our Brains Struck Fire from Each,'" 201.

47. Kaye, "'Determined Raptures.'"

48. Ehnenn, *Women's Literary Collaboration*, 94.

49. Vanita, *Sappho and the Virgin Mary*, 131.

50. Thain, *Michael Field*, 138.

51. White, "Michael Field"; Ehnenn, *Women's Literary Collaboration*, 82.

52. Ehnenn, *Women's Literary Collaboration*, 82.

53. Lysack, *Come Buy, Come Buy*, 111.

54. Ehnenn, Lysack, and Fraser all derive the notion of the "male gaze" from Mulvey, "Visual Pleasure and Narrative Cinema."

55. Ehnenn, *Women's Literary Collaboration*, 78; Lysack, *Come Buy, Come Buy*, 125.

56. Fraser, *Women Writing Art History*, 84.

57. Davis, *Queer Beauty*, 50.

58. Stillman, "Leonardo da Vinci," 839; quoted in Ehnenn, *Women's Literary Collaboration*, 77.

59. Symonds, *Renaissance in Italy*, 317; quoted in Ehnenn, *Women's Literary Collaboration*, 77.

60. Ehnenn, *Women's Literary Collaboration*, 77.

61. Psomiades, *Body's Beauty*, 202.
62. Davis, *Queer Beauty*, 50.

Coda

1. Wilde, *The Picture of Dorian Gray*, 19.
2. Amin, Musser, and Pérez, "Queer Form," 227.
3. Clare Barlow, introduction to *Queer British Art*, 12.
4. Barlow, introduction to *Queer British Art*, 14.
5. Barlow, introduction to *Queer British Art*, 14.
6. Cole, *The Birth of Theory*, 21.
7. See, of course, Susan Sontag, "Notes on Camp."
8. Barlow, introduction to *Queer British Art*, 16.
9. Coombs and Coriale, "V21 Forum on Strategic Presentism," 88.

Ablow, Rachel. "Reading and Re-reading: Wilde, Newman, and the Fiction of Belief," in *The Feeling of Reading: Affective Experience and Victorian Literature*, ed. Rachel Ablow (Ann Arbor: University of Michigan Press, 2010), 157–78.

Adams, James Eli. *Dandies and Desert Saints: Styles of Victorian Masculinity* (Ithaca: Cornell University Press, 1995).

Adorno, Theodor W. *Aesthetic Theory*, trans. Robert Hullot-Kentor (Minneapolis: University of Minnesota Press, 1997).

Adorno, Theodor W. *Beethoven: The Philosophy of Music*, ed. Rolf Tiedeman, trans. Edmund Jephcott (Stanford: Stanford University Press, 1998).

Allan, Amy. "The Anti-subjective Hypothesis: Michel Foucault and the Death of the Subject," *Philosophical Forum* 31.2 (2000), 113–30.

Amin, Kadji, Amber Jamilia Musser, and Roy Pérez. "Queer Form: Aesthetics, Race, and the Violences of the Social," *ASAP/Journal* 2.2 (2017), 227–39.

Andrews, Kit. "The Figure of Watteau in Walter Pater's 'Prince of Court Painters' and Michael Field's *Sight and Song*," *English Literature in Transition, 1880–1920* 53.4 (2010), 451–84.

Andrews, Kit. "Walter Pater as Oxford Hegelian: *Plato and Platonism* and T. H. Green's *Prolegomena to Ethics*," *Journal of the History of Ideas* 72.3 (2011), 437–59.

Anonymous. "An Alexandrian Age," *Macmillan's Magazine* 55 (1886), 27–35.

Anonymous. "New Views of Shakespeare's Sonnets: The 'Other Poet' Identified," *Blackwood's Edinburgh Magazine* 135.824 (June 1884), 727–61.

Anonymous. "New Views of Shakespeare's Sonnets: The 'Other Poet' Identified. II.-Resemblances," *Blackwood's Edinburgh Magazine* 137: 836 (June 1885), 774–800.

Arata, Stephen. *Fictions of Loss in the Victorian Fin de Siècle* (Cambridge: Cambridge University Press, 1996).

Arata, Stephen. "The Impersonal Intimacy of *Marius the Epicurean*," in *The Feeling of Reading: Affective Experience and Victorian Literature*, ed. Rachel Ablow (Ann Arbor: University of Michigan Press, 2010), 131–56.

Arnold, Matthew. *The Complete Prose Works of Matthew Arnold*, vol. 3, ed. R. H. Super (Ann Arbor: University of Michigan Press, 1965).

Arnold, Matthew. *Culture and Anarchy and Other Writings*, ed. Stefan Collini (Cambridge: Cambridge University Press, 1993).

Arnold, Matthew. *Essays in Criticism* (London: Macmillan, 1865).

Ashton, Rosemary. *The German Idea: Four English Writers and the Reception of German Thought 1800–1860* (Cambridge: Cambridge University Press, 1980).

Austin, J. L. *How to Do Things with Words* (Cambridge, MA: Harvard University Press, 1962).

Badiou, Alain. *The Rational Kernel of the Hegelian Dialectic*, trans. Tzuchien Tho (Melbourne: Re.Press, 2011).

Barlow, Clare (ed.). *Queer British Art, 1861–1967* (London: Tate Enterprises, 2017).

Barthes, Roland. *Writing Degree Zero*, trans. Annette Lavers and Colin Smith (New York: Hill and Wang, 1968).

Bashford, Bruce. *Oscar Wilde: The Critic as Humanist* (Cranbury: Associated University Presses, 1999).

Bassett, Sharon. "'Golden Mediocrity': Pater's Marcus Aurelius and the Making of Decadence," in *Perennial Decay: On the Aesthetics and Politics of Decadence*, ed. Liz Constable, Dennis Denisoff, and Matthew Potolsky (Philadelphia: University of Pennsylvania Press, 1999), 254–67.

Bauer, Heike. *English Literary Sexology: Translations of Inversion, 1860–1930* (Basingstoke: Palgrave Macmillan, 2009).

Behlman, Lee. "Burning, Burial, and the Critique of Stoicism in Pater's *Marius the Epicurean*," *Nineteenth-Century Prose* 31.1 (2004), 133–69.

Benson, A. C. *Walter Pater* (London: Macmillan, 1906).

Bersani, Leo. *The Culture of Redemption* (Cambridge, MA: Harvard University Press, 1990).

Bersani, Leo. *Homos* (Cambridge, MA: Harvard University Press, 1995).

Bersani, Leo. "Is the Rectum a Grave?," *October* 43 (1987), 197–222.

Bosanquet, Bernard. *A History of Aesthetic* (London: Swan Sonnenschein, 1892).

Bourdieu, Pierre. *Distinction: A Social Critique of the Judgment of Taste*, trans. Richard Nice (Cambridge, MA: Harvard University Press, 1984).

Brady, Sean. *John Addington Symonds and Homosexuality: A Critical Edition of Sources* (Basingstoke: Palgrave Macmillan, 2012).

Brake, Laurel. *Print in Transition: Studies in Media and Book History* (Basingstoke: Palgrave Macmillan, 2001).

Brake, Laurel. "Vernon Lee and the Pater Circle," in *Vernon Lee: Decadence, Ethics, Aesthetics*, ed. Catherine Maxwell and Patricia Pulham (Basingstoke: Palgrave Macmillan, 2006), 40–56.

Bristow, Joseph. "'A Complex, Multiform Creature'—Wilde's Sexual Identities," in *The Cambridge Companion to Oscar Wilde*, ed. Peter Raby (Cambridge: Cambridge University Press, 1997), 195–219.

Bristow, Joseph. "Vernon Lee's Art of Feeling," *Tulsa Studies in Women's Literature* 25.1 (2006), 1–23.

Brown, Julia Prewitt. *Cosmopolitan Criticism: Oscar Wilde's Philosophy of Art* (Charlottesville: University of Virginia Press, 1997).

Budick, Sanford, and Wolfgang Iser (eds.). *Languages of the Unsayable: The Play of Negativity in Literature and Literary Theory* (New York: Columbia University Press, 1988).

Burdett, Carolyn. "'The Subjective Inside Us Can Turn into the Objective Outside':

Vernon Lee's Psychological Aesthetics," *19: Interdisciplinary Studies in the Long Nineteenth Century* 12 (2011), 287–94, http://doi.org/10.16995/ntn.610.

Bürger, Peter. *Theory of the Avant-Garde* (Minneapolis: University of Minnesota Press, 1984.

Butler, Judith. *Bodies That Matter* (New York: Routledge, 1993).

Butler, Judith. *Gender Trouble* (New York: Routledge, 1990).

Butler, Judith. *Precarious Life: The Power of Mourning and Violence* (London: Verso, 2004).

Butler, Judith. *Subjects of Desire: Hegelian Reflections in Twentieth-Century France* (New York: Columbia University Press, 1987).

Butler, Judith. *Undoing Gender* (New York: Routledge, 2004).

Cameron, S. Brooke. "The Pleasures of Looking and the Feminine Gaze in *Sight and Song*," *Victorian Poetry* 51.2 (2013), 147–75.

Camlot, Jason. "The Victorian Critic as Naturalizing Agent," *ELH* 73.2 (2006), 489–518.

Carlyle, Thomas. *On Heroes, Hero-Worship and the Heroic in History* (Lincoln: University of Nebraska Press, 1966).

Caserio, Robert L., Lee Edelman, Judith Halberstam, José Esteban Muñoz, and Tim Dean. "The Antisocial Thesis in Queer Theory: A Roundtable," *PMLA* 121.3 (May 2006), 819–28.

Castle, Terry. *The Apparitional Lesbian: Female Homosexuality and Modern Culture* (New York: Columbia University Press, 1995).

Chauncey, George. "From Sexual Inversion to Homosexuality: Medicine and the Changing Conceptualization of Female Deviance," *Salmagundi* 58/59 (1982–83), 114–46.

Chedgzoy, Kate. *Shakespeare's Queer Children: Sexual Politics and Contemporary Culture* (Manchester: Manchester University Press, 1995).

Christensen, Peter G. "Cultural Decline and Alienation in Vernon Lee's 'Prince Alberic and the Snake Lady,'" in *Decadences: Morality and Aesthetics in British Literature*, ed. Paula Fox (Stuttgart: Ibidem, 2006), 63–89.

Clark, Kenneth. Introduction to *The Renaissance: Studies in Art and Poetry* (London: Fontana/Collins, 1961), 11–26.

Coates, John. "Pater and the Myth of Dionysus," *English* 56 (Autumn 2007), 265–82.

Cohen, Ed. *Talk on the Wilde Side: Towards a Genealogy of Discourse on Male Sexualities* (New York: Routledge, 1993).

Cohen, William. *Sex Scandal: The Private Parts of Victorian Fiction* (Durham: Duke University Press, 1996).

Cohn, Elisha. "'One Single Ivory Cell': Oscar Wilde and the Brain," *Journal of Victorian Culture* 17.2 (2012), 183–205.

Colby, Vineta. *Vernon Lee: A Literary Biography* (Charlottesville: University of Virginia Press, 2003).

Cole, Andrew. *The Birth of Theory* (Chicago: University of Chicago Press, 2014).

Connor, Steven. "Myth and Meta-myth in Max Müller and Walter Pater," in *The Sun Is God: Painting, Literature, and Mythology in the Nineteenth Century*, ed. J. B. Bullen (Oxford: Clarendon Press, 1989), 199–222.

Connor, Steven. "Myth as Multiplicity in Pater's *Greek Studies* and 'Denys L'Auxerrois,'" *Review of English Studies* 34.133 (1983), 28–42.

Coole, Diana. *Negativity and Politics: Dionysus and Dialectics from Kant to Poststructuralism* (London: Routledge, 2000).

Coombs, David Sweeney, and Danielle Coriale. "V21 Forum on Strategic Presentism: Introduction," *Victorian Studies* 59.1 (2016), 87–89.

Crawford, Robert. "Pater's Renaissance, Andrew Lang, and Anthropological Romanticism," *ELH* 53.4 (1986), 849–79.

Danson, Lawrence. *Wilde's Intentions: The Artist in His Criticism* (Oxford: Oxford University Press, 1997).

Davis, Michael F. "Walter Pater's 'Latent Intelligence' and the Conception of Queer 'Theory,'" in *Walter Pater: Transparencies of Desire*, ed. Laurel Brake, Leslie Higgins, and Carolyn Williams (Greensboro, NC: ELT Press, 2002), 261–85.

Davis, Whitney. *Queer Beauty: Sexuality and Aesthetics from Winckelmann to Freud and Beyond* (New York: Columbia University Press, 2010).

Dawson, Gowan. *Darwin, Literature and Victorian Respectability* (Cambridge: Cambridge University Press, 2010).

de Grazia, Margreta. "The Scandal of Shakespeare's Sonnets," in *Shakespeare's Sonnets: Critical Essays* (New York: Garland, 1999), 89–112.

DeLaura, David. *Hebrew and Hellene in Victorian England: Newman, Arnold, and Pater* (Austin: University of Texas Press, 1969).

Dellamora, Richard. "The Androgynous Body in Pater's 'Winckelmann,'" *Browning Institute Studies* 11 (1983), 51–68.

Dellamora, Richard. "Critical Impressionism as Anti-phallogocentric Strategy," in *Pater in the 1990s*, ed. Laurel Brake and Ian Small (Greensboro, NC: ELT Press, 1991), 127–42.

Dellamora, Richard. *Masculine Desire: The Sexual Politics of Victorian Aestheticism* (Chapel Hill: University of North Carolina Press, 1990).

de Man, Paul. *Aesthetic Ideology* (Minneapolis: University of Minnesota Press, 1996).

Den Otter, Sandra M. *British Idealism and Social Explanation: A Study in Late Victorian Thought* (Oxford: Oxford University Press, 1996).

Denisoff, Dennis. *Aestheticism and Sexual Parody 1840–1940* (Cambridge: Cambridge University Press, 2001).

Denisoff, Dennis. "The Dissipating Nature of Decadent Paganism from Pater to Yeats," *Modernism/Modernity* 15.3 (2008), 431–46.

Denisoff, Dennis. *Sexual Visuality from Literature to Film, 1850–1950* (Basingstoke: Palgrave Macmillan, 2004).

De Quincey, Thomas. "Style," *Blackwood's Edinburgh Magazine* 47 (1840), 1–17.

Derrida, Jacques. *Limited Inc.* (Evanston: Northwestern University Press, 1988).

Donoghue, Denis. *Walter Pater: Lover of Strange Souls* (New York: Knopf, 1996).

Dowling, Linda. *Hellenism and Homosexuality in Victorian Oxford* (Ithaca: Cornell University Press, 1994).

Dowling, Linda. "Imposture and Absence in Oscar Wilde's 'Portrait of Mr. W.H.,'" *Victorian Newsletter* 58 (1980), 26–29.

Dowling, Linda. *Language and Decadence in the Victorian Fin de Siècle* (Princeton: Princeton University Press, 1986).

Dowling, Linda. "Ruskin's Pied Beauty and the Constitution of a 'Homosexual' Code," *Victorian Newsletter* 75 (April 1989), 1–8.

Dowling, Linda. *The Vulgarization of Art: The Victorians and Aesthetic Democracy* (Charlottesville: University of Virginia Press, 1996).

Eagleton, Terry. *The Ideology of the Aesthetic* (Oxford: Blackwell, 1990).

Eastham, Andrew. *Aesthetic Afterlives: Irony, Literary Modernity, and the Ends of Beauty* (London, Continuum, 2011).

Eastham, Andrew. "Walter Pater's Acoustic Space: 'The School of Giorgione,' Dionysian 'Anders-streben,' and the Politics of Soundscape," *Yearbook of English Studies* 40.1/2 (2010), 196–216.

Edelman, Lee. *Homographesis: Essays in Gay Literary and Cultural Theory* (New York: Routledge, 1994).

Edelman, Lee. *No Future: Queer Theory and the Death Drive* (Durham: Duke University Press, 2004).

Ehnenn, Jill. "'Our Brains Struck Fire from Each': Disidentification, Difference, and Desire in the Collaborative Aesthetics of Michael Field," in *Economies of Desire in the Victorian Fin de Siècle*," ed. Jane Ford, Kim Edwards Keates, and Patricia Pulham (New York: Routledge, 2016), 180–204.

Ehnenn, Jill. *Women's Literary Collaboration, Queerness, and Late-Victorian Culture* (Burlington, VT: Ashgate, 2008).

Ellis, Havelock. "Autoeroticism: A Psychological Study," *The Alienist and Neurologist: A Quarterly Journal of Scientific, Clinical, and Forensic Psychiatry and Neurology* 19 (1898), 260–99.

Ellmann, Richard. *Oscar Wilde* (New York: Vintage, 1988).

Engelstein, Stefani. "The Allure of Wholeness: The Eighteenth-Century Organism and the Same-Sex Marriage Debate," *Critical Inquiry* 39.4 (2013), 754–76.

Eribon, Dider. *Insult and the Making of the Gay Self*, trans. Michael Lucey (Durham: Duke University Press, 2004).

Evangelista, Stefano. *British Aestheticism and Ancient Greece: Hellenism, Reception, Gods in Exile*. Palgrave Studies in Nineteenth-Century Writing and Culture (Basingstoke, UK: Palgrave Macmillan, 2009).

Evangelista, Stefano. "Vernon Lee and the Gender of Aestheticism," in *Vernon Lee: Decadence, Ethics, Aesthetics*, ed. Catherine Maxwell and Patricia Pulham (Basingstoke, UK: Palgrave Macmillan, 2006), 91–111.

Evangelista, Stefano. "Vernon Lee in the Vatican: The Uneasy Alliance of Aestheticism and Archeology," *Victorian Studies* 52.1 (2009), 31–41.

Evangelista, Stefano. "Walter Pater: The Queer Reception," *Pater Newsletter* 52 (2007), 19–24.

Felman, Shoshana. *The Scandal of the Speaking Body: Don Juan with J. L. Austin, or Seduction in Two Languages*, trans. Catherine Porter (Stanford: Stanford University Press, 2003).

Felski, Rita. *Uses of Literature* (Oxford: Blackwell, 2008).

Field, Michael [Katharine Bradley and Edith Cooper]. Journals, British Library.

Field, Michael [Katharine Bradley and Edith Cooper]. *Michael Field, the Poet: Published and Manuscript Materials*, ed. Marion Thain and Ana Parejo Vadillo (Peterborough, ON: Broadview Press, 2009).

Field, Michael [Katharine Bradley and Edith Cooper]. *Sight and Song* (London: Elkin Mathews and John Lane, 1892).

Field, Michael [Katharine Bradley and Edith Cooper]. *Uncertain Rain: Sundry Spells of Michael Field*, ed. Ivor Treby (Bury St. Edmunds: De Blackland, 2002).

Field, Michael [Katharine Bradley and Edith Cooper]. *Works and Days: From the Journal of Michael Field*, ed. T. Sturge Moore and D. C. Sturge Moore (London: John Murray, 1933).

Fineman, Joel. *Shakespeare's Perjured Eye: The Invention of Poetic Subjectivity in the Sonnets* (Berkeley: University of California Press, 1986).

Fluck, Winfried. "The Search for Distance: Negation and Negativity in Wolfgang Iser's Literary Theory," *New Literary History* 31.1 (2000), 175–210.

Fluhr, Nicole. "Empathy and Identity in Vernon Lee's *Hauntings*," *Victorian Studies* 48.2 (2006), 287–94.

Fone, Byrne. *A Road to Stonewall: Homosexuality and Homophobia in British and American Literature, 1750–1969* (New York: Twayne, 1995).

Foucault, Michel. *The Foucault Reader*, ed. Paul Rabinow (New York: Pantheon Books, 1984).

Foucault, Michel. *The History of Sexuality*, vol. 1: *An Introduction*, trans. Robert Hurley (London: Penguin, 1978).

Foucault, Michel. *The Order of Things: An Archeology of the Human Sciences*, trans. Alan Sheridan (New York: Vintage Books, 1970).

Frankel, Nicholas. "The Concrete Poetics of Michael Field's *Sight and Song*," in *Michael Field and Their World*, ed. Margaret D. Stetz and Cheryl A. Wilson (High Wycombe: Rivendale Press, 2007), 211–21.

Fraser, Hilary. "A Visual Field: Michael Field and the Gaze," *Victorian Literature and Culture* 34.2 (2006), 553–71.

Fraser, Hilary. *Women Writing Art History: Looking Like a Woman* (Cambridge: Cambridge University Press, 2014).

Freccero, Carla. "Queer Times," *South Atlantic Quarterly* 106.3 (2007), 485–94.

Freedman, Jonathan. *Professions of Taste: Henry James, British Aestheticism, and Commodity Culture* (Stanford: Stanford University Press, 1990).

Freeman, Elizabeth. *Time Binds: Queer Temporalities, Queer Histories* (Durham: Duke University Press, 2010).

Gagnier, Regenia. *Idylls of the Marketplace: Oscar Wilde and the Victorian Public* (Stanford: Stanford University Press, 1986).

Gardner, Burdett. *The Lesbian Imagination (Victorian Style), A Psychological and Critical Study of 'Vernon Lee'* (New York: Garland, 1987).

Gee, Stephen. "Gay Activism," in *Homosexuality: Power and Politics*, ed. Gay Left Collective (London: Alison and Busby, 1980), 198–204.

Glavey, Brian. *The Wallflower Avant-Garde: Modernism, Sexuality, and Queer Ekphrasis* (Oxford: Oxford University Press, 2015).

Goldberg, Jonathan. *Sodometries: Renaissance Texts, Modern Sexualities* (Stanford: Stanford University Press, 1992).

Goldstone, Andrew. *Modernist Fictions of Autonomy: Modernism for Wilde to de Man* (Oxford: Oxford University Press, 2013).

Halberstam, Jack. *The Queer Art of Failure* (Durham: Duke University Press, 2010).

Hallam, Henry. *Introduction to the Literature of Europe in the Fifteenth, Sixteenth, and Seventeenth Centuries*, 4 vols. (London: John Murray, 1839).

Halpern, Richard. *Shakespeare's Perfume: Sodomy and Sublimity in the Sonnets, Wilde, Freud, and Lacan* (Philadelphia: University of Pennsylvania Press, 2002).

Harris, Wendell V. "Arnold, Pater, Wilde, and the Object as in Themselves They See It," *Studies in English Literature 1500–1900* 11.4 (1971), 733–47.

Hassall, Christopher. *Rupert Brooke: A Biography* (London: Faber and Faber, 1964).

Heffernan, James. *Museum of Words: The Poetics of Ekphrasis from Homer to Ashbery* (Chicago: University of Chicago Press, 1993).

Hegel, George Wilhelm Friedrich. *The Encyclopaedia Logic: Part 1 of the Encyclopaedia of Philosophical Sciences with the Zusätze*, trans. T. F. Geraets, W. A. Suchting, and H. S. Harris (Indianapolis: Hackett, 1991).

Hegel, George Wilhelm Friedrich. *Hegel's Aesthetics: Lectures on Fine Art*, vol. 2, trans. T. M. Knox (New York: Clarendon, 1998).

Hegel, George Wilhelm Friedrich. *Hegel's Preface to the "Phenomenology of Spirit,"* trans. Yirmiyahu Yovel (Princeton: Princeton University Press, 2005).

Hegel, George Wilhelm Friedrich. *Phenomenology of Mind*, trans. J. B. Baillie (London: Harper & Row, 1967).

Hegel, George Wilhelm Friedrich. *Science of Logic*, trans. A. V. Miller (London: Allen & Unwin, 1969).

Hegel, George Wilhelm Friedrich. *Vorlesungen über die Ästhetik (Berlin, 1820–1)*, ed. Helmut Schneider (Frankfurt a.M.: Peter Lang, 1995).

Heraud, John A. "A New View of Shakespeare's Sonnets: An Inductive Critique," *Temple Bar* 5 (July 1862), 53–66.

Hext, Kate. "The Limitations of Schilleresque Self-Culture in Pater's Individualist Aesthetics," in *Victorian Aesthetic Conditions: Pater Across the Arts*, ed. Elicia Clements and Lesley J. Higgins (Basingstoke: Palgrave Macmillan, 2010), 205–19.

Hext, Kate. *Walter Pater: Individualism and Aesthetic Philosophy* (Edinburgh: Edinburgh University Press, 2013).

Higgins, Lesley. "No Time for Pater: The Silenced Other of Masculinist Modernism," in *Walter Pater: Transparencies of Desire*, ed. Laurel Brake, Lesley Higgins, and Carolyn Williams (Wilmington, NC: ELT Press, 2002), 37–54.

Hotchkiss, Jane. "(P)revising Freud: Vernon Lee's Castration Phantasy," in *Seeing Double: Revisioning Edwardian and Modernist Literature*, ed. Corola M. Kaplan and Anne B. Simpson (New York: St. Martin's Press, 1996), 21–38.

Hyppolite, Jean. *Logic and Existence*, trans. Leonard Lawlor and Amit Sen (Albany: State University of New York Press, 1997).

Inman, Billie Andrew. "Estrangement and Connection: Walter Pater, Benjamin Jowett, and William M. Hardinge," in *Pater in the 1990s*, ed. Laurel Brake and Ian Small (Greensboro, NC: ELT Press, 1991), 1–20.

Inman, Billie Andrew. "The Intellectual Context of Pater's 'Conclusion,'" *Prose Studies* 4:1 (May 1981), 12–30.

Inman, Billie Andrew. "'Sebastian von Storck': Pater's Exploration into Nihilism," *Nineteenth-Century Fiction* 30 (1976), 457–76.

Inman, Billie Andrew. *Walter Pater and His Reading: 1874–1877, with a Bibliography of His Library Borrowings, 1878–1894* (New York: Garland, 1990).

Inman, Billie Andrew. *Walter Pater's Reading: A Bibliography of His Library Borrowings and Literary References, 1858–1873* (New York: Garland, 1981).

Iser, Wolfgang. *Walter Pater: The Aesthetic Moment* (Cambridge: Cambridge University Press, 1987).

Jameson, Fredric. *The Hegel Variations: On the "Phenomenology of Spirit"* (London: Verso, 2010).

Jameson, Fredric. "Postmodernism and Consumer Society," in *The Cultural Turn: Selected Writings on Postmodernism* (London: Verso, 1998), 1–20.

Jameson, Fredric. *Valences of the Dialectic* (London: Verso, 2010).

Johnson, Wendell. *Living in Sin: The Victorian Sexual Revolution* (Chicago: Nelson-Hall, 1979).

Kane, Mary Patricia. "The Uncanny Mother in Vernon Lee's 'Prince Alberic and the Snake Lady,'" *Victorian Review* 31.1 (2006), 41–62.

Kant, Immanuel. *Critique of Judgment*, trans. Werner S. Pluhar (Indianapolis: Hackett, 1987).

Kant, Immanuel. *Critique of the Power of Judgment*, trans. Paul Guyer and Eric Matthews (Cambridge: Cambridge University Press, 2000).

Kant, Immanuel. *Kant: Political Writings*, ed. Hans Reiss, trans. H. B. Nisbet (Cambridge: Cambridge University Press, 1991).

Kaufman, Robert. "Red Kant, or The Persistence of the Third *Critique* in Adorno and Jameson," *Critical Inquiry* 26.4 (2000), 682–724.

Kaye, Richard A. "'Determined Raptures': Saint Sebastian and the Victorian Discourse of Decadence," *Victorian Literature and Culture* 27.1 (1999), 269–303.

Kaye, Richard A. "Gay Studies / Queer Theory and Oscar Wilde," in *Palgrave Advances in Oscar Wilde Studies*, ed. Frederick S. Roden (Basingstoke: Palgrave Macmillan, 2004), 189–223.

Khalip, Jacques. "Pater's Sadness," *Raritan* 20.2 (2000), 136–58.

Knoepflmacher, U. C. *Religious Humanism and the Victorian Novel: George Eliot, Walter Pater, and Samuel Butler* (Princeton: Princeton University Press, 1965).

Kurnick, David. "Embarrassment and the Forms of Redemption," *PMLA* 125.2 (2010), 398–403.

Kurrik, Marie Jaanus. *Literature and Negation* (New York: Columbia University Press, 1979).

Lacan, Jacques. *On Feminine Sexuality, The Limits of Love and Knowledge, 1972–1973*, vol. 20 of *The Seminar of Jacques Lacan*, ed. Jacques-Alain Miller, trans. Robert Fink (New York: Norton, 1998).

Lanser, Susan. *The Sexuality of History: Modernity and the Sapphic, 1565–1830* (Chicago: University of Chicago Press, 2014).

Lanzoni, Susan. "Practicing Psychology in the Art Gallery: Vernon Lee's Aesthetics of Empathy," *Journal of the History of Behavioral Sciences* 45.4 (2009), 330–54.

Lecourt, Sebastian. *Cultivating Belief: Victorian Anthropology, Liberal Aesthetics, and the Secular Imagination* (Oxford: Oxford University Press, 2018).

Lee, Vernon. *Belcaro: Being Essays on Sundry Aesthetical Questions* (London: Satchell, n.d. [1880]).

Lee, Vernon. *Euphorion: Being Studies of the Antique and the Mediaeval in the Renaissance* (London: T. Fisher Unwin, 1884).

Lee, Vernon. *The Handling of Words* (London: John Lane, 1923).

Lee, Vernon. *Hauntings and Other Fantastic Tales*, ed. Catherine Maxwell and Patricia Pulham (Peterborough: Broadview Press, 2006).

Lee, Vernon. *Renaissance Fancies and Studies: Being a Sequel to Euphorion* (London: Smith, Elder, 1895).

le Gallienne, Richard. "Pictures Done into Verse," *Daily Chronicle* (7 June 1892).

Leighton, Angela. *On Form: Poetry, Aestheticism, and the Legacy of the Word* (Oxford: Oxford University Press, 2007).

Leighton, Angela. *Victorian Women Poets: Writing against the Heart* (Charlottesville: University Press of Virginia, 1992).

Levey, Michael. *The Case of Walter Pater* (London: Thames and Hudson, 1978).

Levine, George (ed.). *Aesthetics and Ideology* (New Brunswick: Rutgers University Press, 1994).

Livesey, Ruth. "Morris, Carpenter, Wilde, and the Political Aesthetics of Labor," *Victorian Literature and Culture* 32.2 (2004), 601–16.

Loesberg, Jonathan. *Aestheticism and Deconstruction: Pater, Derrida, and de Man* (Princeton: Princeton University Press, 1991).

Loesberg, Jonathan. *A Return to Aesthetics: Irony, Indifference, and Postmodernism* (Stanford: Stanford University Press, 2005).

Logan, Peter Melville. "On Culture: Edward B. Tylor's *Primitive Culture*, 1871," in *BRANCH: Britain, Representation and Nineteenth-Century History*, ed. Dino Franco Felluga. Extension of *Romanticism and Victorianism on the Net*, http://www.branchcollective.org/?ps_articles=peter-logan-on-culture-edward-b-tylors-primitive-culture-1871, accessed June 1, 2017.

Love, Heather K. "Exemplary Ambivalence," *Pater Newsletter* 50 (2007), 25–30.

Love, Heather K. *Feeling Backward: Loss and the Politics of Queer History* (Cambridge, MA: Harvard University Press, 2007).

Lyons, Sara. *Algernon Swinburne and Walter Pater: Victorian Aestheticism, Doubt, and Secularisation* (Oxford: Legenda, 2015).

Lysack, Krista. *Come Buy, Come Buy: Shopping and the Culture of Consumption in Victorian Women's Writing* (Athens: Ohio University Press, 2008).

Mahoney, Kristin. "Haunted Collections: Vernon Lee and Ethical Consumption," *Criticism* 48.1 (2007), 39–67.

Mallock, W. H. *The New Republic: Or Culture, Faith, and Philosophy in an English Country House*, ed. J. Max Patrick (Gainesville: University of Florida Press, 1950).

Maltz, Diana. *British Aestheticism and the Urban Working Classes, 1870–1900: Beauty for the People* (New York: Palgrave Macmillan, 2006).

Maltz, Diana. "Engaging 'Delicate Brains': From Working-Class Enculturation to Upper-Class Lesbian Liberation in Vernon Lee and Kit Anstruther-Thomson's Psychological Aesthetics," in *Women and British Aestheticism*, ed. Kathy Alexis Psomiades and Talia Schaffer (Charlottesville: University of Virginia Press, 1999), 211–29.

Marcus, Sharon. *Between Women: Friendship, Desire, and Marriage in Victorian England* (Princeton: Princeton University Press, 2007).

Martin, Robert K. "The Paterian Mode in Forster's Fiction: *The Longest Journey* to *Pharos and Pharillon*," in *E. M. Forster: Centenary Revaluations*, ed. Judith Scherer Herz and Robert K. Martin (Toronto: University of Toronto Press, 1982), 99–112.

Matz, Jesse. *Literary Impressionism and Modernist Aesthetics* (Cambridge: Cambridge University Press, 2001).

Matz, Robert. "The Scandals of Shakespeare's Sonnets," *ELH* 77.2 (Summer 2010), 477–508.

Maxwell, Catherine. *Second Sight: The Visionary Imagination in Late-Victorian Literature* (Manchester: Manchester University Press, 2008).

Maxwell, Catherine, and Patricia Pulham. Introduction to *Vernon Lee: Decadence, Ethics, Aesthetics*, ed. Catherine Maxwell and Patricia Pulham (Basingstoke, UK: Palgrave Macmillan, 2006), 1–20.

McGrath, F. C. *The Sensible Spirit: Walter Pater and the Modernist Paradigm* (Tampa: University of South Florida Press, 1986).

McLynn, Frank. *Marcus Aurelius: A Life* (Cambridge, MA: Da Capo Press, 2009).

Menon, Madhavi. *Unhistorical Shakespeare: Queer Theory in Shakespearean Literature and Film* (New York: Palgrave, 2008).

Merquior, José Guilherme. *Foucault* (Berkeley: University of California Press, 1985).

Mieszkowski, Jan. "Derrida, Hegel, and the Language of Finitude," *Postmodern Culture* 15.3 (2005), n.p.

Mill, John Stuart. *On Liberty and Other Writings*, ed. Stefan Collini (Cambridge: Cambridge University Press, 1989).

Miller, D. A. "*Foutre! Bougre! Ecriture!*" *Yale Journal of Criticism* 14.2 (2001), 503–11.

Monsman, Gerald. "Old Mortality at Oxford," *Studies in Philology* 67.3 (1970), 359–90.

Monsman, Gerald. "Pater's Aesthetic Hero," *University of Toronto Quarterly* 40 (1971), 136–51.

Monsman, Gerald. *Pater's Portraits: Mythic Patterns in the Fictions of Walter Pater* (Baltimore: Johns Hopkins University Press, 1967).

Monsman, Gerald. *Walter Pater* (Boston: Twayne, 1977).

Montgomery, Edmund. "The Unity of the Organic Individual," *Mind* 5.19 (1880), 318–36.

Morgan, Benjamin. "Aesthetic Freedom: Walter Pater and the Politics of Autonomy," *ELH* 77.3 (2010), 731–56.

Morgan, Benjamin. *The Outward Mind: Materialist Aesthetics in Victorian Science and Literature* (Chicago: University of Chicago Press, 2017).

Morgan, Thaïs. "Reimagining Masculinity in Victorian Criticism: Swinburne and Pater," *Victorian Studies* 36.3 (1993), 315–32.

Morley, Henry. "Euphuism," *Quarterly Review* 109 (1861), 350–83.

Muldoon, James. "Foucault's Forgotten Hegelianism," *Parrhesia* 21 (2014), 102–12.

Mulvey, Laura. "Visual Pleasure and Narrative Cinema," *Screen* 16.3 (1975), 6–18.

Muñoz, José Esteban. *Cruising Utopia: The Then and There of Queer Futurity* (New York: New York University Press, 2009).

Nealon, Christopher. *Foundlings: Gay and Lesbian Historical Emotion before Stonewall* (Durham: Duke University Press, 2001).

Newman, Sally. "The Archival Traces of Desire: Vernon Lee's Failed Sexuality and the Interpretation of Letters in Lesbian History," *Journal of the History of Sexuality* 14.1/2 (2005), 51–75.

Norris, Christopher. " 'What Is Enlightenment?' Kant and Foucault," in *The Cambridge Companion to Michel Foucault*, ed. Christopher Norris (Cambridge: Cambridge University Press, 2012), 159–96.

Ohi, Kevin. *Henry James and the Queerness of Style* (Minneapolis: University of Minnesota Press, 2011).

Østermark-Johansen, Lene. "The Death of Euphues: Euphuism and Decadence in Late-Victorian Literature," *English Literature in Transition (1880–1920)* 45 (2002), 4–25.

Parker, Christopher. *The English Idea of History from Coleridge to Collingwood* (Aldershot: Ashgate, 2000).

Parkes, Adam. *A Sense of Shock: The Impact of Impressionism on Modern British and Irish Writing* (Oxford: Oxford University Press, 2011).

Pater, Walter. *Appreciations, with an Essay on Style* (London: Macmillan, 1889).

Pater, Walter. "Coleridge's Writings," *Westminster Review* n.s. 29 (January 1866), 106–32.

Pater, Walter. *Greek Studies: A Series of Essays*, ed. Charles L. Shadwell (London: Macmillan, 1894).

Pater, Walter. "The History of Philosophy," unpublished manuscript, Houghton Library, Harvard University, Cambridge, MA, 6.

Pater, Walter. *Marius the Epicurean: His Sensations and Ideas*, ed. Michael Levey (London, Penguin Books, 1985).

Pater, Walter. *Miscellaneous Studies* (London: Macmillan, 1895).

Pater, Walter. "On Wordsworth," *Fortnightly Review* 15 (1874), 455–65.

Pater, Walter. *Plato and Platonism: A Series of Essays* (London: Macmillan, 1893).

Pater, Walter. "Poems by William Morris," *Westminster Review* n.s. 90 (1868), 300–12.

Pater, Walter. *The Renaissance: Studies in Art and Poetry: The 1893 Text*, ed. Donald L. Hill (Berkeley: University of California Press, 1980).

Pater, Walter. "Winckelmann," *Westminster Review* n.s. 31 (January 1867), 80–110.

Pease, Alison. "Aestheticism and Aesthetic Theory," in *Palgrave Advances in Oscar Wilde Studies*, ed. Frederick S. Roden (Basingstoke: Palgrave Macmillan, 2004), 96–118.

Peckham, Morse. *The Triumph of Romanticism: Collected Essays* (Columbia: University of South Carolina Press, 1970).

Pippin, Robert. *Hegel on Self-Consciousness: Desire and Death in the "Phenomenology of Spirit"* (Princeton: Princeton University Press, 2010).

Potts, Alex. *Flesh and the Ideal: Winckelmann and the Origins of Art History* (New Haven: Yale University Press, 1994).

Price, Matthew Burroughs. "A Genealogy of Queer Detachment," *PMLA* 130.3 (2015), 648–55.

Prins, Yopie. *Victorian Sappho* (Princeton: Princeton University Press, 1999).

Psomiades, Kathy Alexis. *Body's Beauty: Femininity and Representation in British Aestheticism* (Stanford: Stanford University Press, 1997).

Psomiades, Kathy Alexis. "'Still Burning from This Strangling Embrace': Vernon Lee on Desire and Aesthetics," in *Victorian Sexual Dissidence*, ed. Richard Dellamora (Chicago: University of Chicago Press, 1997), 21–41.

Psomiades, Kathy Alexis, and Talia Schaffer (eds.). *Women and British Aestheticism* (Charlottesville: University of Virginia Press, 1999).

Pulham, Patricia. *Art and the Transitional Object in Vernon Lee's Supernatural Tales* (Aldershot, UK: Ashgate, 2008).

Rancière, Jacques. *Aisthesis: Scenes from the Aesthetic Regime of Art* (London: Verso, 2013).

Rancière, Jacques. *The Emancipated Spectator*, trans. Gregory Elliot (London: Verso, 2009).

Reed, Christopher. *Art and Homosexuality: A History of Ideas* (Oxford: Oxford University Press, 2011).

Robbins, Bruce. "'I Couldn't Possibly Love Such a Person': Judith Butler on Hegel," *Minnesota Review* 52–54 (2001), 263–9.

Robbins, Ruth. "Vernon Lee: Decadent Woman?," in Fin de Siècle / Fin du Globe: *Fears and Fantasies of the Late Nineteenth Century*, ed. John Stokes (New York: St. Martin's Press, 1992), 139–61.

Roellinger, Francis. "Intimations of Winckelmann in Pater's 'Diaphaneitè,'" *English Language Notes* 2 (1965), 277–82.

Rosenthal, Jesse. *Good Form: The Ethical Experience of the Victorian Novel* (Princeton: Princeton University Press, 2017).

Ruehl, Sonja. "Inverts and Experts: Radclyffe Hall and the Lesbian Identity," in *Feminist Criticism and Social Change: Sex, Class, and Race in Literature and Culture*, ed. Judith Newton and Deborah Rosenfelt (New York: Methuen, 1985), 165–80.

Ruskin, John. *The Works of John Ruskin* (Library Edition), ed. E. T. Cook and A. Wedderburn, vol. 3 (London: George Allen, 1903–12).

Ruti, Mari. *The Ethics of Opting Out: Queer Theory's Defiant Subjects* (New York: Columbia University Press, 2017).

Rutter, Benjamin. *Hegel on the Modern Arts* (Cambridge: Cambridge University Press, 2010).

Saint-Amour, Paul K. *The Copywrights: Intellectual Property and the Literary Imagination* (Ithaca: Cornell University Press, 2003).

Saville, Julia F. "The Poetic Imaging of Michael Field," in *The Fin de Siècle Poem*, ed. Joseph Bristow (Athens: Ohio University Press, 2005), 178–206.

Schaffer, Talia. *The Forgotten Female Aesthetes: Literary Culture in Late-Victorian England* (Charlottesville: University of Virginia Press, 2000).

Schmidgall, Gary. *The Stranger Wilde: Interpreting Oscar* (New York: Dutton, 1994).

Schroeder, Horst. *"The Portrait of Mr. W.H.": Its Composition, Publication, and Reception* (Braunschweig: Technische Universität Carolo-Wilhelmina zu Braunschweig, 1984).

Sedgwick, Eve Kosofsky. "Around the Performative: Periperformative Vicinities in Nineteenth-Century Narrative," in *Touching Feeling: Affect, Pedagogy, Performativity* (Durham: Duke University Press, 2003), 67–92.

Sedgwick, Eve Kosofsky. *Epistemology of the Closet* (Berkeley: University of California Press, 1991).

Sedgwick, Eve Kosofsky. "How to Bring Your Kids Up Gay," *Social Text* 29 (1991), 18–27.

Sedgwick, Eve Kosofsky. "Queer and Now," in *Tendencies* (Durham: Duke University Press, 1993), 1–8.

Sedgwick, Eve Kosofsky. "Shame, Theatricality, and Queer Performativity: Henry James's *The Art of the Novel*," in *Touching Feeling* (Durham: Duke University Press, 2003), 35–66.

Seppä, Anita. "Foucault, Enlightenment, and the Aesthetics of the Self," *Contemporary Aesthetics* 2 (2004), https://quod.lib.umich.edu/c/ca/7523862.0002.004/--foucault-enlightenment-and-the-aesthetics-of-the-self?rgn=main;view=fulltext.

Shakespeare, William. *The Riverside Shakespeare*, 2nd ed. (Boston: Houghton Mifflin, 1997).

Shewan, Rodney. *Oscar Wilde: Art and Egotism* (New York: Barnes and Noble, 1977).

Shorter, Edward. *A Historical Dictionary of Psychiatry* (Oxford: Oxford University Press, 2005).

Shrimpton, Nicholas. "The Old Aestheticism and the New," *Literature Compass* 2.1 (2005), https://doi.org/10.1111/j.1741-4113.2005.00150.x.

Shuter, William F. "History as Palingenesis in Pater and Hegel," *PMLA* 86 (1971), 411–21.

Shuter, William F. "The 'Outing' of Walter Pater," *Nineteenth Century Literature* 48.4 (March 1994), 480–506.

Shuter, William F. *Rereading Walter Pater* (Cambridge: Cambridge University Press, 1997).

Siegel, Jonah. *Desire and Excess: The Nineteenth-Century Culture of Art* (Princeton: Princeton University Press, 2000).

Siegel, Jonah. "The Material of Form: Vernon Lee at the Vatican and Out of It," *Victorian Studies* 55.2 (2013), 189–201.

Sinfield, Alan. *The Wilde Century: Effeminacy, Oscar Wilde, and the Queer Moment* (London: Cassell, 1994).

Smith, Andrew. *The Victorian Ghost Story 1840–1920: A Cultural History* (Manchester: Manchester University Press, 2010.

Smith, John H. "U-Topian: Dialectic and Its Other in Poststructuralism," *German Quarterly* 60.2 (1987), 237–61.

Smith, Philip E. "Philosophical Approaches to Interpretation of Oscar Wilde," in *Palgrave Advances in Oscar Wilde Studies*, ed. Frederick S. Roden (Basingstoke: Palgrave Macmillan, 2004), 143–66.

Smith, Philip E., and Michael S. Helfand. *Oscar Wilde's Oxford Notebooks: A Portrait of a Mind in the Making* (Oxford: Oxford University Press, 1989).

Snediker, Michael. *Queer Optimism: Lyric Personhood and Other Felicitous Persuasions* (Minneapolis: University of Minnesota Press, 2009).

Sontag, Susan. "Notes on Camp," in *Against Interpretation* (New York: Farrar, Straus and Giroux, 1966), 105–19.

Stetz, Margaret. "The Snake Lady and the Bruised Bodley Head: Vernon Lee and Oscar Wilde in the *Yellow Book*," in *Vernon Lee: Decadence, Ethics, Aesthetics*, ed. Catherine Maxwell and Patricia Pulham (Basingstoke: Palgrave Macmillan, 2006), 112–22.

Stillman, W. J. "Leonardo da Vinci 1452–1519," *Century* 41(1891), 838–42.

Stirling, John Hutchison. *Jerrold, Tennyson, and Macaulay* (Edinburgh: Edmonston & Douglas, 1868).

Stocking, George W. *After Tylor: British Social Anthropology, 1888–1951* (Madison: University of Wisconsin Press, 1995).

Stocking, George W. *Victorian Anthropology* (New York: Free Press, 1987).

Symonds, John Addington. *The Letters of John Addington Symonds* (3 vols.), ed.

Herbert M. Schuller and Robert L. Peters (Detroit: Wayne State University Press, 1967–69), vol. 2.

Symonds, John Addington. *Renaissance in Italy* (London: Smith, Elder, 1875–86).

Symonds, John Addington. *Shakespeare's Predecessors in the English Drama* (London: Smith, Elder, 1884).

Tate, Carolyn. "Lesbian Incest as Queer Kinship," *Victorian Review* 39.2 (2013), 181–99.

Taussig, Michael. *Defacement: Public Secrecy and the Labor of the Negative* (Stanford: Stanford University Press, 1999).

Temple, Ruth Z. "Truth in Labeling: Pre-Raphaelitism, Aestheticism, Decadence, Fin-de-Siècle," *English Literature in Transition* 17 (1974), 201–22.

Thain, Marion. *"Michael Field": Poetry, Aestheticism, and the* Fin de Siècle (Cambridge: Cambridge University Press, 2007).

Thomas, David Wayne. *Cultivating Victorians: Liberal Culture and the Aesthetic* (Philadelphia: University of Pennsylvania Press, 2003).

Toews, John. "Transformations of Hegelianism, 1805–1846," in *The Cambridge Companion to Hegel*, ed. Frederick C. Beiser (Cambridge: Cambridge University Press, 1993), 378–413.

Traub, Valerie. "The New Unhistoricism in Queer Studies," *PMLA* 128.1 (2013), 21–39.

Traub, Valerie. *Thinking Sex with the Early Moderns* (Philadelphia: University of Pennsylvania Press, 2016).

Turner, Frank M. *Contesting Cultural Authority: Essays in Victorian Intellectual Life* (Cambridge: Cambridge University Press, 1993).

Turner, Frank M. *The Greek Heritage in Victorian Britain* (New Haven: Yale University Press, 1981).

Turner, Frank M. "Why the Greeks and Not the Romans in Victorian Britain?," in *Rediscovering Hellenism: The Hellenic Inheritance and the English Imagination*, ed. G. W. Clarke and J. C. Eade (Cambridge: Cambridge University Press, 1989), 61–82.

Tylor, Edward B. *Primitive Culture: Researches into the Development of Mythology, Philosophy, Religion, Art, and Custom*, 2 vols. (London: John Murray, 1871).

Tylor, Edward B. "The Religion of Savages," *Fortnightly Review* 6 (1866), 71–86.

Tyrwhitt, Richard St. John. "The Greek Spirit in Modern Literature," *Contemporary Review* 29 (March 1877), 552–66.

Vadillo, Ana Parejo. "Sight and Song: Transparent Translations and a Manifesto for the Observer," *Victorian Poetry* 38.1 (2000), 15–34.

Vadillo, Ana Parejo. *Women Poets and Urban Aestheticism: Passengers of Modernity* (Basingstoke: Palgrave Macmillan, 2005).

Vanita, Ruth. *Sappho and the Virgin Mary: Same-Sex Love and the English Literary Imagination* (New York: Columbia University Press, 1996).

Varty, Anne. "The Crystal Man: A Study of "Diaphaneitè," in *Pater in the 1990s*, ed. Laurel Brake and Ian Small (Greensboro, NC: ELT Press, 1991), 205–15.

Vicinus, Martha. "The Adolescent Boy: *Fin de Siècle* Femme Fatale?," in *Victorian Sexual Dissidence*, ed. Richard Dellamora (Chicago: University of Chicago Press, 1997), 83–108.

Vicinus, Martha. *Intimate Friends: Women Who Loved Women, 1778–1928* (Chicago: University of Chicago Press, 2004).

Vicinus, Martha. "'A Legion of Ghosts': Vernon Lee (1856–1935) and the Art of Nostalgia," *GLQ: A Journal of Lesbian and Gay Studies* 10.4 (2004), 599–616.

Virno, Paolo. *Multitude: Between Innovation and Negation*, trans. Isabella Bertoletti, James Cascaito, and Andrea Casson (New York: Semiotext[e], 2008).

Vrettos, Athena. "'In the Clothes of Dead People': Vernon Lee and Ancestral Memory," *Victorian Studies* 55.2 (2013), 202–11.

Walkowitz, Rebecca. *Cosmopolitan Style: Modernism Beyond the Nation* (New York: Columbia University Press, 2006).

Wallace, Diana. *Female Gothic Histories: Gender, History, and the Gothic* (Cardiff: University of Wales Press, 2013).

Wallen, Jeffrey. "Reflection and Self-Reflection: Narcissistic or Aesthetic Criticism?," *Texas Studies in Literature and Language* 34.3 (1992), 301–22.

Ward, Anthony. *Walter Pater: The Idea in Nature* (London: MacGibbon & Kee, 1966).

Ward, James. "Psychological Principles," *Mind* 23 (1883), 465–86.

Watson, W. E. "Life of Bishop John Wordsworth" (1915), quoted in *Walter Pater: The Critical Heritage*, ed. R. M. Seiler (London: Routledge & Kegan Paul, 1980), 61–62.

Wellek, René. *A History of Modern Criticism*, vol. 4: *The Later Nineteenth Century* (New Haven: Yale University Press, 1965).

White, Christine. "Michael Field: Tiresian Poet," in *Victorian Women Poets: A Critical Reader*, ed. Angela Leighton (Oxford: Blackwell, 1996), 148–61.

White, Christine. "'Poets and Lovers Evermore': Interpreting Female Love in the Poetry and Journals of Michael Field," *Textual Practice* 4.2 (1990), 197–212.

White, Hayden. *Metahistory: The Historical Imagination in Nineteenth-Century Europe* (Baltimore: Johns Hopkins University Press, 1973).

Whiteley, Giles. *Aestheticism and the Philosophy of Death: Walter Pater and Post-Hegelianism* (London: Legenda, 2010).

Wilde, Oscar. *De Profundis* (New York: Modern Library, 2000).

Wilde, Oscar. "Essay on Chatterton," unpublished manuscript, William Andrews Clark Memorial Library, University of California, Los Angeles, Wilde W6721M3.E78 [1886?].

Wilde, Oscar. *The Picture of Dorian Gray*, ed. Joseph Bristow (Oxford: Oxford University Press, 2006).

Wilde, Oscar. *The Soul of Man under Socialism and Selected Critical Prose*, ed. Linda Dowling (London: Penguin, 2001).

Wilhelm, Lindsey P. "Evolutionary Science and Aestheticism: A Survey and a Suggestion," *Literature Compass* 13.2 (2016), 88–97.

Williams, Carolyn. "On Pater's Late Style," *Nineteenth-Century Prose* 24.2 (1997), 143–60.

Williams, Carolyn. *Transfigured World: Walter Pater's Aesthetic Historicism* (Ithaca: Cornell University Press, 1989).

Willis, Kirk. "The Introduction and Critical Reception of Hegelian Thought in Britain 1830–1900," *Victorian Studies* 32.1 (1988), 85–111.

Wordsworth, William. *The Prose Works of William Wordsworth*, ed. W. J. B. Owen and Jane Worthington Smyser (Oxford: Clarendon Press, 1974), vol. 1.

Wright, Thomas. *Life of Walter Pater* (London: Everet, 1907).

Yannis, Kanarakis. "The Aesthete as Scientist: Walter Pater and Nineteenth Century Science," *Victorian Network* 2.1 (2010), 88–105.

Žižek, Slavoj. *Tarrying with the Negative: Kant, Hegel, and the Critique of Ideology* (Durham: Duke University Press, 1993).

Zorn, Christa. *Vernon Lee: Aesthetics, History, and the Victorian Female Intellectual* (Athens: Ohio University Press, 2003).

www.ingramcontent.com/pod-product-compliance
Ingram Content Group UK Ltd.
Pitfield, Milton Keynes, MK11 3LW, UK
UKHW042310250425
457898UK00001B/25